Human Rights

Status
of International Instruments

United Nations
New York.1987

UNITED NATIONS PUBLICATION

Sales No. E.87.XIV.2

ISBN 92-1-154063-1
ISSN 1014-3629

03000P

Foreword

The present booklet is published within the programme of activities carried out by the Centre for Human Rights in commemoration of the 40th Anniversary Year of the Universal Declaration of Human Rights. It updates and revises a previous publication entitled *Human Rights—International Instruments: Signatures, Ratifications, Accessions, etc.* (ST/HR/4 and Rev.1-5), which was first issued in 1978 and subsequently in 1979, 1980, 1981, 1982 and 1983.

This booklet, while retaining a format similar to that of its predecessor, endeavours to provide more information on the main body of international human rights law. In this connection, extensive details are given on each of the twenty-two human rights instruments covered, with their status updated as of 1 September 1987.

In addition, a chart of ratification is available in the inside pocket of the booklet. The Centre for Human Rights intends to update this chart periodically, in order to record developments in the field of human rights as they take place. This, in turn, will make information on the progress of the international community in this field even more timely and accessible.

All the information contained in the booklet is based on the United Nations publication *Multilateral Treaties Deposited with the Secretary-General, Status as at 31 December 1986* (ST/LEG/SER.E/5, Sales No. E.87.V.6) and brought up to date as of 1 September 1987.

Chapter I

INTERNATIONAL COVENANT ON ECONOMIC, SOCIAL AND CULTURAL RIGHTS

Adopted by the General Assembly of the United Nations on 16 December 1966

ENTRY INTO FORCE: 3 January 1976, in accordance with article 27.[1,*]

Participant	Signature	Ratification, accession (a) succession (d)
Afghanistan		24 Jan. 1983 *a*
Algeria	10 Dec. 1968	
Argentina	19 Feb. 1968	8 Aug. 1986
Australia	18 Dec. 1972	10 Dec. 1975
Austria	10 Dec. 1973	10 Sep. 1978
Barbados		5 Jan. 1973 *a*
Belgium	10 Dec. 1968	21 Apr. 1983
Bolivia		12 Aug. 1982 *a*
Bulgaria	8 Oct. 1968	21 Sep. 1970
Byelorussian SSR	19 Mar. 1968	12 Nov. 1973
Cameroon		27 June 1984 *a*
Canada		19 May 1976 *a*
Central African Republic		8 May 1981 *a*
Chile	16 Sep. 1969	10 Feb. 1972
China[2]		
Colombia	21 Dec. 1966	29 Oct. 1969
Congo		5 Oct. 1983 *a*
Costa Rica	19 Dec. 1966	29 Nov. 1968
Cyprus	9 Jan. 1967	2 Apr. 1969
Czechoslovakia	7 Oct. 1968	23 Dec. 1975
Democratic Kampuchea[3]	17 Oct. 1980	
Democratic People's Republic of Korea		14 Sep. 1981 *a*
Democratic Yemen		9 Feb. 1987 *a*

Participant	Signature	Ratification, accession (a) succession (d)
Denmark	20 Mar. 1968	6 Jan. 1972
Dominican Republic		4 Jan. 1978 *a*
Ecuador	29 Sep. 1967	6 Mar. 1969
Egypt	4 Aug. 1967	14 Jan. 1982
El Salvador	21 Sep. 1967	30 Nov. 1979
Finland	11 Oct. 1967	19 Aug. 1975
France		4 Nov. 1980 *a*
Gabon		21 Jan. 1983 *a*
Gambia		29 Dec. 1978 *a*
German Democratic Republic	27 Mar. 1973	8 Nov. 1973
Germany, Federal Republic of[4]	9 Oct. 1968	17 Dec. 1973
Greece		16 May 1985 *a*
Guinea	28 Feb. 1967	24 Jan. 1978
Guyana	22 Aug. 1968	15 Feb. 1977
Honduras	19 Dec. 1966	17 Feb. 1981
Hungary	25 Mar. 1969	17 Jan. 1974
Iceland	30 Dec. 1968	22 Aug. 1979
India		10 Apr. 1979 *a*
Iran (Islamic Republic of)	4 Apr. 1968	24 June 1975
Iraq	18 Feb. 1969	25 Jan. 1971
Ireland	1 Oct. 1973	
Israel	19 Dec. 1966	
Italy	18 Jan. 1967	15 Sep. 1978
Jamaica	19 Dec. 1966	3 Oct. 1975
Japan	30 May 1978	21 June 1979
Jordan	30 June 1972	28 May 1975
Kenya		1 May 1972 *a*
Lebanon		3 Nov. 1972 *a*
Liberia	18 Apr. 1967	
Libyan Arab Jamahiriya		15 May 1970 *a*
Luxembourg	26 Nov. 1974	18 Aug. 1983
Madagascar	14 Apr. 1970	22 Sep. 1971
Mali		16 July 1974 *a*
Malta	22 Oct. 1968	
Mauritius		12 Dec. 1973 *a*
Mexico		23 Mar. 1981 *a*
Mongolia	5 June 1968	18 Nov. 1974
Morocco	19 Jan. 1977	3 May 1979
Netherlands	25 June 1969	11 Dec. 1978
New Zealand	12 Nov. 1968	28 Dec. 1978

Participant	Signature	Ratification, accession (a) succession (d)
Nicaragua		12 Mar. 1980 *a*
Niger		7 Mar. 1985 *a*
Norway	20 Mar. 1968	13 Sep. 1972
Panama	27 July 1976	8 Mar. 1977
Peru	11 Aug. 1977	28 Apr. 1978
Philippines	19 Dec. 1966	7 June 1974
Poland	2 Mar. 1967	18 Mar. 1977
Portugal	7 Oct. 1976	31 July 1978
Romania	27 June 1968	9 Dec. 1974
Rwanda		16 Apr. 1975 *a*
Saint Vincent and the Grenadines		9 Nov. 1981 *a*
San Marino		18 Oct. 1985 *a*
Senegal	6 July 1970	13 Feb. 1978
Solomon Islands		17 Mar. 1982 *d*[5]
Spain	28 Sep. 1976	27 Apr. 1977
Sri Lanka		11 June 1980 *a*
Sudan		18 Mar. 1986 *a*
Suriname		28 Dec. 1976 *a*
Sweden	29 Sep. 1967	6 Dec. 1971
Syrian Arab Republic		21 Apr. 1969 *a*
Togo		24 May 1984 *a*
Trinidad and Tobago		8 Dec. 1978 *a*
Tunisia	30 Apr. 1968	18 Mar. 1969
Uganda		21 Jan. 1987 *a*
Ukrainian SSR	20 Mar. 1968	12 Nov. 1973
Union of Soviet Socialist Republics	18 Mar. 1968	16 Oct. 1973
United Kingdom	16 Sep. 1968	20 May 1976
United Republic of Tanzania		11 June 1976 *a*
United States of America	5 Oct. 1977	
Uruguay	21 Feb. 1967	1 Apr. 1970
Venezuela	24 June 1969	10 May 1978
Viet Nam		24 Sep. 1982 *a*
Yugoslavia	8 Aug. 1967	2 June 1971
Zaire		1 Nov. 1976 *a*
Zambia		10 Apr. 1984 *a*

DECLARATIONS AND RESERVATIONS

(Unless otherwise indicated, the declarations and reservations were made upon ratification, accession or succession. For objections thereto and territorial applications see hereinafter.)

Afghanistan

Declaration:

The presiding body of the Revolutionary Council of the Democratic Republic of Afghanistan declares that the provisions of article 48, paragraphs 1 and 3, of the International Covenant on Civil and Political Rights and provisions of article 26, paragraphs 1 and 3, of the International Covenant on Economic, Social and Cultural Rights, according to which some countries cannot join the aforesaid Covenants, contradict the international character of the aforesaid treaties. Therefore, according to the equal rights of all States to sovereignty, both Covenants should be left open for the purpose of the participation of all States.

Barbados

"The Government of Barbados states that it reserves the right to postpone

"(*a*) The application of article 7, subparagraph (*a*) (1), of the Covenant in so far as it concerns the provision of equal pay to men and women for equal work;

"(*b*) The application of article 10 (2) in so far as it relates to the special protection to be accorded mothers during a reasonable period during and after childbirth; and

"(*c*) The application of article 13 (2) (*a*) of the Covenant, in so far as it relates to primary education, since, while the Barbados Government fully accepts the principles embodied in the same articles and undertakes to take the necessary steps to apply them in their entirety, the problems of implementation are such that full application of the principles in question cannot be guaranteed at this stage."

Belgium

Interpretative declaration:

1. With respect to article 2, paragraph 2, the Belgian Government interprets non-discrimination as to national origin as not necessarily implying an obligation on States automatically to guarantee to foreigners the same rights as to their nationals. The term should be understood to refer to the elimination of any arbitrary behaviour but not of differences in treatment based on objective and reasonable considerations, in conformity with the principles prevailing in democratic societies.

2. With respect to article 2, paragraph 3, the Belgian Government understands that this provision cannot infringe the principle of fair compensation in the event of expropriation or nationalization.

Bulgaria

"The People's Republic of Bulgaria deems it necessary to underline that the provisions of article 48, paragraphs 1 and 3, of the International Covenant on Civil and Political Rights, and article 26, paragraphs 1 and 3, of the International Covenant on Economic, Social and Cultural Rights, under which a number of States are deprived of the opportunity to become parties to the Covenants, are of a discriminatory nature. These provisions are inconsistent with the very nature of the Covenants, which are universal in character and should be open for accession by all States. In accordance with the principle of sovereign equality, no State has the right to bar other States from becoming parties to a covenant of this kind."

Byelorussian Soviet Socialist Republic

Declaration made upon signature and confirmed upon ratification:

The Byelorussian Soviet Socialist Republic declares that the provisions of article 26, paragraph 1, of the International Covenant on Economic, Social and Cultural Rights and of article 48, paragraph 1, of the International Covenant on Civil and Political Rights, under which a number of States cannot become parties to these Covenants, are of a discriminatory nature and considers that the Covenants, in accordance with the principle of sovereign equality of States, should be open for participation by all States concerned without any discrimination or limitation.

Congo

Reservation:

The Government of the People's Republic of the Congo declares that it does not consider itself bound by the provisions of article 13, paragraphs 3 and 4.

Article 13, paragraphs 3 and 4, of the International Covenant on Economic, Social and Cultural Rights embody the principle of freedom of education by allowing parents the liberty to choose for their children schools other than those established by the public authorities. Those provisions also authorize individuals to establish and direct educational institutions.

In our country, such provisions are inconsistent with the principle of nationalization of education and with the monopoly granted to the State in that area.

Czechoslovakia

Upon signature:

The Czechoslovak Socialist Republic declares that the provision of article 26, paragraph 1, of the International Covenant on Economic, Social and Cultural Rights is in contradiction with the principle that all States have the right to become parties to multilateral treaties governing matters of general interest.

Upon ratification:

The provision of article 26, paragraph 1, of the Covenant is in contradiction with the principle that all States have the right to become parties to multilateral treaties regulating matters of general interest.

Democratic Yemen

The accession of the People's Democratic Republic of Yemen to the International Covenant on Economic, Social and Cultural Rights shall in no way signify recognition of Israel or serve as grounds for the establishment of relations of any sort with Israel.

Denmark [6]

"The Government of Denmark cannot, for the time being, undertake to comply entirely with the provision of article 7 (*d*) on remuneration for public holidays."

France

Declarations:

(1) The Government of the Republic considers that, in accordance with Article 103 of the Charter of the United Nations, in case of conflict between its obligations under the Covenant and its obligations under the Charter (especially Articles 1 and 2 thereof), its obligations under the Charter will prevail.

(2) The Government of the Republic declares that articles 6, 9, 11 and 13 are not to be interpreted as derogating from provisions governing the access of aliens to employment or as establishing residence requirements for the allocation of certain social benefits.

(3) The Government of the Republic declares that it will implement the provisions of article 8 in respect of the right to strike in conformity with article 6, paragraph 4, of the European Social Charter according to the interpretation thereof given in the annex to that Charter.

German Democratic Republic

The German Democratic Republic considers that article 26, paragraph 1, of the Covenant runs counter to the principle that all States which are guided in their policies by the purposes and principles of the Charter of the United Nations have the right to become parties to conventions which affect the interests of all States.

The German Democratic Republic has ratified the two Covenants in accordance with the policy it has so far pursued with the view to safeguarding human rights. It is convinced that these Covenants promote the world-wide struggle for the enforcement of human rights, which is an integral part of the struggle for the maintenance and strengthening of peace. On the occasion of the 25th anniversary of the Universal Declaration of Human Rights it thus contributes to the peaceful international co-operation of States, to the promotion of human rights and to the joint struggle against their violation by aggressive policies, colonialism and *apartheid,* racism and other forms of assaults on the right of the peoples to self-determination.

The Constitution of the German Democratic Republic guarantees the political, economic, social and cultural rights to every citizen independent of race, sex and religion. Socialist democracy has created the conditions for every citizen not only to enjoy these rights but also to take an active part in their implementation and enforcement.

Such fundamental human rights as the right to peace, the right to work and social security, the equality of women, and the right to education have been fully implemented in the German Democratic Republic. The Government of the German Democratic Republic has always paid great attention to the material prerequisites for guaranteeing above all the social and economic rights. The welfare of the working people and its continuous improvement are the leitmotiv of the entire policy of the Government of the German Democratic Republic.

The Government of the German Democratic Republic holds that the signing and ratification of the two International Covenants on Human Rights by further Member States of the United Nations would be an important step to implement the aims for respecting and promoting the human rights, the aims proclaimed in the Charter of the United Nations.

Guinea

In accordance with the principle whereby all States whose policies are guided by the purposes and principles of the Charter of the United Nations are entitled to become parties to covenants affecting the interests of the international community, the Government of the Republic of Guinea considers that the provision of article 26, paragraph 1, of the International Covenant on Economic, Social and Cultural Rights is contrary to the principle of the universality of international treaties and the democratization of international relations.

The Government of the Republic of Guinea likewise considers that article 1, paragraph 3, and the provision of article 14 of that instrument are contrary to the provisions of the Charter of the United Nations, in general, and United Nations resolutions on the granting of independence to colonial countries and peoples, in particular.

The above provisions are contrary to the Declaration on Principles of International Law concerning Friendly Relations and Co-operation among States contained in General Assembly resolution 2625 (XXV), pursuant to which every State has the duty to promote realization of the principle of equal rights and self-determination of peoples in order to put an end to colonialism.

Hungary

Upon signature:

"The Government of the Hungarian People's Republic declares that article 26, paragraph 1, of the International Covenant on Economic, Social and Cultural Rights and article 48, paragraph 1, of the International Covenant on Civil and Political Rights according to which certain States may not become signatories to the said Covenants are of a discriminatory nature and are contrary to the basic principle of international law that all States are entitled to become signatories to general multilateral treaties. These discriminatory provisions are incompatible with the objectives and purposes of the Covenants."

Upon ratification:

"The Presidential Council of the Hungarian People's Republic declares that the provisions of article 48, paragraphs 1 and 3, of ... the International Covenant on Civil and Political Rights, and article 26, paragraphs 1 and 3, of the International Covenant on Economic, Social and Cultural Rights are inconsistent with the universal character of the Covenants. It follows from the principle of sovereign equality of States that the Covenants should be open for participation by all States without any discrimination or limitation."

India

Declarations:

"I. With reference to article 1 of the International Covenant on Economic, Social and Cultural Rights, ... the Government of the Republic of India declares that the words 'the right of self-determination' appearing in [this article] apply only to the peoples under foreign domination and that these words do not apply to sovereign independent States or to a section of a people or nation—which is the essence of national integrity.

"II. With reference to article 9 of the International Covenant on Civil and Political Rights, the Government of the Republic of India takes the position that the provisions of the article shall be so applied as to be in consonance with the provisions of clauses (3) to (7) of article 22 of the Constitution of India. Further, under the Indian Legal System, there is no enforceable right to compensation for persons claiming to be victims of unlawful arrest or detention against the State.

"III. With respect to article 13 of the International Covenant on Civil and Political Rights, the Government of the Republic of India reserves its right to apply its law relating to foreigners.

"IV. With reference to articles 4 and 8 of the International Covenant on Economic, Social and Cultural Rights, the Government of the Republic of India declares that the provisions of the said [article] shall be so applied as to be in conformity with the provisions of article 19 of the Constitution of India.

"V. With reference to article 7 (c) of the International Covenant on Economic, Social and Cultural Rights, the Government of the Republic of India declares that the provisions of the said article shall be so applied as to be in conformity with the provisions of article 16 (4) of the Constitution of India."

Iraq[7]

Upon signature and confirmed upon ratification:

The entry of the Republic of Iraq as a party to the International Covenant on Economic, Social and Cultural Rights and the International Covenant on Civil and Political Rights shall in no way signify recognition of Israel nor shall it entail any obligation towards Israel under the said two Covenants."

"The entry of the Republic of Iraq as a party to the above two Covenants shall not constitute entry by it as a party to the Optional Protocol to the International Covenant on Civil and Political Rights."

Upon ratification:

"Ratification by Iraq ... shall in no way signify recognition of Israel nor shall it be conducive to entry with her into such dealings as are regulated by the said [Covenant]."

Japan

Reservations and declarations made upon signature and confirmed upon ratification:

"1. In applying the provision of article 7, paragraph (d), of the International Covenant on Economic, Social and Cultural Rights, Japan reserves the right not to be bound by "remuneration for public holidays" referred to in the said provision.

"2. Japan reserves the right not to be bound by the provision of article 8, paragraph 1, subparagraph (*d*), of the International Covenant on Economic, Social and Cultural Rights, except in relation to the sectors in which the right referred to in the said provision is accorded in accordance with the laws and regulations of Japan at the time of ratification of the Covenant by the Government of Japan.

"3. In applying the provisions of article 13, paragraph 2, subparagraphs (*b*) and (*c*), of the International Covenant on Economic, Social and Cultural Rights, Japan reserves the right not to be bound 'in particular by the progressive introduction of free education' referred to in the said provisions.

"4. Recalling the position taken by the Government of Japan, when ratifying the Convention (No. 87) concerning Freedom of Association and Protection of the Right to Organise, that 'the police' referred to in article 9 of the said Convention be interpreted to include the fire service of Japan, the Government of Japan declares that 'members . . . of the police' referred to in article 8, paragraph 2, of the International Covenant on Economic, Social and Cultural Rights as well as in article 22, paragraph 2, of the International Covenant on Civil and Political Rights be interpreted to include fire service personnel of Japan."

Kenya

"While the Kenya Government recognizes and endorses the principles laid down in article 10, paragraph 2, of the Covenant, the present circumstances obtaining in Kenya do not render necessary or expedient the imposition of those principles by legislation."

Libyan Arab Jamahiriya[7]

"The acceptance and the accession to this Covenant by the Libyan Arab Republic shall in no way signify a recognition of Israel or be conducive to entry by the Libyan Arab Republic into such dealings with Israel as are regulated by the Covenant."

Madagascar

The Government of Madagascar states that it reserves the right to postpone the application of article 13, paragraph 2, of the Covenant, more particularly in so far as it relates to primary education, since, while the Malagasy Government fully accepts the principles embodied in the said paragraph and undertakes to take the necessary steps to apply them in their entirety at the earliest possible date, the problems of implementation, and particularly the financial implications, are such that full application of the principles in question cannot be guaranteed at this stage.

Malta

Upon signature:

"The Government of Malta recognises and endorses the principles laid down in article 10, paragraph 2, of the Covenant. However, the present circumstances obtaining in Malta do not render necessary and do not render expedient the imposition of those principles by legislation."

Mexico

Interpretative statement:

The Government of Mexico accedes to the International Covenant on Economic, Social and Cultural Rights with the understanding that article 8 of the Covenant shall be applied in the Mexican Republic under the conditions and in conformity with the procedure established in the applicable provisions of the Political Constitution of the United Mexican States and the relevant implementing legislation.

Mongolia

Declaration made upon signature and confirmed upon ratification:

The Mongolian People's Republic declares that the provisions of article 26, paragraph 1, of the International Covenant on Economic, Social and Cultural Rights and of article 48, paragraph 1, of the International Covenant on Civil and Political Rights, under which a number of States cannot become parties to these Covenants, are of a discriminatory nature and considers that the Covenants, in accordance with the principle of sovereign equality of States, should be open for participation by all States concerned without any discrimination or limitation.

Netherlands

Reservation with respect to article 8, paragraph 1 (d)

"The Kingdom of the Netherlands does not accept this provision in the case of the Netherlands Antilles with regard to the latter's central and local government bodies."

Explanation

"[The Kingdom of the Netherlands] clarifies that although it is not certain whether the reservation [...] is necessary, [it] has preferred the form of a reservation to that of a declaration. In this way the Kingdom of the Netherlands wishes to ensure that the relevant obligation under the Covenant does not apply to the Kingdom as far as the Netherlands Antilles is concerned.

New Zealand

"The Government of New Zealand reserves the right not apply article 8 to the extent that existing legislative measures, enacted to ensure effective trade union representation and encourage orderly industrial relations, may not be fully compatible with that article.

"The Government of New Zealand reserves the right to postpone, in the economic circumstances foreseeable at the present time, the implementation of article 10 (2) as it relates to paid maternity leave or leave with adequate social security benefits."

Norway

Subject to reservations to article 8, paragraph 1 (*d*) "to the effect that the current Norwegian practice of referring labour conflicts to the State Wages Board (a permanent tripartite arbitral commission in matters of wages) by Act of Parliament for the particular conflict, shall not be considered incompatible with the right to strike, this right being fully recognized in Norway."

Romania

Upon signature:

The Government of the Socialist Republic of Romania declares that the provision of article 26, paragraph 1, of the International Covenant on Economic, Social and Cultural Rights is at variance with the principle that all States have the right to become parties to multilateral treaties governing matters of general interest.

Upon ratification:

(*a*) The State Council of the Socialist Republic of Romania considers that the provision of article 26 (1) of the International Covenant on Economic, Social and Cultural Rights is inconsistent with the principle that multilateral international treaties whose purposes concern the international community as a whole must be open to universal participation.

(*b*) The State Council of the Socialist Republic of Romania considers that the maintenance in a state of dependence of certain territories referred to in articles 1 (3) and 14 of the International Covenant on Economic, Social and Cultural Rights is inconsistent with the Charter of the United Nations and the instruments adopted by the Organization on the granting of independence to colonial countries and peoples, including the Declaration on Principles of International Law concerning Friendly Relations and Co-operation among States in accordance with the Charter of the United Nations, adopted unanimously by the United Nations General Assembly in its resolution 2625 (XXV) of 1970, which solemnly proclaims the duty of States to promote the realization of the principle of equal rights and self-determination of peoples in order to bring a speedy end to colonialism.

Rwanda

The Rwandese Republic [is] bound, however, in respect of education, only by the provisions of its Constitution.

Sweden

Sweden enters a reservation in connection with article 7 (*d*) of the Covenant in the matter of the right to remuneration for public holidays.

Syrian Arab Republic[7]

1. The accession of the Syrian Arab Republic to these two Covenants shall in no way signify recognition of Israel or entry into a relationship with it regarding any matter regulated by the said two Covenants.

2. The Syrian Arab Republic considers that article 26, paragraph 1, of the International Covenant on Economic, Social and Cultural Rights and article 48, paragraph 1, of the International Covenant on Civil and Political Rights are incompatible with the purposes and objectives of the said Covenants, inasmuch as they do not allow all States, without distinction or discrimination, the opportunity to become parties to the said Covenants.

Trinidad and Tobago

In respect to article 8 (1) (d) *and 8 (2):*

"The Government of Trinidad and Tobago reserves the right to impose lawful and/or reasonable restrictions on the exercise of the aforementioned rights by personnel engaged in essential services under the Industrial Relations Act or under any Statute replacing same which has been passed in accordance with the provisions of the Trinidad and Tobago Constitution.

Ukrainian Soviet Socialist Republic

Declaration made upon signature and confirmed upon ratification:

The Ukrainian Soviet Socialist Republic declares that the provisions of article 26, paragraph 1, of the International Covenant on Economic, Social and Cultural Rights and of article 48, paragraph 1, of the International Covenant on Civil and Political Rights, under which a number of States cannot become parties to these Covenants, are of a discriminatory nature and considers that the Covenants, in accordance with the principle of sovereign equality of States, should be open for participation by all States concerned without any discrimination or limitation.

Union of Soviet Socialist Republics

Declaration made upon signature and confirmed upon ratification:

The Union of Soviet Socialist Republics declares that the provisions of article 26, paragraph 1, of the International Covenant on Economic, Social and Cultural Rights and of article 48, paragraph 1, of the International Covenant on Civil and Political Rights, under which a number of States cannot become parties to these Covenants, are of a discriminatory nature and considers that the Covenants, in accordance with the principle of sovereign equality of States, should be open for participation by all States concerned without any discrimination or limitation.

United Kingdom of Great Britain and Northern Ireland

Upon signature:

"First, the Government of the United Kingdom declare their understanding that, by virtue of Article 103 of the Charter of the United Nations, in the event of any conflict between their obligations under article 1 of the Covenant and their obligations under the Charter (in particular, under Articles 1, 2 and 73 thereof) their obligations under the Charter shall prevail.

"Secondly, the Government of the United Kingdom declare that they must reserve the right to postpone the application of article 7, subparagraph (*a*) (i), of the Covenant in so far as it concerns the provision of equal pay to men and women for equal work, since, while they fully accept this principle and are pledged to work towards its complete application at the earliest possible time, the problems of implementation are such that complete application cannot be guaranteed at present.

"Thirdly, the Government of the United Kingdom declare that, in relation to article 8 of the Covenant, they must reserve the right not to apply paragraph 1, subparagraph (*b*), in Hong Kong, in so far as it may involve the right of trade unions not engaged in the same trade or industry to establish federations or confederations.

"Lastly, the Government of the United Kingdom declare that the provisions of the Covenant shall not apply to Southern Rhodesia unless and until they inform the Secretary-General of the United Nations that they are in a position to ensure that the obligations imposed by the Covenant in respect of that territory can be fully implemented."

Upon ratification:

"First, the Government of the United Kingdom maintain their declaration in respect of article 1 made at the time of signature of the Covenant.

"The Government of the United Kingdom declare that for the purposes of article 2 (3) the British Virgin Islands, the Cayman Islands, the Gilbert Islands, the Pitcairn Islands Group, St. Helena and Dependencies, the Turks and Caicos Islands and Tuvalu are developing countries.

"The Government of the United Kingdom reserve the right to interpret article 6 as not precluding the imposition of restrictions, based on place of birth or residence qualifications, on the taking of employment in any particular region or territory for the purpose of safeguarding the employment opportunities of workers in that region or territory.

"The Government of the United Kingdom reserve the right to postpone the application of article 7, paragraph (*a*), subparagraph (i), in so far as it concerns the provision of equal pay to men and women for equal work in the private sector in Jersey, Guernsey, the Isle of Man, Bermuda, Hong Kong and the Solomon Islands.

"The Government of the United Kingdom reserve the right not to apply article 8, subparagraph 1 (*b*), in Hong Kong.

"The Government of the United Kingdom while recognizing the right of everyone to social security in accordance with article 9 reserve the right to postpone implementation of the right in the Cayman Islands and the Falkland Islands because of shortage of resources in these territories.

"The Government of the United Kingdom reserve the right to postpone the application of article 10, paragraph 1, in regard to a small number of customary marriages in the Solomon Islands and the application of article 10, paragraph 2, in so far as it concerns paid maternity leave in Bermuda and the Falkland Islands.

"The Government of the United Kingdom maintain the right to postpone the application of article 13, paragraph 2, subparagraph (*a*), and article 14, in so far as they require compulsory primary education, in the Gilbert Islands, the Solomon Islands and Tuvalu.

"Lastly, the Government of the United Kingdom declare that the provisions of the Covenant shall not apply to Southern Rhodesia unless and until they inform the Secretary-General of the United Nations that they are in a position to ensure that the obligations imposed by the Covenant in respect of that territory can be fully implemented."

Viet Nam

Declaration:

That the provisions of article 48, paragraph 1, of the International Covenant on Civil and Political Rights, and of article 26, paragraph 1, of the International Covenant on Economic, Social and Cultural Rights, under which a number of States are deprived of the opportunity to become parties to the Covenants, are of a discriminatory nature. The Government of the Socialist Republic of Viet Nam considers that the Covenants, in accordance with the principle of sovereign equality of States, should be open for participation by all States without any discrimination or limitation.

Zambia

Reservation:

The Government of the Republic of Zambia states that it reserves the right to postpone the application of article 13 (2) (*a*) of the Covenant, in so far as it relates to primary education; since, while the Government of the Republic of Zambia fully accepts the principles embodied in the same article and undertakes to take the necessary steps to apply them in their entirety, the problems of implementation, and particularly the financial implications, are such that full application of the principles in question cannot be guaranteed at this stage.

OBJECTIONS

(Unless otherwise indicated, the objections were made
upon ratification, accession or succession.)

France

The Government of the Republic takes objection to the reservation entered by the Government of India to article 1 of the International Covenant on Economic, Social and Cultural Rights, as this reservation attaches conditions not provided for by the Charter of the United Nations to the exercise of the right of self-determination. The present declaration will not be deemed to be an obstacle to the entry into force of the Covenant between the French Republic and the Republic of India.

Germany, Federal Republic of

15 August 1980

"The Government of the Federal Republic of Germany strongly objects, ... to the declaration made by the Republic of India in respect of article 1 of the International Covenant on Economic, Social and Cultural Rights and of article 1 of the International Covenant on Civil and Political Rights.

"The right of self-determination as enshrined in the Charter of the United Nations and as embodied in the Covenants applies to all peoples and not only to those under foreign domination. All peoples, therefore, have the inalienable right freely to determine their political status and freely to pursue their economic, social and cultural development. The Federal Government cannot consider as valid any interpretation of the right of self-determination which is contrary to the clear language of the provisions in question. It moreover considers that any limitation of their applicability to all nations is incompatible with the object and purpose of the Covenants."

Netherlands

12 January 1981

"The Government of the Kingdom of the Netherlands objects to the declaration made by the Government of the Republic of India in relation to article 1 of the International Covenant on Civil and Political Rights and article 1 of the International Covenant on Economic, Social and Cultural Rights, since the right of self-determination as embodied in the Covenants is conferred upon all peoples. This follows not only from the very language of article 1 common to the two Covenants but as well from the most authoritative statement of the law concerned, i.e. the Declaration on Principles of International Law concerning Friendly Relations and Co-operation among States in accordance with the Charter of the United Nations. Any attempt to limit the scope of this right or to attach conditions not provided for in the relevant instruments would undermine the concept of self-determination itself and would thereby seriously weaken its universally acceptable character."

TERRITORIAL APPLICATIONS

Participant	Date of receipt of the notification	Territories
United Kingdom .	20 May 1976	The Bailiwick of Guernsey, the Bailiwick of Jersey, the Isle of Man, Belize, Bermuda, the British Virgin Islands, the Cayman Islands, the Falkland Islands and Dependencies[8], Gibraltar, the Gilbert Islands, Hong Kong, Montserrat, the Pitcairn Group, St. Helena and Dependencies, the Solomon Islands, the Turks and Caicos Islands and Tuvalu
Netherlands . . .	11 Dec. 1978	Netherlands Antilles

NOTES

[1] The thirty-fifth instrument of ratification or accession was deposited with the Secretary-General on 3 October 1975. The Contracting States did not object to having those instruments accompanied with reservations taken into account under article 27 (1) for the purpose of determining the date of general entry into force of the Covenant.

[2] Signed on behalf of the Republic of China on 5 October 1967.

On 29 September 1972, a communication was received by the Secretary-General from the Minister for Foreign Affairs of the People's Republic of China stating:

"1. With regard to the multilateral treaties signed, ratified or acceded to by the defunct Chinese Government before the establishment of the Government of the People's Republic of China, my Government will examine their contents before making a decision in the light of the circumstances as to whether or not they should be recognized.

"2. As from 1 October 1949, the day of the founding of the People's Republic of China, the Chiang Kai-shek clique has no right at all to represent China. Its signature and ratification of, or accession to, any multilateral treaties by usurping the name of 'China' are all illegal and null and void. My Government will study these multilateral treaties before making a decision in the light of the circumstances as to whether or not they should be acceded to."

All entries recorded throughout this publication in respect of China refer to actions taken by the authorities representing China in the United Nations at the time of those actions.

With reference to the above-mentioned signature, communications have been addressed to the Secretary-General by the Permanent Representatives or Permanent Missions to the United Nations of Bulgaria, Byelorussian SSR, Czechoslovakia, Mongolia, Romania, the Ukrainian SSR, the Union of Soviet Socialist Republics and Yugoslavia, stating that their Governments did not recognize the said signature as valid since the only Government authorized to represent China and to assume obligations on its behalf was the Government of the People's Republic of China.

In letters addressed to the Secretary-General in regard to the above-mentioned communications, the Permanent Representative of China to the United Nations stated that the Republic of China, a sovereign State and Member of the United Nations, had attended the twenty-first regular session of the General Assembly of the United Nations and contributed to the formulation of, and signed the Covenants and the Optional Protocol concerned, and that "any statements or reservations relating to the above-mentioned Covenants and Optional Protocol that are incompatible with or derogatory to the legitimate position of the Government of the Republic of China shall in no way affect the rights and obligations of the Republic of China under these Covenants and Optional Protocol".

[3] With respect to the signature by Democratic Kampuchea the Secretary-General received, on 5 November 1980, the following communication from the Government of Mongolia:

"The Government of the Mongolian People's Republic considers that only the People's Revolutionary Council of Kampuchea as the sole authentic and lawful representative of the Kampuchean people has the right to assume international obligations on behalf of the Kampuchean people. Therefore, the Government of the Mongolian People's Republic considers that the signature of the International Covenants on Human Rights by the representative of the so-called Democratic Kampuchea, a régime that ceased to exist as a result of the people's revolution in Kampuchea, is null and void.

"The signing of the International Covenants on Human Rights by an individual, whose régime during its short period of reign in Kampuchea had exterminated about 3 million people and had thus grossly violated the elementary norms of human rights, each and every provision of the International Covenants on Human Rights is a regrettable precedence, which discredits the noble aims and lofty principles of the Charter of the United Nations, the very spirit of the above-mentioned Covenants and gravely impairs the prestige of the United Nations."

Thereafter, similar communications were received from the Governments of the following States on the dates indicated:

State	Date of receipt
German Democratic Republic	11 Dec 1980
Poland	12 Dec 1980
Ukrainian SSR	16 Dec 1980
Hungary	19 Jan 1981
Bulgaria	29 Jan 1981
Union of Soviet Socialist Republics	18 Feb 1981
Byelorussian SSR	18 Feb 1981
Czechoslovakia	10 Mar 1981

The text of the said objections were circulated as depositary notifications or, at the request of the States concerned, as official documents of the General Assembly (A/33/781 and A/35/784).

⁴ With the following declaration: ". . . The said Covenant shall also apply to Berlin (West) with effect from the date on which it enters into force for the Federal Republic of Germany except as far as allied rights and responsibilities are affected."

In this connection, the Secretary-General received on 5 July 1974 a communication from the Government of the Union of Soviet Socialist Republics which states in part as follows:

"By reason of their material content, the International Covenant on Civil and Political Rights and the International Covenant on Economic, Social and Cultural Rights of 19 December 1966 directly affect matters of security and status. With this in mind the Soviet Union considers the statement made by the Federal Republic of Germany concerning the extension of the operation of these Covenants to Berlin (West) to be illegal and to have no force in law, since, under the Quadripartite Agreement of 3 September 1971, the treaty obligations of the Federal Republic of Germany affecting matters of security and status may not be extended to the Western Sectors of Berlin."

Communications identical in essence, *mutatis mutandis,* were received from the Governments of the German Democratic Republic (12 August 1974) and of the Ukrainian Soviet Socialist Republic (16 August 1974).

In this regard, the Governments of France, the United Kingdom and the United States of America, in a communication received on 5 November 1974, made the following declaration:

"The Governments of France, the United Kingdom of Great Britain and Northern Ireland and the United States of America wish to bring to the attention of the States parties to the Covenants that the extension of the Covenants to the Western Sectors of Berlin received the prior authorization, under established procedures, of the authorities of France, the United Kingdom and the United States on the basis of their supreme authority in those Sectors.

"The Governments of France, the United Kingdom and the United States wish to point out that the International Covenant on Economic, Social and Cultural Rights and the International Covenant on Civil and Political Rights, the primary purpose of both of which is the protection of the rights of the individual, are not treaties which 'by reason of their material content, directly affect matters of security and status'.

"As for the references to the Quadripartite Agreement of 3 September 1971 which are contained in the communication made by the Government of the Union of Soviet Socialist Republics referred to in the Legal Counsel's Note, the Governments of France, the United Kingdom and the United States wish to point out that, in a communication to the Government of the Union of Soviet Socialist Republics which is an integral part (Annex IV A) of the Quadripartite Agreement, they reaffirmed that, provided that matters of security and status are not affected, international agreements and arrangements entered into by the Federal Republic of Germany may be extended to the Western Sectors of Berlin. For its part the Government of the Union of Soviet Socialist Republics, in a communication to the Governments of France, the United Kingdom and the United States which is similarly an integral part (Annex IV B) of the Quadripartite Agreement, affirmed that it would raise no objection to such extension.

"In authorizing the extension of the Covenants to the Western Sectors of Berlin, as mentioned above, the authorities of France, the United Kingdom and the United States took all necessary measures to ensure that the Covenants cannot be applied in the Western Sectors of Berlin in such a way as to affect matters of security and status. Accordingly, the application of the Covenants to the Western Sectors of Berlin continues in full force and effect."

In a communication received on 6 December 1974, the Government of the Federal Republic of Germany stated in part:

"By their note of 4 November 1974, circulated to all States parties to either of the Covenants by C.N.306.1974. TREATIES-7 of 19 November 1974, the Governments of France, the United Kingdom and the United States answered the assertions made in the communication of the Government of the Union of Soviet Socialist Republics referred to above. The Government of the Federal Republic of Germany shares the position set out in the note of the Three Powers. The extension of the Covenants to Berlin (West) continues in full force and effect."

On the same subject, the Secretary-General received the following communications:
Union of Soviet Socialist Republics (13 February 1975):

"The Soviet Union deems it essential to reassert its view that the extension by the Federal Republic of Germany of the operation of the International Covenant on Civil and Political Rights and the International Covenant on Economic, Social and Cultural Rights of 19 December 1966 to Berlin (West) is illegal as stated in the note dated 4 July 1974 addressed to the Secretary-General (C.N.145.1974. TREATIES-3) of 5 August 1974."

France, United Kingdom of Great Britain and Northern Ireland and United States of America (8 July 1975—in relation to the declarations by the German Democratic Republic and by the Ukrainian Soviet Socialist Republic received on 12 and 16 August 1974, respectively):

"The communications mentioned in the notes listed above refer to the Quadripartite Agreement of 3 September 1971. This Agreement was concluded in Berlin between the Governments of the French Republic, the Union of Soviet Socialist Republics, the United Kingdom of Great Britain and Northern Ireland and the United States of America. The Governments sending these communications are not parties to the Quadripartite Agreement and are therefore not competent to make authoritative comments on its provisions.

"The Governments of France, the United Kingdom and the United States wish to bring the following to the attention of the States parties to the instruments referred to in the above-mentioned communications. When authorizing the extension of these instruments to the Western Sectors of Berlin, the authorities of the Three Powers, acting in the exercise of their supreme authority, ensured in accordance with established procedures that those instruments are applied in the Western Sectors of Berlin in such a way as not to affect matters of security and status.

"Accordingly, the application of these instruments to the Western Sectors of Berlin continues in full force and effect.

"The Governments of France, the United Kingdom and the United States do not consider it necessary to respond to any further communications of a similar nature by States which are not signatories to the Quadripartite Agreement. This should not be taken to imply any change in the position of those Governments in this matter."

Federal Republic of Germany (19 September 1975—in relation to the declarations by the German Democratic Republic and the Ukrainian Soviet Socialist Republic received on 12 and 16 August 1974, respectively):

"By their note of 8 July 1975, disseminated by circular note ... C.N.198.1975. TREATIES-6 of 13 August 1975, the Governments of France, the United Kingdom and the United States answered the assertions made in the communications referred to above. The Government of the Federal Republic of Germany, on the basis of the legal situation set out in the note of the Three Powers, wishes to confirm that the application in Berlin (West) of the above-mentioned instruments extended by it under the established procedures continues in full force and effect.

"The Government of the Federal Republic of Germany wishes to point out that the absence of a response to further communications of a similar nature should not be taken to imply any change of its position in this matter."

[5] In a communication received on 10 May 1982, the Government of Solomon Islands declared that Solomon Islands maintains the reservations entered by the United Kingdom save in so far as the same cannot apply to Solomon Islands.

[6] In a communication received on 14 January 1976, the Government of Denmark notified the Secretary-General that it withdraws its reservation made prior with regard to article 7 (*a*) (i) on equal pay for equal work.

[7] In two communications received by the Secretary-General on 10 July 1969 and 23 March 1971 respectively, the Government of Israel declared that it "has noted the political character of the declaration made by the Government of Iraq on signing and ratifying the above Covenants. In the view of the Government of Israel, these two Covenants are not the proper place for making such political pronouncements. The Government of Israel will, in so far as concerns the substance of the matter, adopt towards the Government of Iraq an attitude of complete reciprocity.

Identical communications, *mutatis mutandis,* were received by the Secretary-General from the Government of Israel on 9 July 1969 in respect of the declaration made on accession by the Government of Syria, and on 29 June 1970 in respect of the declaration made on accession by the Government of Libya. In the latter communication, the Government of Israel moreover stated that the declaration concerned "cannot in any way affect the obligations of the Libyan Arab Republic already existing under general international law".

[8] On 3 October 1983 the Secretary-General received from the Government of Argentina the following objection:

[The Government of Argentina makes a] formal objection to the [declaration] of territorial extension issued by the United Kingdom with regard to the Malvinas Islands (and dependencies), which that country is illegally occupying and refers to as the "Falkland Islands".

The Argentine Republic rejects and considers null and void the [said declaration] of territorial extension. See also note 14 in chapter II.

Subsequently, upon ratification, the Government of Argentina made the following declaration:

"The Argentine Republic rejects the extension, notified to the Secretary-General of the United Nations on 20 May 1976 by the United Kingdom of Great Britain and Northern Ireland, of the application of the International Covenant on Economic, Social and Cultural Rights, adopted by the General Assembly of the United Nations on 16 December 1966, to the Malvinas, South Georgia and South Sandwich Islands, and reaffirms its sovereign rights to those archipelagos, which form an integral part of its national territory.

The General Assembly of the United Nations had adopted resolutions 2065 (XX), 3160 (XXVIII), 31/49, 37/9, 38/12, 39/6 and 40/21 in which it recognizes the existence of a sovereignty dispute regarding the question of the Falkland Islands (Malvinas) and urges the Argentine Republic and the United Kingdom of Great Britain and Northern Ireland to pursue negotiations in order to find as soon as possible a peaceful and definitive solution to the dispute, through the good offices of the Secretary-General of the United Nations, who shall inform the General Assembly of the progress made."

Chapter II

INTERNATIONAL COVENANT ON CIVIL AND POLITICAL RIGHTS

Adopted by the General Assembly of the United Nations on 16 December 1966

ENTRY INTO FORCE: 23 March 1976, in accordance with article 49, for all provisions except those of article 41; 28 March 1979 for the provisions of article 41 (Human Rights Committee), in accordance with paragraph 2 of the said article 41.

Participant	Signature	Ratification, accession (a)
Afghanistan		24 Jan. 1983 *a*
Algeria	10 Dec. 1968	
Argentina	19 Feb. 1968	8 Aug. 1986
Australia	18 Dec. 1972	13 Aug. 1980
Austria	10 Dec. 1973	10 Sep. 1978
Barbados		5 Jan. 1973 *a*
Belgium	10 Dec. 1968	21 Apr. 1983
Bolivia		12 Aug. 1982 *a*
Bulgaria	8 Oct. 1968	21 Sep. 1970
Byelorussian SSR	19 Mar. 1968	12 Nov. 1973
Cameroon		27 June 1984 *a*
Canada		19 May 1976 *a*
Central African Republic		8 May 1981 *a*
Chile	16 Sep. 1969	10 Feb. 1972
China[1,*]		
Colombia	21 Dec. 1966	29 Oct. 1969
Congo		5 Oct. 1983 *a*
Costa Rica	19 Dec. 1966	29 Nov. 1968
Cyprus	19 Dec. 1966	2 Apr. 1969
Czechoslovakia	7 Oct. 1968	23 Dec. 1975
Democratic Kampuchea[2]	17 Oct. 1980	

---

* For notes, see end of chapter.

Participant	Signature	Ratification, accession (a)
Democratic People's Republic of Korea		14 Sep. 1981 *a*
Democratic Yemen		9 Feb. 1987 *a*
Denmark	20 Mar. 1968	6 Jan. 1972
Dominican Republic		4 Jan. 1978 *a*
Ecuador	4 Apr. 1968	6 Mar. 1969
Egypt	4 Aug. 1967	14 Jan. 1982
El Salvador	21 Sep. 1967	30 Nov. 1979
Finland	11 Oct. 1967	19 Aug. 1975
France		4 Nov. 1980 *a*
Gabon		21 Jan. 1983 *a*
Gambia		22 Mar. 1979 *a*
German Democratic Republic	27 Mar. 1973	8 Nov. 1973
Germany, Federal Republic of[3]	9 Oct. 1968	17 Dec. 1973
Guinea	28 Feb. 1967	24 Jan. 1978
Guyana	22 Aug. 1968	15 Feb. 1977
Honduras	19 Dec. 1966	
Hungary	25 Mar. 1969	17 Jan. 1974
Iceland	30 Dec. 1968	22 Aug. 1979
India		10 Apr. 1979 *a*
Iran (Islamic Republic of)	4 Apr. 1968	24 June 1975
Iraq	18 Feb. 1969	25 Jan. 1971
Ireland	1 Oct. 1973	
Israel	19 Dec. 1966	
Italy	18 Jan. 1967	15 Sep. 1978
Jamaica	19 Dec. 1966	3 Oct. 1975
Japan	30 May 1978	21 June 1979
Jordan	30 June 1972	28 May 1975
Kenya		1 May 1972 *a*
Lebanon		3 Nov. 1972 *a*
Liberia	18 Apr. 1967	
Libyan Arab Jamahiriya		15 May 1970 *a*
Luxembourg	26 Nov. 1974	18 Aug. 1983
Madagascar	17 Sep. 1969	21 June 1971
Mali		16 July 1974 *a*
Mauritius		12 Dec. 1973 *a*
Mexico		23 Mar. 1981 *a*
Mongolia	5 June 1968	18 Nov. 1974
Morocco	19 Jan. 1977	3 May 1979
Netherlands	25 June 1969	11 Dec. 1978

Participant	Signature	Ratification, accession (a)
New Zealand	12 Nov. 1968	28 Dec. 1978
Nicaragua		12 Mar. 1980 *a*
Niger		7 Mar. 1986 *a*
Norway	20 Mar. 1968	13 Sep. 1972
Panama	27 July 1976	8 Mar. 1977
Peru	11 Aug. 1977	28 Apr. 1978
Philippines	19 Dec. 1966	23 Oct. 1986
Poland	2 Mar. 1967	18 Mar. 1977
Portugal	7 Oct. 1976	15 June 1978
Romania	27 June 1968	9 Dec. 1974
Rwanda		16 Apr. 1975 *a*
Saint Vincent and the Grenadines		9 Nov. 1981 *a*
San Marino		18 Oct. 1985 *a*
Senegal	6 July 1970	13 Feb. 1978
Spain	28 Sep. 1976	27 Apr. 1977
Sri Lanka		11 June 1980 *a*
Sudan		18 Mar. 1986 *a*
Suriname		28 Dec. 1976 *a*
Sweden	29 Sep. 1967	6 Dec. 1971
Syrian Arab Republic		21 Apr. 1969 *a*
Togo		24 May 1984 *a*
Trinidad and Tobago		21 Dec. 1978 *a*
Tunisia	30 Apr. 1968	18 Mar. 1969
Ukrainian SSR	20 Mar. 1968	12 Nov. 1973
Union of Soviet Socialist Republics	18 Mar. 1968	16 Oct. 1973
United Kingdom	16 Sep. 1968	20 May 1976
United Republic of Tanzania		11 June 1976 *a*
United States of America	5 Oct. 1977	
Uruguay	21 Feb. 1967	1 Apr. 1970
Venezuela	24 June 1969	10 May 1978
Viet Nam		24 Sep. 1982 *a*
Yugoslavia	8 Aug. 1967	2 June 1971
Zaire		1 Nov. 1976 *a*
Zambia		10 Apr. 1984 *a*

DECLARATIONS AND RESERVATIONS
(Unless otherwise indicated, the declarations and
reservations were made upon ratification or accession.
For objections thereto, see hereinafter.)

Afghanistan

[*See chapter I.*]

Argentina

Understanding:

The Argentine Government states that the application of the second part of article 15 of the International Covenant on Civil and Political Rights shall be subject to the principle laid down in article 18 of the Argentine National Constitution.

Australia [4]

Article 10

"In relation to paragraph 2 (*a*) the principle of segregation is accepted as an objective to be achieved progressively. In relation to paragraphs 2 (*b*) and 3 (second sentence) the obligation to segregate is accepted only to the extent that such segregation is considered by the responsible authorities to be beneficial to the juveniles or adults concerned."

Article 14

"Australia makes the reservation that the provision of compensation for miscarriage of justice in the circumstances contemplated in article 14, paragraph 6, may be by administrative procedures rather than pursuant to specific legal provision."

Article 20

"Australia interprets the rights provided for by articles 19, 21 and 22 as consistent with article 20; accordingly, the Commonwealth and the constituent States, having legislated with respect to the subject-matter of the article in matters of practical concern in the interest of public order (*ordre public*), the right is reserved not to introduce any further legislative provision on these matters."

Declaration:

"Australia has a federal constitutional system in which legislative, executive and judicial powers are shared or distributed between the Commonwealth and the constituent States. The implementation of the treaty throughout Australia will be effected by the Commonwealth, State and Territory authorities having regard to their respective constitutional powers and arrangements concerning their exercise."

Austria

1. Article 12, paragraph 4, of the Covenant will be applied provided that it will not affect the Act of 3 April 1919, State Law Gazette No. 209, concerning the Expulsion and the Transfer of Property of the House of Habsburg-Lorraine as amended by the Act of 30 October 1919, State Law Gazette No. 501, the Federal Constitutional Act of 30 July 1925, Federal Law Gazette No. 292, and the Federal Constitutional Act of 26 January 1928, Federal Law Gazette No. 30, read in conjunction with the Federal Constitutional Act of 4 July 1963, Federal Law Gazette No. 172.

2. Article 9 and article 14 of the Covenant will be applied provided that legal regulations governing the proceedings and measures of deprivation of liberty as provided for in the Administrative Procedure Acts and in the Financial Penal Act remain permissible within the framework of the judicial review by the Federal Administrative Court or the Federal Constitutional Court as provided by the Austrian Federal Constitution.

3. Article 10, paragraph 3, of the Covenant will be applied provided that legal regulations allowing for juvenile prisoners to be detained together with adults under 25 years of age who give no reason for concern as to their possible detrimental influence on the juvenile prisoner remain permissible.

4. Article 14 of the Covenant will be applied provided that the principles governing the publicity of trials as set forth in article 90 of the Federal Constitutional Law as amended in 1929 are in no way prejudiced and that

(*a*) paragraph 3, subparagraph (*d*), is not in conflict with legal regulations which stipulate that an accused person who disturbs the orderly conduct of the trial or whose presence would impede the questioning of another accused person, of a witness or of an expert can be excluded from participation in the trial;

(*b*) paragraph 5 is not in conflict with legal regulations which stipulate that after an acquittal or a lighter sentence passed by a court of the first instance, a higher tribunal may pronounce conviction or a heavier sentence for the same offence, while they exclude the convicted person's right to have such conviction or heavier sentence reviewed by a still higher tribunal;

(*c*) paragraph 7 is not in conflict with legal regulations which allow proceedings that led up to a person's final conviction or acquittal to be reopened.

5. Articles 19, 21 and 22 in connection with article 2 (1) of the Covenant will be applied provided that they are not in conflict with legal restrictions as provided for in article 16 of the Convention for the Protection of Human Rights and Fundamental Freedoms.

6. Article 26 is understood to mean that it does not exclude different treatment of Austrian nationals and aliens, as is also permissible under article 1, paragraph 2, of the International Convention on the Elimination of All Forms of Racial Discrimination.

Barbados

"The Government of Barbados states that it reserves the right not to apply in full, the guarantee of free legal assistance in accordance with article 14, paragraph 3 (*d*), of the Covenant, since, while accepting the principles contained in the same paragraph, the problems of implementation are such that full application cannot be guaranteed at present."

Belgium

Reservations:

1. With respect to articles 2, 3 and 25, the Belgian Government makes a reservation, in that under the Belgian Constitution the royal powers may be exercised only by males. With respect to the exercise of the functions of the regency, the said articles shall not preclude the application of the constitutional rules as interpreted by the Belgian State.

2. The Belgian Government considers that the provision of article 10, paragraph 2 (*a*), under which accused persons shall, save in exceptional circumstances, be segregated from convicted persons is to be interpreted in conformity with the principle, already embodied in the standard minimum rules for the treatment of prisoners [resolution (73) 5 of the Committee of Ministers of the Council of Europe of 19 January 1973], that untried prisoners shall not be put in contact with convicted prisoners against their will [rules 7 (*b*) and 85 (1)]. If they so request, accused persons may be allowed to take part with convicted persons in certain communal activities.

3. The Belgian Government considers that the provision of article 10, paragraph 3, under which juvenile offenders shall be segregated from adults and be accorded treatment appropriate to their age and legal status refers exclusively to the judicial measures provided for under the régime for the protection of minors established by the Belgian Act relating to the protection of young persons. As regards other juvenile ordinary-law offenders, the Belgian Government intends to reserve the option to adopt measures that may be more flexible and be designed precisely in the interest of the persons concerned.

4. With respect to article 14, the Belgian Government considers that the last part of paragraph 1 of the article appears to give States the option of providing or not providing for certain derogations from the principle that judgements shall be made public. Accordingly, the Belgian constitutional principle that there shall be no exceptions to the public pronouncements of judgements is in conformity with that provision. Paragraph 5 of the article shall not apply to persons who, under Belgian law, are convicted and sentenced at second instance following an appeal against their acquittal of first instance or who, under Belgian law, are brought directly before a higher tribunal such as the Court of Cassation, the Appeals Court or the Assize Court.

5. Articles 19, 21 and 22 shall be applied by the Belgian Government in the context of the provisions and restrictions set forth or authorized in articles 10 and 11 of the Convention for the Protection of Human Rights and Fundamental Freedoms of 4 November 1950, by the said Convention.

Declarations:

6. The Belgian Government declares that it does not consider itself obligated to enact legislation in the field covered by article 20, paragraph 1, and that article 20 as whole shall be applied taking into acount the rights to freedom of thought and religion, freedom of opinion and freedom of assembly and association proclaimed in articles 18, 19 and 20 of the Universal Declaration of Human Rights and reaffirmed in articles 18, 19, 21 and 22 of the Covenant.

7. The Belgian Government declares that it interprets article 23, paragraph 2, as meaning that the right of persons of marriageable age to marry and to found a family presupposes not only that national law shall prescribe the marriageable age but that it may also regulate the exercise of that right.

Bulgaria

[See chapter I.]

Byelorussian Soviet Socialist Republic

*[For the text of the declaration made upon signature
and confirmed upon ratification, see chapter I.]*

Congo

Reservation:

The Government of the People's Republic of the Congo declares that it does not consider itself bound by the provision of article 11 ...

Article 11 of the International Covenant on Civil and Political Rights is quite incompatible with articles 386 *et seq.* of the Congolese Code of Civil, Commercial, Administrative and Financial Procedure, derived from Act 51/83 of 21 April 1983. Under those provisions, in matters of private law, decisions or orders emanating from conciliation proceedings may be enforced through imprisonment for debt when other means of enforcement have failed, when the amount due exceeds 20,000 CFA francs and when the debtor, between 18 and 60 years of age, makes himself insolvent in bad faith.

Czechoslovakia

Upon signature:

The Czechoslovak Socialist Republic declares that the provision of article 48, paragraph 1, of the International Covenant on Civil and Political Rights is in contradiction with the principle that all States have the right to become parties to multilateral treaties governing matters of general interest.

Upon ratification:

The provision of article 48, paragraph 1, is in contradiction with the principle that all States have the right to become parties to multilateral treaties regulating matters of general interest.

Democratic Yemen

The accession of the People's Democratic Republic of Yemen to the International Covenant on Civil and Political Rights shall in no way signify recognition of Israel or serve as grounds for the establishment of relations of any sort with Israel.

Denmark

"1. The Government of Denmark makes a reservation in respect of article 10, paragraph 3, second sentence. In Danish practice, considerable efforts are made to ensure appropriate age distribution of convicts serving sentences of imprisonment, but it is considered valuable to maintain possibilities of flexible arrangements.

"2. (*a*) Article 14, paragraph 1, shall not be binding on Denmark in respect of public hearings. In Danish law, the right to exclude the press and the public from trials may go beyond what is permissible under this Covenant, and the Government of Denmark finds that this right should not be restricted.

"(*b*) Article 14, paragraphs 5 and 7, shall not be binding on Denmark."

[The Danish Administration of Justice Act contains detailed provisions regulating the matters dealt with in these two paragraphs. In some cases, Danish legislation is less restrictive than the Covenant (e.g. a verdict returned by a jury on the question of guilt cannot be reviewed by a higher tribunal, cf. paragraph 5); in other cases, Danish legislation is more restrictive than the Covenant (e.g. with respect to resumption of a criminal case in which the accused party was acquitted, cf. paragraph 7).]

"3. Reservation is further made to article 20, paragraph 1. This reservation is in accordance with the vote cast by Denmark in the sixteenth session of the General Assembly of the United Nations in 1961 when the Danish Delegation, referring to the preceding article concerning freedom of expression, voted against the prohibition against propaganda for war."

Finland

Reservations:

"1. With respect to article 9, paragraph 3, of the Covenant, Finland declares that according to the present Finnish legislation the administrative authorities may take decisions concerning arrest or imprisonment, in which event the case is taken up for decision in court only after a certain time lapse;

"2. With respect to article 10, paragraphs 2 (*b*) and 3, of the Covenant, Finland declares that although juvenile offenders are, as a rule, segregated from adults, it does not deem appropriate to adopt an absolute prohibition not allowing for more flexible arrangements;

"... [5]

"5. With respect to article 14, paragraph 3 (*d*), of the Covenant, Finland declares that the contents of this paragraph do not correspond to the present legislation in Finland inasmuch as it is a question of the defendant's absolute right to have legal assistance already at the stage of preliminary investigations;

"6. With respect to article 14, paragraph 7, of the Covenant, Finland declares that it is going to pursue its present practice, according to which a sentence can be changed to the detriment of the convicted person, if it is established that a member or an official of the court, the prosecutor or the legal counsel have through criminal or fraudulous activities obtained the acquittal of the defendant or a substantially more lenient penalty, or if false evidence has been presented with the same effect, and according to which an aggravated criminal case may be taken up for reconsideration if within a year until then unknown evidence is presented, which would have led to conviction or a substantially more severe penalty;

"7. With respect to article 20, paragraph 1, of the Covenant, Finland declares that it will not apply the provision of this paragraph, this being compatible with the standpoint Finland already expressed at the sixteenth session of the United Nations General Assembly by voting against the prohibition of propaganda for war, on the grounds that this might endanger the freedom of expression referred in article 19 of the Covenant."

France

Declarations and reservations:

(1) The Government of the Republic considers that, in accordance with Article 103 of the Charter of the United Nations, in case of conflict between its obligations under the Convenant and its obligations under the Charter (especially Articles 1 and 2 thereof), its obligations under the Charter will prevail.

(2) The Government of the Republic enters the following reservation concerning article 4, paragraph 1: first, the circumstances enumerated in article 16 of the Constitution in respect of its implementation, in article 1 of the Act of 3 April 1978 and in the Act of 9 August 1849 in respect of the declaration of a state of siege, in article 1 of Act No. 55-385 of 3 April 1955 in respect of the declaration of a state of emergency and which enable these instruments to be implemented, are to be understood as meeting the purpose of article 4 of the Covenant; and, secondly, for the purpose of interpreting and implementing article 16 of the Constitution of the French Republic, the terms

"to the extent strictly required by the exigencies of the situation" cannot limit the power of the President of the Republic to take "the measures required by circumstances."

(3) The Government of the Republic enters a reservation concerning articles 9 and 14 to the effect that these articles cannot impede enforcement of the rules pertaining to the disciplinary régime in the armies.

(4) The Government of the Republic declares that article 13 cannot derogate from chapter IV of Order No. 45-2658 of 2 November 1945 concerning the entry into, and sojourn in, France of aliens, nor from the other instruments concerning the expulsion of aliens in force in those parts of the territory of the Republic in which the Order of 2 November 1945 does not apply.

(5) The Government of the Republic interprets article 14, paragraph 5, as stating a general principle to which the law may make limited exceptions, for example, in the case of certain offences subject to the initial and final adjudication of a police court and of criminal offences. However, an appeal against a final decision may be made to the Court of Cassation which rules on the legality of the decision concerned.

(6) The Government of the Republic declares that articles 19, 21 and 22 of the Covenant will be implemented in accordance with articles 10, 11 and 16 of the Convention for the Protection of Human Rights and Fundamental Freedoms of 4 November 1950.

However, the Government of the Republic enters a reservation concerning article 19 which cannot derogate from the monopoly of the French radio and television broadcasting system.

(7) The Government of the Republic declares that the term "war", appearing in article 20, paragraph 1, is to be understood to mean war in contravention of international law and considers, in any case, that French legislation in this matter is adequate.

(8) In the light of article 2 of the Constitution of the French Republic, the French Government declares that article 27 is not applicable so far as the Republic is concerned.[6]

Gambia

"For financial reasons free legal assistance for accused persons is limited in our Constitution to persons charged with capital offences only. The Government of the Gambia therefore wishes to enter a reservation in respect of article 14 (3) (*d*) of the Covenant in question."

German Democratic Republic

The German Democratic Republic considers that article 48, paragraph 1, of the Covenant runs counter to the principle that all States which are guided in their policies by the purposes and principles of the Charter of the United Nations have the right to become parties to conventions which affect the interests of all States.

[Also see declaration under chapter I.]

Germany, Federal Republic of

"1. Articles 19, 21 and 22 in conjunction with article 2 (1) of the Covenant shall be applied within the scope of article 16 of the Convention for the Protection of Human Rights and Fundamental Freedoms of 4 November 1950.

"2. Article 14 (3) (*d*) of the Covenant shall be applied in such manner that it is for the court to decide whether an accused person held in custody has to appear in person at the hearing before the court of review (*Revisionsgericht*).

"3. Article 14 (5) of the Covenant shall be applied in such manner that:

"(*a*) A further appeal does not have to be instituted in all cases solely on the grounds the accused person—having been acquitted by the lower court—was convicted for the first time in the proceedings concerned by the appellate court.

"(*b*) In the case of criminal offences of minor gravity the review by a higher tribunal of a decision not imposing imprisonment does not have to be admitted in all cases.

"4. Article 15 (1) of the Covenant shall be applied in such manner that when provision is made by law for the imposition of a lighter penalty the hitherto applicable law may for certain exceptional categories of cases remain applicable to criminal offences committed before the law was amended."

Guinea

In accordance with the principle whereby all States whose policies are guided by the purposes and principles of the Charter of the United Nations are entitled to become parties to covenants affecting the interests of the international community, the Government of the Republic of Guinea considers that the provision of article 48, paragraph 1, of the International Covenant on Civil and Political Rights is contrary to the principle of the universality of international treaties and the democratization of international relations.

Guyana

In respect of article 14, paragraph 3, subparagraph (d)

"While the Government of the Republic of Guyana accept the principle of Legal Aid in all appropriate criminal proceedings, are working towards that end and at present apply it in certain defined cases, the problems of implementation of a comprehensive Legal Aid Scheme are such that full application cannot be guaranteed at this time."

In respect of article 14, paragraph 6

"While the Government of the Republic of Guyana accept the principle of compensation for wrongful imprisonment, it is not possible at this time to implement such a principle."

Hungary

[*See chapter I.*]

Iceland

The ratification is accompanied by reservations with respect to the following provisions:

1. Article 8, paragraph 3 (*a*), in so far as it affects the provisions of Icelandic law which provide that a person who is not the main provider of his family may be sentenced to a term at a labour facility in satisfaction of arrears in support payments for his child or children.

2. Article 10, paragraph 2 (*b*), and paragraph 3, second sentence, with respect to the separation of juvenile prisoners from adults. Icelandic law in principle provides for such separation but it is not considered appropriate to accept an obligation in the absolute form called for in the provisions of the Covenant.

3. Article 13, to the extent that it is inconsistent with the Icelandic legal provisions in force relating to the right of aliens to object to a decision on their expulsion.

4. Article 14, paragraph 7, with respect to the resumption of cases which have already been tried. The Icelandic law of procedure has detailed provisions on this matter which it is not considered appropriate to revise.

5. Article 20, paragraph 1, with reference to the fact that a prohibition against propaganda for war could limit the freedom of expression. This reservation is consistent with the position of Iceland at the General Assembly at its sixteenth session.

Other provisions of the Covenant shall be inviolably observed.

India

[See chapter I.]

Iraq

[See chapter I.]

Italy

Article 9, paragraph 5

The Italian Republic, considering that the expression "unlawful arrest or detention" contained in article 9, paragraph 5, could give rise to differences of interpretation, declares that it interprets the aforementioned expression as referring exclusively to cases of arrest or detention contrary to the provisions of article 9, paragraph 1.

Article 12, paragraph 4

Article 12, paragraph 4, shall be without prejudice to the application of transitional provision XIII of the Italian Constitution, respecting prohibition of the entry into and sojourn in the national territory of certain members of the House of Savoy.

Article 14, paragraph 3 (d)

The provision of article 14, paragraph 3 (*d*), is deemed to be compatible with existing Italian provisions governing trial of the accused in his presence and determining the cases in which the accused may present his own defence and those in which legal assistance is required.

Article 14, paragraph 5

Article 14, paragraph 5, shall be without prejudice to the application of existing Italian provisions which, in accordance with the Constitution of the Italian Republic, govern the conduct, at one level only, of proceedings instituted before the Constitutional Court in respect of charges brought against the President of the Republic and its Ministers.

Article 15, paragraph 1

With reference to article 15, paragraph 1, last sentence: "If, subsequent to the commission of the offence, provision is made by law for the imposition of a lighter penalty the offender shall benefit thereby", the Italian Republic deems this provision to apply exclusively to cases in progress.

Consequently, a person who has already been convicted by a final decision shall not benefit from any provision made by law, subsequent to that decision, for the imposition of a lighter penalty.

Article 19, paragraph 3

The provisions of article 19, paragraph 3, are interpreted as being compatible with the existing licensing system for national radio and television and with the restrictions laid down by law for local radio and television companies and for stations relaying foreign programmes.

Japan

[*See chapter I.*]

Libyan Arab Jamahiriya

[*See chapter I.*]

Luxembourg

(*a*) "The Government of Luxembourg considers that article 10, paragraph 3, which provides that juvenile offenders shall be segregated from adults and accorded treatment appropriate to their age and legal status, refers solely to the legal measures incorporated in the system for the protection of minors, which is the subject of the Luxembourg Youth Welfare Act. With regard to other juvenile offenders falling within the sphere of ordinary law, the Government of Luxembourg wishes to retain the option of adopting measures that might be more flexible and be designed to serve the interests of the persons concerned."

(*b*) "The Government of Luxembourg declares that it is implementing article 14, paragraph 5, since that paragraph does not conflict with the relevant Luxembourg legal statutes, which provide that, following an acquittal or a conviction by a court of first instance, a higher tribunal may deliver a sentence, confirm the sentence passed or impose a harsher penalty for the same crime. However, the tribunal's decision does not give the person declared guilty on appeal the right to appeal that conviction to a higher appellate jurisdiction."

"The Government of Luxembourg further declares that article 14, paragraph 3, shall not apply to persons who, under Luxembourg law, are remanded directly to a higher court or brought before the Assize Court."

(*c*) "The Government of Luxembourg accepts the provision in article 19, paragraph 2, provided that it does not preclude it from requiring broadcasting, television and film companies to be licensed."

(*d*) "The Government of Luxembourg declares that it does not consider itself obligated to adopt legislation in the field covered by article 20, paragraph 1, and that article 20 as a whole will be implemented taking into account the rights to freedom of thought, religion, opinion, assembly and association laid down in articles 18, 19 and 20 of the Universal Declaration of Human Rights and reaffirmed in articles 18, 19, 21 and 22 of the Covenant."

Mexico

Interpretative statements:

Article 9, paragraph 5

Under the Political Constitution of the United Mexican States and the relevant implementing legislation, every individual enjoys the guarantees relating to penal matters embodied therein, and consequently no person may be unlawfully arrested or detained. However, if by reason of false accusation or complaint any individual suffers an infringement of this basic right, he has, *inter alia*, under the provisions of the appropriate laws, an enforceable right to just compensation.

Article 18

Under the Political Constitution of the United Mexican States, every person is free to profess his preferred religious belief and to practise its ceremonies, rites and religious acts, with the limitation, with regard to public religious acts, that they must be performed in places of worship and, with regard to education, that studies carried out in establishments designed for the professional education of ministers of religion are not officially recognized. The Government of Mexico believes that these limitations are included among those established in paragraph 3 of this article.

Reservations:

Article 13

The Government of Mexico makes a reservation to this article, in view of the present text of article 33 of the Political Constitution of the United Mexican States.

Article 25, subparagraph (b)

The Government of Mexico also makes a reservation to this provision, since article 130 of the Political Constitution of the United Mexican States provides that ministers of religion shall have neither an active nor a passive vote, nor the right to form associations for political purposes.

Mongolia

[*See chapter I.*]

Netherlands

Reservations:

"*Article 10*

"The Kingdom of the Netherlands subscribes to the principle set out in paragraph 1 of this article, but it takes the view that ideas about the treatment of prisoners are so liable to change that it does not wish to be bound by the obligations set out in paragraph 2 and paragraph 3 (second sentence) of this article.

"*Article 12, paragraph 1*

"The Kingdom of the Netherlands regards the Netherlands and the Netherlands Antilles as separate territories of a State for the purpose of this provision.

"*Article 12, paragraphs 2 and 4*

"The Kingdom of the Netherlands regards the Netherlands and the Netherlands Antilles as separate countries for the purpose of these provisions.

"Article 14, paragraph 3 (d)

"The Kingdom of the Netherlands reserves the statutory option of removing a person charged with a criminal offence from the courtroom in the interests of the proper conduct of the proceedings.

"Article 14, paragraph 5

"The Kingdom of the Netherlands reserves the statutory power of the Supreme Court of the Netherlands to have sole jurisdiction to try certain categories of persons charged with serious offences committed in the discharge of a public office.

"Article 14, paragraph 7

"The Kingdom of the Netherlands accepts this provision only in so far as no obligations arise from it further to those set out in article 68 of the Criminal Code of the Netherlands and article 70 of the Criminal Code of the Netherlands Antilles as they now apply. They read:

"1. Except in cases where court decisions are eligible for review, no person may be prosecuted again for an offence in respect of which a court in the Netherlands or the Netherlands Antilles has delivered an irrevocable judgement.

"2. If the judgement has been delivered by some other court, the same person may not be prosecuted for the same offence in the case of (I) acquittal or withdrawal of proceedings or (II) conviction followed by complete execution, remission or lapse of the sentence.

"Article 19, paragraph 2

"The Kingdom of the Netherlands accepts the provision with the proviso that it shall not prevent the Kingdom from requiring the licensing of broadcasting, television or cinema enterprises.

"Article 20, paragraph 1

"The Kingdom of the Netherlands does not accept the obligation set out in this provision in the case of the Netherlands.

" . . ."7

Explanation:

"[The Kingdom of the Netherlands] clarifies that although the reservations [. . .] are partly of an interpretational nature, [it] has preferred reservations to interpretational declarations in all cases, since if the latter form were used doubt might arise concerning whether the text of the Covenant allows for the interpretation put upon it. By using the reservation form the Kingdom of the Netherlands wishes to ensure in all cases that the relevant obligations arising out of the Covenant will not apply to the Kingdom, or will apply only in the way indicated."

New Zealand

Reservations:

"The Government of New Zealand reserves the right not to apply article 10 (2) (*b*) or article 10 (3) in circumstances where the shortage of suitable facilities makes the mixing of juveniles and adults unavoidable; and further reserves the right not to apply article 10 (3) where the interests of other juveniles in an establishment require the removal of a particular juvenile offender or where mixing is considered to be of benefit to the persons concerned.

"The Government of New Zealand reserves the right not to apply article 14 (6) to the extent that it is not satisfied by the existing system for *ex gratia* payments to persons who suffer as a result of a miscarriage of justice.

"The Government of New Zealand having legislated in the areas of the advocacy of national and racial hatred and the exciting of hostility or ill will against any group of persons, and having regard to the right of freedom of speech, reserves the right not to introduce further legislation with regard to article 20.

"The Government of New Zealand reserves the right not to apply article 22 as it relates to trade unions to the extent that existing legislative measures, enacted to ensure effective trade union representation and encourage orderly industrial relations, may not be fully compatible with that article."

Norway

Subject to reservations to . . .[8] article 10, paragraph 2 (*b*) and paragraph 3, "with regard to the obligation to keep accused juvenile persons and juvenile offenders segregated from adults" and to article 14, paragraphs 5 and 7, and to article 20, paragraph 1.

Romania

Upon signature:

The Government of the Socialist Republic of Romania declares that the provision of article 48, paragraph 1, of the International Covenant on Civil and Political Rights is at variance with the principle that all States have the right to become parties to multilateral treaties governing matters of general interest.

Upon ratification:

(*a*) The State Council of the Socialist Republic of Romania considers that the provision of article 48 (1) of the International Covenant on Civil and Political Rights is inconsistent with the principle that multilateral international treaties whose purposes concern the international community as a whole must be open to universal participation.

(*b*) The State Council of the Socialist Republic of Romania considers that the maintenance in a state of dependence of certain territories referred to in article 1 (3) of the International Covenant on Civil and Political Rights is inconsistent with the Charter of the United Nations and the instruments adopted by the Organization on the granting of independence to colonial countries and peoples, including the Declaration on Principles of International Law concerning Friendly Relations and Co-operation among States in accordance with the Charter of the United Nations, adopted unanimously by the United Nations General Assembly in its resolution 2625 (XXV) of 1970, which solemnly proclaims the duty of States to promote the realization of the principle of equal rights and self-determination of peoples in order to bring a speedy end to colonialism.

Sweden

Sweden reserves the right not to apply the provisions of article 10, paragraph 3, with regard to the obligation to segregate juvenile offenders from adults, the provisions of article 14, paragraph 7, and of article 20, paragraph 1, of the Covenant.

Syrian Arab Republic

[See chapter I.]

Trinidad and Tobago

(i) The Government of the Republic of Trinidad and Tobago reserves the right not to apply in full the provision of article 4, paragraph 2, of the

Covenant since section 7 (3) of its Constitution enables Parliament to enact legislation even though it is inconsistent with sections (4) and (5) of the said Constitution;

(ii) Where at any time there is a lack of suitable prison facilities, the Government of the Republic of Trinidad and Tobago reserves the right not to apply article 10 (2) (*b*) and 10 (3) so far as those provisions require juveniles who are detained to be accommodated separately from adults;

(iii) The Government of the Republic of Trinidad and Tobago reserves the right not to apply article 12, paragraph 2, in view of the statutory provisions requiring persons intending to travel abroad to furnish tax clearance certificates;

(iv) The Government of the Republic of Trinidad and Tobago reserves the right not to apply article 14, paragraph 5, in view of the fact that section 43 of its Supreme Court of Judicature Act No. 12 of 1962 does not confer on a person convicted on indictment an unqualified right of appeal and that in particular cases, appeal to the Court of Appeal can only be done with the leave of the Court of Appeal itself or of the Privy Council;

(v) While the Government of the Republic of Trinidad and Tobago accepts the principle of compensation for wrongful imprisonment, it is not possible at this time to implement such a principle in accordance with article 14, paragraph 6, of the Covenant;

(vi) With reference to the last sentence of article 15, paragraph 1 — "If, subsequent to the commission of the offence, provision is made by law for the imposition of a lighter penalty, the offender shall benefit thereby", the Government of the Republic of Trinidad and Tobago deems this provision to apply exclusively to cases in progress. Consequently, a person who has already been convicted by a final decision shall not benefit from any provision made by law, subsequent to that decision, for the imposition of a lighter penalty;[9]

(vii) The Government of the Republic of Trinidad and Tobago reserves the right to impose lawful and/or reasonable restrictions with respect to the right of assembly under article 21 of the Covenant;

(viii) The Government of the Republic of Trinidad and Tobago reserves the right not to apply the provision of article 26 of the Covenant in so far as it applies to the holding of property in Trinidad and Tobago, in view of the fact that licences may be granted to or withheld from aliens under the Aliens Landholding Act of Trinidad and Tobago.

Ukrainian Soviet Socialist Republic

Declaration made upon signature and confirmed upon ratification:

The Ukrainian Soviet Socialist Republic declares that the provisions of article 26, paragraph 1, of the International Covenant on Economic, Social and Cultural Rights and of article 48, paragraph 1, of the International Covenant on Civil and Political Rights, under which a number of States cannot become parties to these Covenants, are of a discriminatory nature and considers that the Covenants, in accordance with the principle of sovereign equality of States, should be open for participation by all States concerned without any discrimination or limitation.

Union of Soviet Socialist Republics

Declaration made upon signature and confirmed upon ratification:

The Union of Soviet Socialist Republics declares that the provisions of article 26, paragraph 1, of the International Covenant on Economic, Social and Cultural Rights and of article 48, paragraph 1, of the International Covenant on Civil and Political Rights, under which a number of States cannot become parties to these Covenants, are of a discriminatory nature and considers that the Covenants, in accordance with the principle of sovereign equality of States, should be open for participation by all States concerned without any discrimination or limitation.

United Kingdom of Great Britain and Northern Ireland

Upon signature:

"First, the Government of the United Kingdom declare their understanding that, by virtue of Article 103 of the Charter of the United Nations, in the event of any conflict between their obligations under article 1 of the Covenant and their obligations under the Charter (in particular, under Articles 1, 2 and 73 thereof) their obligations under the Charter shall prevail.

"Secondly, the Government of the United Kingdom declare that:

"(*a*) In relation to article 14 of the Covenant, they must reserve the right not to apply, or not to apply in full, the guarantee of free legal assistance contained in paragraph 3, subparagraph (*d*), in so far as the shortage of legal practitioners and other considerations render the application of this guarantee in British Honduras, Fiji and St. Helena impossible;

"(*b*) In relation to article 23 of the Covenant, they must reserve the right not to apply the first sentence of paragraph 4 in so far as it concerns any inequality which may arise from the operation of the law of domicile;

"(*c*) In relation to article 25 of the Covenant, they must reserve the right not to apply:

"(i) Subparagraph (*b*) in so far as it may require the establishment of an elected legislature in Hong Kong and the introduction of equal suffrage, as between different electoral rolls, for elections in Fiji; and

"(ii) Subparagraph (*c*) in so far as it applies to jury service in the Isle of Man and to the employment of married women in the Civil Service of Northern Ireland, Fiji and Hong Kong.

"Lastly, the Government of the United Kingdom declare that the provisions of the Covenant shall not apply to Southern Rhodesia unless and until they inform the Secretary-General of the United Nations that they are in a position to ensure that the obligations imposed by the Covenant in respect of that territory can be fully implemented."

Upon ratification:

"First, the Government of the United Kingdom maintain their declaration in respect of article 1 made at the time of signature of the Covenant.

"The Government of the United Kingdom reserve the right to apply to members of and persons serving with the armed forces of the Crown and to persons lawfully detained in penal establishments of whatever character such laws and procedures as they may from time to time deem to be necessary for the preservation of service and custodial discipline and their acceptance of the provisions of the Covenant is subject to such restrictions as may for these purposes from time to time be authorized by law.

"Where at any time there is a lack of suitable prison facilities or where the mixing of adults and juveniles is deemed to be mutually beneficial, the Government of the United Kingdom reserve the right not to apply article 10 (2) (*b*) and 10 (3), so far as those provisions require juveniles who are detained to be accommodated separately from adults, and not to apply article 10 (2) (*a*) in Gibraltar, Montserrat and the Turks and Caicos Islands in so far as it requires segregation of accused and convicted persons.

"The Government of the United Kingdom reserve the right not to apply article 11 in Jersey.

"The Government of the United Kingdom reserve the right to interpret the provision of article 12 (1) relating to the territory of a State as applying separately to each of the territories comprising the United Kingdom and its dependencies.

"The Government of the United Kingdom reserve the right to continue to apply such immigration legislation governing entry into, stay in and departure from, the United Kingdom as they may deem necessary from time to time and, accordingly, their acceptance of article 12 (4) and of the other provisions of the Covenant is subject to the provisions of any such legislation as regards persons not at the time having the right under the law of the United Kingdom to enter and remain in the United Kingdom. The United Kingdom also reserves a similar right in regard to each of its dependent territories.

"The Government of the United Kingdom reserve the right not to apply article 13 in Hong Kong in so far as it confers a right of review of a decision to deport an alien and a right to be represented for this purpose before the competent authority.

"The Government of the United Kingdom reserve the right not to apply or not to apply in full the guarantee of free legal assistance in article 14, paragraph 3, subparagraph (*d*), in so far as the shortage of legal practitioners renders the application of this guarantee impossible in the British Virgin Islands, the Cayman Islands, the Falkland Islands, the Gilbert Islands, the Pitcairn Islands Group, St. Helena and Dependencies and Tuvalu.

"The Government of the United Kingdom interpret article 20 consistently with the rights conferred by articles 19 and 21 of the Covenant and having legislated in matters of practical concern in the interests of public order (*ordre public*) reserve the right not to introduce any further legislation. The United Kingdom also reserves a similar right in regard to each of its dependent territories.

"The Government of the United Kingdom reserve the right to postpone the application of article 23, paragraph 3, in regard to a small number of customary marriages in the Solomon Islands.

"The Government of the United Kingdom reserve the right to enact such nationality legislation as they may deem necessary from time to time to reserve the acquisition and possession of citizenship under such legislation to those having sufficient connection with the United Kingdom or any of its dependent territories and accordingly their acceptance of article 24 (3) and of the other provisions of the Covenant is subject to the provisions of any such legislation.

"The Government of the United Kingdom reserve the right not to apply article 25, subparagraph (*b*), in so far as it may require the establishment of an elected Executive or Legislative Council in Hong Kong and article 25, subparagraph (*c*), in so far as it relates to jury service in the Isle of Man.

"Lastly, the Government of the United Kingdom declare that the provisions of the Covenant shall not apply to Southern Rhodesia unless and until they inform the Secretary-General of the United Nations that they are in a position to ensure that the obligations imposed by the Covenant in respect of that territory can be fully implemented."

Venezuela

Article 60, paragraph 5, of the Constitution of the Republic of Venezuela establishes that: "No person shall be convicted in a criminal trial unless he has first been personally notified of the charges and heard in the manner prescribed by law. Persons accused of an offence against the *res publica* may be tried *in absentia*, with the guarantees and in the manner prescribed by law." Venezuela is making this reservation because article 14, paragraph 3 (*d*), of the Covenant makes no provision for persons accused of an offence against the *res publica* to be tried *in absentia*.

Viet Nam

[See chapter I.]

OBJECTIONS

(Unless otherwise indicated, the objections were made
upon ratification or accession.)

Belgium

6 November 1984

[The Belgian Government] wishes to observe that the sphere of application of article 11 is particularly restricted. In fact, article 11 prohibits imprisonment only when there is no reason for resorting to it other than the fact that the debtor is unable to fulfil a contractual obligation. Imprisonment is not incompatible with article 11 when there are other reasons for imposing this penalty, for example when the debtor, by acting in bad faith or through fraudulent manœuvres, has placed himself in the position of being unable to fulfil his obligations. This interpretation of article 11 can be confirmed by reference to the *travaux préparatoires* (see document A/2929 of 1 July 1955).

After studying the explanations provided by the Congo concerning its reservation, [the Belgian Government] has provisionally concluded that this reservation is unnecessary. It is its understanding that the Congolese legislation authorizes imprisonment for debt when other means of enforcement have failed when the amount due exceeds 20,000 CFA francs and when the debtor, between 18 and 60 years of age, makes himself insolvent in bad faith. The latter condition is sufficient to show that there is no contradiction between the Congolese legislation and the letter and the spirit of article 11 of the Covenant.

By virtue of article 4, paragraph 2, of the aforementioned Covenant, article 11 is excluded from the sphere of application of the rule which states that in the event of an exceptional public emergency, the States parties to the Covenant may, in certain conditions, take measures derogating from their obligations under the Covenant. Article 11 is one of the articles containing a provision from which no derogation is permitted in any circumstances. Any reservation concerning that article would destroy its effects and would therefore be in contradiction with the letter and the spirit of the Covenant.

Consequently, and without prejudice to its firm belief that Congolese law is in complete conformity with the provision of article 11 of the Covenant, [the Belgian Government] fears that the reservation made by the Congo may, by reason of its very principle, constitute a precedent which might have considerable effects at the international level.

[The Belgian Government] therefore hopes that this reservation will be withdrawn and, as a precautionary measure, wishes to raise an objection to that reservation.

France

The Government of the Republic takes objection to the reservation entered by the Government of the Republic of India to article 1 of the International Covenant on Civil and Political Rights, as this reservation attaches conditions not provided for by the Charter of the United Nations to the exercise of the right of self-determination. The present declaration will not be deemed to be an obstacle to the entry into force of the Covenant between the French Republic and the Republic of India.

Germany, Federal Republic of

[*See chapter I.*]

21 April 1982

"The Government of the Federal Republic of Germany objects to the [reservation (i) by the Government of Trinidad and Tobago]. In the opinion of the Government of the Federal Republic of Germany it follows from the text and the history of the Covenant that the said reservation is incompatible with the object and purpose of the Covenant."

Netherlands

12 June 1980

"In the opinion of the Government of the Kingdom of the Netherlands it follows from the text and the history of the Covenant that [reservation (i) by the Government of Trinidad and Tobago] is incompatible with the object and purpose of the Covenant. The Government of the Kingdom of the Netherlands therefore considers the reservation unacceptable and formally raises an objection to it."

12 January 1981

[*See chapter I.*]

17 September 1981

I. *Reservation by Australia regarding articles 2 and 50*

"The reservation that article 2, paragraphs 2 and 3, and article 50 shall be given effect consistently with and subject to the provision in article 2, paragraph 2, is acceptable to the Kingdom on the understanding that it will in no way impair Australia's basic obligation under international law, as laid down in article 2, paragraph 1, to respect and to ensure to all individuals within its territory and subject to its jurisdiction the rights recognized in the International Covenant on Civil and Political Rights."

II. *Reservation by Australia regarding article 10*

"The Kingdom is not able to evaluate the implications of the first part of the reservation regarding article 10 on its merits, since Australia has given no further explanation on the laws and lawful arrangements, as referred to in the text of the reservation. In expectation of further clarification by Australia, the Kingdom for the present reserves the right to raise objection to the reservation at a later stage."

III. *Reservation by Australia regarding "Convicted Persons"*

"The Kingdom finds it difficult, for the same reasons as mentioned in its commentary on the reservation regarding article 10, to accept the declaration by Australia that it reserves the right not to seek amendment of laws now in force in Australia relating to the rights of persons who have been convicted of serious criminal offences. The Kingdom expresses the hope it will be possible to gain a more detailed insight in the laws now in force in Australia, in order to facilitate a definitive opinion on the extent of this reservation."

6 November 1984

[*Same objection as the one made by Belgium.*]

DECLARATIONS RECOGNIZING THE COMPETENCE OF THE HUMAN RIGHTS COMMITTEE UNDER ARTICLE 41 [10]

(Unless otherwise indicated, the declarations were
made upon ratification or accession)

Argentina

The instrument contains a declaration under article 41 of the Covenant by which the Government of Argentina recognizes the competence of the Human Rights Committee established by virtue of the International Covenant on Civil and Political Rights.

Austria

10 September 1978

[The Government of the Republic of Austria] declares under article 41 of the International Covenant on Civil and Political Rights that Austria recognizes the competence of the Human Rights Committee to receive and consider communications to the effect that a State party claims that another State party is not fulfilling its obligations under the International Covenant on Civil and Political Rights.

Belgium

5 March 1987

The Kingdom of Belgium declares that it recognizes the competence of the Human Rights Committee under article 41 of the International Covenant on Civil and Political Rights.

18 June 1987

The Kingdom of Belgium declares, under article 41 of the International Covenant on Civil and Political Rights, that it recognizes the competence of the Human Rights Committee established under article 28 of the Covenant to receive and consider communications submitted by another State party, provided that such State party has, not less than twelve months prior to the submission by it of a communication relating to Belgium, made a declaration under article 41 recognizing the competence of the Committee to receive and consider communications relating to itself.

Canada

29 October 1979

"The Government of Canada declares, under article 41 of the International Covenant on Civil and Political Rights, that it recognizes the competence of the Human Rights Committee referred to in article 28 of the said Covenant to receive and consider communications submitted by another State party, provided that such State party has, not less than twelve months prior to the submission by it of a communication relating to Canada, made a declaration under article 41 recognizing the competence of the Committee to receive and consider communications relating to itself."

Denmark

19 April 1983[11]

"[The Government of Denmark] recognizes, in accordance with article 41 of the International Covenant on Civil and Political Rights, opened for signature in New York on 19 December 1966, the competence of the Committee referred to in article 41 to receive and consider communications to the effect that a State party claims that another State party is not fulfilling its obligations under the Covenant."

Ecuador

6 August 1984

... The Government of Ecuador recognizes the competence of the Human Rights Committee to receive and consider communications to the effect that a State party claims that another State party is not fulfilling its obligations under the aforementioned Covenant, as provided for in paragraph 1 (*a*), (*b*), (*c*), (*d*), (*e*), (*f*), (*g*) and (*h*) of that article.

This recognition of competence is effective for an indefinite period and is subject to the provisions of article 41, paragraph 2, of the International Covenant on Civil and Political Rights.

Finland

19 August 1975

"Finland declares, under article 41 of the International Covenant on Civil and Political Rights that it recognizes the competence of the Human Rights Committee referred to in article 28 of the said Covenant, to receive and consider communications to the effect that a State party claims that another State party is not fulfilling its obligation under this Covenant."

Germany, Federal Republic of[12]

24 March 1986[13]

The Federal Republic of Germany, in accordance with article 41 of the said Covenant, recognizes for a further five years from the date of expiry of the declaration of 28 March 1981 the competence of the Human Rights Committee to receive and consider communications from the State party in so far as that State party has recognized in regard to itself the competence of the Committee and as corresponding obligations have been assumed under the Covenant by the Federal Republic of Germany and by the State party concerned.

Iceland

22 August 1979

"The Government of Iceland ... recognizes in accordance with article 41 of the International Covenant on Civil and Political Rights the competence of the Human Rights Committee referred to in article 28 of the Covenant to receive and consider communications to the effect that a State party claims that another State party is not fulfilling its obligations under the Covenant."

Italy

15 September 1978

The Italian Republic recognizes the competence of the Human Rights Committee, elected in accordance with article 28 of the Covenant, to receive and consider communications to the effect that a State party claims that another State party is not fulfilling its obligations under the Covenant.

Luxembourg

18 August 1983

"The Government of Luxembourg recognizes, in accordance with article 41, the competence of the Human Rights Committee referred to in article 28 of the Covenant to receive and consider communications to the effect that a State party claims that another State party is not fulfilling its obligations under the Covenant."

Netherlands

11 December 1978

"The Kingdom of the Netherlands declares under article 41 of the International Covenant on Civil and Political Rights that it recognizes the competence of the Human Rights Committee referred to in article 28 of the Covenant to receive and consider communications to the effect that a State party claims that another State party is not fulfilling its obligations under the Covenant."

New Zealand

28 December 1978

"The Government of New Zealand declares under article 41 of the International Covenant on Civil and Political Rights that it recognises the competence of the Human Rights Committee to receive and consider communications from another State party which has similarly declared under article 41 its recognition of the Committee's competence in respect to itself except where the declaration by such a State party was made less than twelve months prior to the submission by it of a complaint relating to New Zealand."

Norway

31 August 1972

"Norway recognizes the competence of the Human Rights Committee referred to in article 28 of the Covenant, to receive and consider communications to the effect that a State party claims that another State party is not fulfilling its obligations under the Covenant."

Peru

9 April 1984

Peru recognizes the competence of the Human Rights Committee to receive and consider communications to the effect that a State party claims that another State party is not fulfilling its obligations under the International Covenant on Civil and Political Rights, in accordance with article 41 of the said Covenant.

Philippines

"The Philippine Government, in accordance with article 41 of the said Covenant, recognizes the competence of the Human Rights Committee set up in the aforesaid Covenant, to receive and consider communications to the effect that a State party claims that another State party is not fulfilling its obligations under the Covenant."

Senegal

5 January 1981

The Government of Senegal declares, under article 41 of the International Covenant on Civil and Political Rights, that it recognizes the competence of the Human Rights Committee referred to in article 28 of the said Covenant to receive and consider communications submitted by another

State party, provided that such State party has, not less than twelve months prior to the submission by it of a communication relating to Senegal, made a declaration under article 41 recognizing the competence of the Committee to receive and consider communications relating to itself.

Spain

25 January 1985

The Spanish Government declares, with reference to the provisions of article 41 of the International Covenant on Civil and Political Rights, that it recognizes, for a period of three years starting on the date of the deposit of this Declaration, the competence of the Human Rights Committee to receive and consider communications to the effect that a State party claims that another State party is not fulfilling its obligations under the Covenant.

Sri Lanka

11 June 1980

"The Government of the Democratic Socialist Republic of Sri Lanka declares under article 41 of the International Covenant on Civil and Political Rights that it recognizes the competence of the Human Rights Committee to receive and consider communications to the effect that a State party claims that another State party is not fulfilling its obligations under the Covenant, from another State party which has similarly declared under article 41 its recognition of the Committee's competence in respect to itself."

Sweden

26 November 1971

"Sweden recognizes the competence of the Human Rights Committee referred to in article 28 of the Covenant to receive and consider communications to the effect that a State Party claims that another State party is not fulfilling its obligations under the Covenant."

United Kingdom of Great Britain
and Northern Ireland

"The Government of the United Kingdom declare under article 41 of this Covenant that they recognize the competence of the Human Rights Committee to receive and consider communications submitted by another State party, provided that such other State party has, not less than twelve months prior to the submission by it of a communication relating to the United Kingdom made a declaration under article 41 recognizing the competence of the Committee to receive and consider communications relating to itself."

NOTIFICATIONS UNDER ARTICLE 4 (3) OF THE COVENANT (DEROGATIONS)

Bolivia

1 October 1985

[Dated 27 September 1985]

By Supreme Decree No. 21069, the Government of Bolivia declared a temporary state of siege throughout the country, with effect from 18 September 1985.

The notification specifies that the Government of Bolivia has been compelled to declare a temporary state of siege in order to discharge its obligation to ensure the maintenance of the rule of law, the constitutional system, democratic continuity and the safeguarding of the country's institutions and public order, these being essential to the life of the Republic and to the process of economic recovery initiated by the Government so as to save Bolivia from the scourge of hyperinflation, which had come to threaten the very life of the country.

The notification further specifies that the measure was adopted to counter the social unrest which sought to supplant the legitimately constituted authorities by establishing itself as an authority which publicly proclaimed the repudiation of the law and openly called for subversion, and to counter the occupation of State facilities and buildings and the interruption of services which are essential to the normal pursuit of all public activities.

In a complementary notification dated 28 October 1985, received on 29 October 1985, the Government of Bolivia indicated that the provisions of the Covenant from which it is derogated from concern articles 9, 12 and 21.

9 January 1986

[6 January 1986]

Notification to the effect that at the end of the constitutional period of 90 days the Supreme Government has not found it necessary to prolong the emergency situation and that the guarantees and rights of citizens had been fully restored throughout the national territory, with effect from 19 December 1985 and advising that, accordingly, the provisions of the Covenant were again being implemented in accordance with the stipulations of its relevant articles.

29 August 1986

[28 August 1986]

The notification indicates that the state of emergency was proclaimed because of serious political and social disturbances, *inter alia:* a general strike in Potosi and Druro which paralysed illegally those cities; the hyperinflationary crisis suffered by the country; the need for rehabilitation of the Bolivian mining structures; the subversive activities of the extreme left; the desperate reaction of the drug trafficking mafia in response to the successful government campaign of eradication; and in general plans aiming to overthrow the constitutional Government.

28 November 1986

[Dated 28 November 1986]

Notification, identical in essence, *mutatis mutandis,* as that of 9 January 1986. With effect from 29 November 1986.

Chile

7 September 1976

[Chile] has been under a state of siege for reasons of internal defence since 11 March 1976; the state of siege was legally proclaimed by Legislative Decree No. 1369.

The proclamation was made in accordance with the constitutional provisions concerning state of siege, which have been in force since 1925, in view of the inescapable duty of the government authorities to preserve public order and the fact that there continue to exist in Chile extremist seditious groups whose aim is to overthrow the established Government.

As a consequence of the proclamation of the state of siege, the rights referred to in articles 9, 12, 13, 19 and 25 (*b*) of the International Covenant on Civil and Political Rights have been restricted in Chile.

23 September 1986

[Dated 16 September 1986]

By Decree No. 1037, the Government of Chile declared a state of siege throughout the national territory from 8 September to 6 December 1986, for as long as circumstances warrant. The notification specifies that Chile has been subjected to a wave of terrorist aggression of alarming proportions, that an alarming number of attacks have taken the lives of a significant number of citizens and armed forces personnel, massive stockpiles of weapons were discovered in terrorists' hands, and that for the first time in the history of the Republic, a terrorist attack was launched on H. E. the President of the Republic.

The notification specifies that the rights set forth in articles 9, 12, 13 and 19 of the Covenant would be derogated from.

29 October 1986

[Dated 28 October 1986]

Termination of state of siege by Decree No. 1074 of 26 September 1986 in the Eleventh Region and by Decree No. 1155 of 16 October 1986 in the Twelfth Region (with the exception of the Commune of Punta Arenas), in the province of Chiloé in the Tenth Region, and in the province of Parinacota in the First Region.

20 November 1986

[Dated 20 November 1986]

Termination of the state of siege in the provinces of Cardenal Caro in the Sixth Region, Arauco in the Eighth Region and Palena in the Tenth Region.

29 January 1987

[Dated 20 January 1987]

Termination of the state of siege throughout Chile as at 6 January 1987.

Colombia

18 July 1980

The Government, by Decree No. 2131 of 1976, declared that public order had been disturbed and that all of the national territory was in a state of siege, the requirements of the Constitution having been fulfilled, and that in the face of serious events that disturbed the public peace, it had become necessary to adopt extraordinary measures within the framework of the legal régime provided for in the National Constitution for such situations (art. 121 of the National Constitution).

The events disturbing the public peace that led the President of the Republic to take that decision are a matter of public knowledge. Under the stage of siege (art. 121 of the National Constitution) the Government is empowered to suspend, for the duration of the state of siege, those provisions that are incompatible with the maintenance and restoration of public order.

On many occasions the President of the Republic has informed the country of his desire to terminate the state of siege when the necessary circumstances prevail.

It should be observed that, during the state of siege in Colombia, the institutional order has remained unchanged, with the Congress and all public bodies functioning normally. Public freedoms were fully respected during the most recent elections, both the election of the President of the Republic and the election of members of elective bodies.

11 October 1982

By Decree No. 1674 of 9 June 1982, the state of siege was terminated on 20 June 1982.

11 April 1984

[Dated 30 March 1984]

The Government of Colombia had declared a breach of the peace and a state of siege in the territory of the Departments of Caquetá, Huila, Meta and Cauca in response to the activities in those Departments of armed groups which were seeking to undermine the constitutional system by means of repeated public disturbances.

Further to Decree No. 615, Decrees Nos. 666, 667, 668, 669 and 670 had been enacted on 21 March 1984 to restrict certain freedoms and to take other measures aimed at restoring public order. (For the provisions which were derogated from, see *in fine* notification of 8 June 1984 hereinafter.)

8 June 1984

[Dated 7 May 1984]

The Government of Colombia indicated that it had, through Decree No. 1038 of 1 May 1984, declared a state of siege in the territory of the Republic of Colombia owing to the assassination in April of the Minister of Justice and to recent disturbances of the public order that occurred in the cities of Bogotá, Cali, Barranquilla, Medellín, Acevedo (Department of Santander), Giraldo (Department of Antioquia) and Miraflores (*Comisaría* of Guaviare).

Pursuant to the above-mentioned Decree No. 1038, the Government had issued Decrees Nos. 1039 and 1040 of 1 May 1984 and Decree No. 1042 of 2

May 1984, restricting certain freedoms and enacting other measures to restore public order. (Following inquiries made by the Secretary-General, in keeping with the purpose of article 4 (3) of the Covenant, as to which articles of the Covenant were being derogated from, the Government of Colombia, in a communication dated 23 November 1984, which was received by the Secretary-General on that date, indicated that the decrees affected the rights referred to in articles 12 and 21 of the Covenant.)

12 December 1984

[Dated 11 December 1984]

Termination of derogation from article 21.

Ecuador

12 May 1983

The Government declared the extension of the state of emergency as from 20 to 25 October 1982 by Executive Decree No. 1252 of 20 October 1982 and derogation from article 12 (1) owing to serious disorders brought about by the suppression of subsidies, and termination of the state of emergency by Executive Decree No. 1274 of 27 October 1982.

20 March 1984

Derogation from articles 9 (1) and (2); 12 (1) and (3); 17; 19 (2) and 21 in the provinces of Napo and Esmeraldas by Executive Decree No. 2511 of 16 March 1984 owing to destruction and sabotage in these areas.

29 March 1984

Termination of the state of emergency by Executive Decree No. 2537 of 27 March 1984.

17 March 1986

[Dated 14 March 1986]

Declaration of the state of emergency in the provinces of Pichincha and Manabi due to the acts of subversion and armed uprising by a high-ranking officer no longer on active service, backed by extremist groups; thereby derogations from articles 12, 21 and 22, it being understood that no Ecuadorian may be exiled or deported outside the capitals of the provinces or to a region other than the one in which he lives.

19 March 1986

[Dated 18 March 1986]

End of state of emergency as from 17 March 1986.

El Salvador

14 November 1983

[Dated 3 November 1983]

The Government has declared an extension for a period of 30 days of the suspension of constitutional guarantees by Legislative Decree No. 329 dated 28 October 1983. The constitutional guarantees have been suspended in accordance with article 175 of the Political Constitution because of disruption of public order.

In a complementary notification dated 23 January 1984 and received on 24 January 1984, the Government of El Salvador specified the following:

1. The provisions of the Covenant from which it is derogated are articles 12 and 19 by Decree No. 329 of 28 August 1983, and article 17 (in respect of interference with correspondence);

2. The constitutional guarantees were first suspended by Decree No. 155 dated 6 March 1980, with further extensions of the suspension for a total of 24 months. Decree No. 155 was modified by Decree No. 999 dated 24 February 1982, which expired on 24 March 1982. By Decree No. 1089 dated 20 April 1982, the Revolutionary Government Junta again suspended the constitutional guarantees. By Legislative Decree No. 7 dated 20 May 1982, the Constituent Assembly extended the suspension for an additional period of 30 days. The said Legislative Decree No. 7 was itself extended several times until the adoption of the above-mentioned Decree No. 329 dated 28 October 1983, which took effect on that date.

3. The reasons for the adoption of the initial suspension decree (No. 155 of 6 March 1980) were the same as for the adoption of the subsequent decrees.

18 June 1984

[Dated 14 June 1984]

By Legislative Decree No. 28 of 27 January 1984, previous measures were amended to the effect that political parties would be permitted to conduct electoral campaigns, and were thus authorized to engage in partisan campaigning and electoral propaganda activities. The said Decree was extended for successive 30-day periods until the promulgation of Decree No. 97 of 17 May 1984, which rescinded the aforementioned change which had allowed political parties to conduct electoral campaigns.

The provisions of the Covenant from which it is derogated are articles 12, 19, 17 (in respect of interference with correspondence) and 21 and 22. As regards article 22, the suspension refers to the right of association in general, but does not affect the right to join professional associations (the right to form and join trade union).

2 August 1985

[Dated 31 July 1985)

[. . .] the Government of El Salvador has for successive periods extended martial law by the following legislative decrees:

> Decrees No. 127 of 21 June 1984, No. 146 of 19 July 1984, No. 175 of 24 August 1984, No. 210 of 18 September 1984, No. 234 of 21 October 1984, No. 261 of 20 November 1984, No. 277 of 14 December 1984, No. 322 of 18 January 1985, No. 335 of 21 February 1985, No. 351 of 14 March 1985, No. 386 of 18 April 1985, No. 10 of 21 May 1985, No. 38 of 13 June 1985, and the most recent, Decree No. 96 of 11 July 1985 which extended the martial law for an additional period of 30 days beyond that date.

The provisions of the Covenant that are thus suspended are those of articles 12, 17 (in respect of interference with correspondence) and 19 (2).

The notification specifies that the reasons for the suspension of constitutional guarantees continue to be those originally indicated, namely: the need to maintain a climate of peace and tranquility, which had been disturbed through the commission of acts designed to create a state of instability and social unrest which affected the economy and the public peace by persons seeking to obstruct the process of structural change, thus seriously disrupting public order.

Nicaragua

4 June 1980

The Governing Junta for National Reconstruction of the Republic of Nicaragua by Decree No. 383 of 29 April 1980, rescinded the National Emergency Act promulgated on 22 July 1979 and revoked the state of emergency extended by Decree No. 365 of 11 April 1980.

14 April 1982

Suspension of articles 1-5, 8 (3), 10, 12-14, 17, 19-22, 26 and 27 in accordance with Decree No. 996 of 15 March 1982 (national emergency) from 15 March to 14 April 1982. Extension of the suspension to 14 May 1982.

8 June 1982

Extension of the suspension to 14 June 1982.

26 August 1982

Suspension of the above-mentioned articles of the Covenant in accordance with Decree No. 1082 of 26 July 1982 from 26 July 1982 to 26 January 1983.

14 December 1982

Extension of the suspension to 30 May 1983.

8 June 1984

Extension of the state of emergency for fifty days beginning on 31 May 1984 and derogation from article 2, paragraph 3; articles 9, 12 and 14; article 19, paragraphs 2 and 3; and article 21 of the Covenant.

1 August 1984

[Dated 10 June 1984]

Extension of the state of emergency until 30 May 1984 by Decree No. 1255 of 26 May 1984 and derogations from articles 1 to 5; article 8, paragraph 3; articles 9, 10, 12, 13, 14, 19 to 22; and articles 26 and 27.

22 August 1984

[Dated 2 August 1984]

Extension of the state of emergency until 20 October 1984 and derogation from articles 2 (3), 9 and 14 of the Covenant by Legislative Decree No. 1477 of 19 July 1984.

[Dated 9 August 1984]

Derogation from the implementation of articles 2 (3), 9 and 14 of the Covenant from 6 August to 20 October 1984, in respect of persons committing or suspected of committing the offences referred to in articles 1 and 2 of the Act concerning the Maintenance of Order and Public Security.

13 November 1985

[Dated 11 November 1985]

... In accordance with article 4 of the International Covenant on Civil and Political Rights [the] Government [of Nicaragua] has been obliged, as a result of the foreign aggression to which it is being subjected, to suspend the application of certain of the provisions of the Covenant throughout the national territory, for a period of one year starting on 30 October 1985.

The reasons for this suspension are [the following]: the Government of the United States of America, against the express will of the majority of the world's governments and peoples and in violation of the norms of international law has continued its unjust, unlawful and immoral aggression against the Nicaraguan people and their revolutionary Government.

The political and diplomatic efforts exerted by [the] Government [of Nicaragua], by the nations of the Contadora Group and by other peace-loving countries to change this criminal and aggressive policy have all proved fruitless.

The Government of the United States, instead of scaling down its aggression, has in the past few months intensified it, supplying the bands of mercenaries with more and improved weapons so that they can go on committing murder, destroying productive infrastructure through terrorist attacks, in short, bringing more pain, grief, death and economic difficulties to the Nicaraguan people. This intensification of terrorist acts is due in part to the fact that the United States Government has started to distribute to the counter-revolutionary bands the $27 million that was authorized by the United States Congress in June 1985 as "humanitarian aid".

... The following provisions of the Covenant [are suspended] throughout the national territory for the period of one year, starting on 29 October 1985:

Article 8 (3); article 9; article 10, except paragraph 1; article 12 (2) and (4); article 14, except paragraphs 2 and 5 and subparagraphs (a), (b), (d) and (g) of paragraph 3; article 17; article 19; article 21 and article 22.

Article 2 (2) remains in force for those rights that have not been suspended, and paragraph 3 of the same remains in force for all those offences which do not affect national security and public order.

30 January 1987

Re-establishment as of 9 January 1987 of the state of national emergency with suspension of the following provisions of the Covenant throughout the territory of Nicaragua until 8 January 1988:

Article 2 (3) is suspended in respect of acts which undermine national security and public order and of the rights and guarantees set forth in those provisions of the Covenant which have been suspended;

Article 9, although the recourse referred to in paragraph 4 is suspended solely for offences against national security and public order. Article 12 and article 14 (3) (c); article 17, in so far as it relates to home and correspondence, with the other rights remaining in effect; and articles 19, 21 and 22.

13 May 1987

[Dated 9 April 1987]

Further extension of the state of emergency:

"... it [is] advisable and necessary to adduce as evidence the events which have prompted [the] Government to renew the state of national emergency.

"In this regard, [the Government would] like to refer to the most recent report of the Inter-American Commission on Human Rights (ICHR), issued in 1986, which acknowledges the justice of the Nicaraguan Government's promulgation of the state of national emergency, in view of the seriousness and scope of the situation prevailing in the country as a result of the cruel, illegal and immoral war of aggression imposed on Nicaragua by the United States.

"That aggressive policy is still being pursued, as is shown by the funds and military equipment recently supplied by the Reagan Administration to the mercenary forces who, using terrorist methods, have escalated their attacks on the civilian population and civilian targets, as can be seen from the recent attacks using C-4 explosives, which destroyed two electricity pylons at Peñas Blancas and, on a previous occasion, destroyed an electricity pylon near Nicaragua's northern border using similar methods.

"These events have been denounced in international forums and by the world community at large, and [the] Government has repeatedly requested the United States Government to cease its aggression against [our] country and comply with the judgment of 27 June 1986 of the International Court of Justice.

"The conflict that Nicaragua is facing has already claimed more than 33,000 victims and is all the more serious and detrimental because the parties are clearly unevenly matched. This is aggression directed, organized and financed by one of the major military and economic Powers in the world, which is attacking the impoverished, underdeveloped and tiny country of Nicaragua which, only seven years ago, waged a bloody war of national liberation in which more than 50,000 Nicaraguans lost their lives.

"Few countries in the world have suffered aggression of the scale and scope of that confronting Nicaragua; this aggression has been condemned by the International Court of Justice and justifies the strict suspension of the guarantees provided under article 4 of the International Covenant on Civil and Political Rights. [The] Government has, however, tried to maintain in force the maximum number of guarantees possible in the current circumstances.

"Moreover, it should be noted that of the 66 articles combined in Title IV of the Political Constitution of Nicaragua, dealing with civil and political rights, 54 cannot be affected by the state of emergency. In fact, of the 12 articles suspended, 6 are totally suspended and the remaining 6 are only partially suspended.

"In view of the foregoing, ... a state of national emergency has been established in the Republic of Nicaragua, in accordance with article 4 of the Covenant, under which the following provisions thereof are suspended throughout the territory of Nicaragua for a period of one year, as of 28 February 1987:

"Article 2, paragraph 3, in which we draw a distinction between administrative *amparo* which is suspended in respect of the rights and guarantees provided in the Covenant, which have been suspended, and the remedy of *habeas corpus,* which is not applicable to offences against national security and public order;

"Article 9. It should be understood that the remedy referred to in paragraph 4 is suspended solely in respect of offences against national security and public order;

"Article 12, regarding the right of residence, liberty of movement and freedom to enter and leave the country;

"Article 14, paragraph 3 (*c*), regarding the right to be tried without undue delay;

"Article 17, in respect of the inviolability of the home and correspondence, with the other rights remaining in effect;

"Article 19, paragraphs 1 and 2, regarding the right to hold opinions and freedom of expression."

Panama

12 June 1987

[Dated 11 June 1987]

Communication received to the effect that the Government of Panama had declared a state of emergency throughout the territory of the Republic of Panama.

The notification specifies that the state of emergency was declared since, on 9 and 10 June 1987, there were outbreaks of violence, clashes between demonstrators and units of defence forces, and incitement to violence by individuals and political groups resulting in personal injury and considerable material damage. The measure was taken with a view to restoring law and order and safeguarding the life, the dignity and the property of Panamanian nationals and of foreigners living in Panama.

The notification further specifies that this exceptional measure will apply as long as reasons for the disruption of law and order remain. The articles of the Covenant being derogated from are articles 12, paragraph 1; 17, with regard only to the inviolability of correspondence; 19 and 21.

1 July 1987

[Dated 30 June 1987]

Notification that, by a resolution of the Legislative Assembly dated 30 June 1987, all constitutional guarantees suspended on 11 June 1987 had been reinstated.

The notification further informs that, in the text of the resolution reinstating the aforementioned guarantees, the Legislative Assembly states that "at national level, there has been a marked improvement in the situation which prompted the declaration of the state of emergency and the suspension of individual guarantees" and that "the country is now facing foreign aggression through the United States Senate".

Peru

22 March 1983

[Dated 18 March 1983]

First notification

The Government has declared the extension of the state of emergency in the provinces of Huanta, La Mar, Cangallo, Víctor Fajardo and Huamanga, in the Department of Ayacucho, Andahuaylas in the Department of Apurímac, and Angaraes, Tayacaja and Acobamba in the Department of Huancavelica and for a period of 60 days from the date of the issue of the Supreme Decree No. 003-83-IN of 25 February 1983.

Suspension of the constitutional guarantees provided for in article 2, paragraphs 7, 9, 10 and 20 (*g*) of the Political Constitution of Peru, which relate to the inviolability of the home, liberty of movement in the national territory, the right of peaceful assembly and the right to liberty and security of person.

Second notification

Extension of a state of emergency in the Department of Lima by Supreme Decree No. 005-83-IN of 9 March [1983], and suspension for a period of five days of the constitutional guarantees provided for in article 2, paragraphs 9, 10 and 20 (*g*) of the Political Constitution of Peru relating to liberty of movement in the national territory, the right of peaceful assembly and the right to liberty and security of persons.

Suspension of the state of emergency as from 14 March 1983. In a communication received by the Secretary-General on 4 April 1983, the Government of Peru specified that the state of emergency extended by Supreme Decree No. 003-83-IN of 25 February 1983 was originally proclaimed by Supreme Decree No. 026-81-IN of 12 October 1981. It further specified that the provisions of the Covenant from which it was derogated by reason of the proclamation of the state of emergency were articles 9, 12, 17 and 21.

3 May 1983

[Dated 27 April 1983]

Extension of derogations (articles 9, 12, 17 and 21) for a further 60 days by Supreme Decree No. 014-83-IN of 22 April 1983 and extension of the suspension of constitutional guarantees provided for in article 2, paragraphs 7, 9, 10 and 20 (*g*) of the Political Constitution of Peru, which correspond to articles 17, 12, 21, and 9 of the Covenant.

2 June 1983

[Dated 28 May 1983]

Extension of the state of emergency for a period of three days in Lima and in the province of Callao by Supreme Decree No. 020-83 of 25 May 1983, and derogations from articles 9, 12, 17 and 21 of the Covenant.

[Dated 31 May 1983]

Extension of the state of emergency for a period of 60 days throughout the Republic by Supreme Decree No. 022-83 of 30 May 1983 and derogations from articles 9, 12, 17 and 21 of the Covenant.

9 August 1983

[Dated 8 August 1983]

Further extension of the state of emergency in its national territory for 60 days by Supreme Decree No. 036-83 of 2 August 1983, and derogations from articles 9, 12, 17 and 21 of the Covenant.

29 September 1983

Termination as from 9 September 1983 of the state of emergency and of the derogations with the exceptions of the Departments of Huancavelica, Ayacucho and Apurímac.

9 November 1983

[Dated 3 November 1983]

Extension of the state of emergency in the provinces of Huanta, La Mar, Cangallo, Victor Fajardo and Huamanga (Department of Ayacucho), Andahuaylas (Department of Apurímac), Angaraes, Tayacaja and Acobamba (Department of Huancavelica) by Supreme Decree No. 054-83 of 22 October 1983 and continuation of the derogations from articles 9, 12, 17 and 21 of the Covenant.

20 December 1983

[Dated 19 December 1983]

Extension of the state of emergency in the provinces of Lucanas and Ayacucho (Department of Ayacucho) and the province of Huancavelica (Department of Huancavelica) by Supreme Decree No. 061-83-IN of 6 December 1983, and derogations from articles 9, 12, 17 and 21 of the Covenant.

13 February 1984

[Dated 31 January 1984]

Extension of the state of emergency for 60 days in the provinces of Huanta, La Mar, Cangallo, Víctor Fajardo and Huamanga (Department of Ayacucho), Andahuaylas (Department of Apurímac), Angaraes, Tayacaja and Acobamba (Department of Huancavelica), and in the districts of Querobamba and Cabana (Department of Ayacucho), and throughout the provinces of Lucanas (Department of Ayacucho) and Huancavelica (Department of Huancavelica) by Supreme Decree No. 061-83-IN of 6 December 1983, and derogations from articles 9, 12, 17 and 21 of the Covenant in the above-mentioned provinces and districts.

28 March 1984

[Dated 26 March 1984]

Extension of state of emergency throughout Peru from 21 to 23 March 1984, and derogations from articles 9, 12, 17 and 21 of the Covenant.

14 May 1984

[Dated 19 April 1984]

Continuation of state of emergency for a period of 60 days in the provinces of Huanta, La Mar, Cangallo, Víctor Fajardo and Huamanga and Lucanas (Department of Ayacucho); Andahuaylas and Chincheros (Department of Apurímac); Angaraes, Tayacaja, Acobamba, Huancavelica and Castrovirreyna (Department of Huancavelica) by Decree No. 031-84-IN of 17 April 1984 and derogations from articles 9, 12, 17 and 21 of the Covenant.

18 June 1984

[Dated 15 June 1984]

Declaration of the state of emergency for a period of 30 days, starting from 8 June 1984, in the whole of the territory of the Republic of Peru and derogations from articles 9, 12, 17 and 21 of the Covenant.

9 August 1984

[Dated 12 July 1984]

Extension of the state of emergency as at 8 July 1984, for a period of 30 days, throughout the territory of the Republic of Peru and derogations from articles 9, 12, 17 and 21.

14 August 1984

Extension of the state of emergency throughout Peru for a period of 60 days, starting from 7 August 1984 and extension of the said derogations.

25 October 1984

[Dated 22 October 1984]

By Supreme Decree No. 052-84-IN of 5 October 1984 termination of the state of emergency in the territory of the Republic excepting the following provinces and departments, where the state of emergency has been extended for 60 days as of 5 October 1984:

The Department of Huánuco; the province of Mariscal Cáceres (Department of San Martín); the provinces of Huanta, La Mar, Cangallo, Víctor Fajardo, Huamanga and Lucanas (Department of Ayacucho); the provinces of Andahuaylas and Chincheros (Department of Apurímac); the provinces of Angaraes, Tayacaja, Acobamba, Huancavelica and Castrovirreyna (Department of Huancavelica), and

Derogations from articles 9, 12, 17 and 21 of the Covenant in the above-mentioned departments and provinces.

21 December 1984

[Dated 19 December 1984]

By Supreme Decree No. 063-84-IN, the Government of Peru had extended the state of emergency as at 3 December 1984, for a period of 60 days, in the Departments of Huánuco and San Martín and the province of Mariscal Cáceres. The said extension had been declared owing to the continued terrorist acts of violence and sabotage in those regions and, as a result, the Government of Peru continued to derogate from articles 9, 12, 17 and 21 of the Covenant.

[Dated 21 December 1984]

By Supreme Decree No. 065-84-IN, the Government of Peru had found it necessary to extend the state of emergency for a period of 60 days, starting from 7 December 1984, in the following provinces:

Department of Ayacucho: Cangallo, Huamanga, Huanta, La Mar, Lucanas, Víctor Fajardo, Huanca Sancos and Vilcashuamán;

Department of Huancavelica: Acobamba, Angaraes, Castrovirreyna, Huancavelica, Tayacaja and Huaytará;

Department of Apurímac: Andahuaylas and Chincheros.

The notification specifies that the extension of the state of emergency was decided because of the continued terrorist acts of violence and sabotage in the said provinces and that it was necessary to continue to derogate from articles 9, 12, 17 and 21 of the Covenant.

8 February 1985

[Dated 7 February 1985]

By Supreme Decree No. 001-85-IN, extension of the state of emergency as of 3 February 1985 in the Department of San Martín, including the province of Tocache and excluding the province of Mariscal Cáceres, and Huánuco, excluding the provinces of Puerto Inca and Pachitea.

By Supreme Decree No. 001-85-IN, exclusion of the state of emergency as of 3 February 1985 in the Department of San Martín, including the province of Tocache and excluding the province of Mariscal Cáceres, and Huánuco, excluding the provinces of Puerto Inca and Pachitea. The said extension had been declared owing to the continued terrorist acts of violence and sabotage in those regions and, as a result, the Government of Peru continued to derogate from articles 9, 12, 17 and 21 of the Covenant.

12 April 1985

[Dated 9 April 1985]

By Supreme Decree No. 012-85-IN, extension of the state of emergency as of 1 April 1985 in the Department of San Martín including the province of Tocache, and in the Department of Huánuco, except in the provinces of Puerto Inca and Pachitea.

The said extension has been declared owing to the continued terrorist acts of violence and sabotage in those regions and, as a result, the Government of Peru continued to derogate from articles 9, 12, 17 and 21 of the Covenant.

18 June 1985

[14 June 1985]

By Supreme Decree No. 020-85-IN, the state of emergency in the province of Pasco (Department of Pasco) has been declared for a period of 60 days, starting from 10 May 1985.

By Supreme Decree No. 021-85-IN the state of emergency in the Department of San Martín, including the province of Tocache and in the Department of Huánuco, except in the provinces of Puerto Inca and Pachitea, has been extended for a period of 60 days, starting from 1 June 1985.

By Supreme Decree No. 022-85-IN the state of emergency in the province of Daniel Alcides Carrión (Department of Pasco) has been extended for a period of 60 days, starting from 4 June 1985.

By Supreme Decree No. 023-85-IN, the state of emergency has been extended for a period of 60 days starting from 5 June 1985 in the following provinces:

Department of Ayacucho: Cangallo, Huamanga, Huanta, La Mar, Lucanas, Víctor Fajardo, Huanca Sancos and Vilcashuamán;

Department of Huancavelica: Acobamba, Angaraes, Castrovirreyna, Huancavelica, Tayacaja, Huaytará and Churcampa;

Department of Apurímac: Andahuaylas and Chincheros.

The above-mentioned notifications specify that the state of emergency had been declared or extended as indicated above owing to the continued terrorist acts of violence and sabotage.

As a result, articles 9, 12, 17 and 21 of the Covenant are being or still being derogated from in the regions in question for the said periods of time.

24 July 1985

[Dated 23 July 1985]

By Supreme Decree No. 031-85, the state of emergency in the province of Pasco (Department of Pasco) has been extended for a period of 60 days, starting from 10 July 1985.

6 August 1985

[Dated 31 July 1985]

By Supreme Decree No. 033-85-IN, the state of emergency in the province of Yauli (Department of Junín) has been declared for a period of 12 days, starting from 19 July 1985.

12 August 1985

[Dated 12 August 1985]

By Supreme Decree No. 042-85-IN, the state of emergency has been extended for a period of 60 days starting from 6 August 1985 in the following provinces and departments:

    (i) the province of Tocache (Department of San Martín);

    (ii) the Department of Huánuco, except the provinces of Puerto Inca and Pachitea;

    (iii) the province of Daniel Alcides Carrión (Department of Pasco);

    (iv) the provinces of Cangallo, Huamanga, Huanta, La Mar, Lucanas, Víctor Fajardo, Huanca Sancos and Vilcashuamán (Department of Ayacucho);

    (v) the provinces of Acobamba, Angaraes, Castrovirreyna, Huancavelica, Andahuaylas and Chincheros (Department of Apurímac).

As a result, articles 9, 12, 17 and 21 of the Covenant are being or still being derogated from in the regions in question for the said periods.

13 December 1985

[Dated 11 December 1985]

Extension of the state of emergency for a period of 60 days in the following provinces, in accordance with Decree No. 052-85-IN as of 5 December 1985 (derogation to articles 9, 12, 17, and 21 of the Covenant), owing to continued terrorist actions in the said regions:

Provinces of Cangallo, Huamanga, Huanta, La Mar, Víctor Fajardo, Huanca Sancos and Vilcashuamán (Department of Ayacucho);

Provinces of Acobamba, Angaraes, Castrovirreyna, Huancavelica, Tayacaja, Huaytará and Churcampa (Department of Huancavelica);

Provinces of Huayabamba, Huamalíes, Dos de Mayo and Ambo (Department of Huánuco);

Province of Chincheros (Department of Apurímac).

21 February 1986

[Dated 14 February 1986]

First notification

Extension as of 5 February 1986 by Decree No. 001-86 of the state of emergency for a period of 60 days in the same provinces as declared by Decree No. 052-85-IN (see notification of 13 December 1985).

Second notification

Extension of the state of emergency for a period of 60 days in the city of Lima and the constitutional province of Callao for a period of 60 days starting from 7 February 1986, in accordance with Decree No. 002-86.

The notifications specify that the extension was decided owing to continued terrorist actions and that articles 9, 12, 17 and 21 of the Covenant continue to be derogated from.

24 April 1986

[Dated 14 April 1986]

Extension of the state of emergency for a period of 60 days in the same provinces and city as declared by Decrees Nos. 001-86 and 002-86 (see notifications of 21 February 1986), in accordance with Decrees Nos. 004-86 and 005-86-IN as of 3 April 1986.

5 June 1986

[Dated 4 June 1986]

By Supreme Decree No. 012-86-IN, extension of the state of emergency in the city of Lima and the constitutional province of Callao for a period of 60 days, starting from 2 June 1986.

9 June 1986

[Dated 6 June 1986]

By Supreme Decree No. 013-86-IN, extension of the state of emergency for a period of 60 days, starting from 4 June 1986, in the provinces stated in the notification received on 21 February 1986.

23 June 1986

[Dated 20 June 1986]

By Supreme Decree No. 015-86-IN, declaration of the state of emergency in the provinces of Daniel Alcides Carrión and Pasco (Department of Pasco) for a period of 60 days, starting from 18 June 1986.

The Government of Peru specified that the said extensions and declaration of a state of emergency had been declared owing to the continuation or occurrence of terrorist acts and sabotage. As a result, articles 9, 12, 17 and 21 of the Covenant are being or still being derogated from in the regions in question for the said period of time.

6 August 1986

[Dated 5 August 1986]

By Supreme Decree No. 019-86-IN, extension of the state of emergency in the province of Lima and the constitutional province of Callao for a period of 30 days starting from 2 August 1986.

8 August 1986

[Dated 7 August 1986]

By Supreme Decree No. 020-86-IN, for a period of 60 days starting from 3 August 1986, extension of the state of emergency in the same provinces as under notification of 18 June 1985 and the Department of Huánuco (provinces of Huayabamba, Huamalíes, Dos de Mayo and Ambo).

25 August 1986

[Dated 19 August 1986]

By Supreme Decree No. 023-86-IN, in the provinces of Daniel Alcides Carrión and Pasco (Department of Pasco) for a period of 60 days, starting from 19 August 1986.

The notifications specify that the said extensions had been declared as indicated above owing to the continued terrorist acts of violence and sabotage.

As a result, articles 9, 12, 17 and 21 of the Covenant have continued to be derogated from in the regions in question for the said period of time.

5 September 1986

[Dated 4 September 1986]

By Supreme Decree No. 026-86-IN, extension of the state of emergency for a period of 60 days starting 1 September 1986 in the province of Lima and the constitutional province of Callao.

The notification specifies that the said extension had been declared owing to persistent acts of violence in the above-mentioned provinces.

The notification specifies that inasmuch as the municipal election process has begun, and in order to facilitate campaigning by political parties and independent candidates, without adversely affecting the security measures necessitated by the state of emergency, the prefectural authority, during the state of emergency, shall issue the appropriate regulations for governing the exercise of the right of assembly and the liberty of movement is partially re-established. In accordance with the said Decree, articles 9, 12, 17 and 21 of the Covenant continue to be derogated from, within the limits indicated above.

8 October 1986

[Dated 3 October 1986]

By Supreme Decree No. 029-86-IN, extension of the state of emergency for a period of 60 days, starting on 1 October 1986, in the same provinces as those indicated under the notification of 8 August 1986 (see above).

The notification specifies that the said extension of the state of emergency had been declared owing to the continued terrorist acts of violence and sabotage.

As a result, articles 9, 12, 17 and 21 of the Covenant will continue to be derogated from in the regions in question for the said period of time.

22 October 1986

[Dated 17 October 1986]

By Supreme Decree No. 03-86-IN, extension of the state of emergency for a period of 60 days, starting from 16 October 1986, in the provinces of Daniel Alcides Carrión and Pasco (Department of Pasco). The reasons of the extension and the articles of the Covenant from which it is derogated are identical to those indicated in the notification of 8 October 1986 above. The notification further specifies that, during the state of emergency, the prefectoral authority shall issue the appropriate regulations for governing the exercise of the right of assembly.

5 November 1986

[Dated 3 November 1986]

By Supreme Decree No. 03-86-IN, extension of the state of emergency for a period of 60 days, starting from 16 October 1986, in the provinces of Daniel Alcides Carrión and Pasco (Department of Pasco) and starting from 29 October 1986, in the provinces of Lima and Callao. The reasons for the extension, the articles of the Covenant which are derogated from and the intervention of the prefectoral authority are identical in essence, *mutatis mutandis,* to those indicated in the notification of 22 October 1986 (see above). The notification further specifies that, the armed forces shall continue to maintain responsibility for public order in the provinces concerned.

18 December 1986

[Dated 16 December 1986]

By Supreme Decree No. 036-86-IN, extension of the state of emergency in the provinces of Daniel Alcides Carrión and Pasco (Department of Pasco) for a period of 60 days, starting from 19 August 1986.

The notifications specify that the said extension had been declared as indicated above owing to the continued terrorist acts of violence and sabotage.

As a result, articles 9, 12, 17 and 21 of the Covenant have continued to be derogated from in the regions in question for the said period of time.

2 February 1987

[Dated 30 January 1987]

Extension of the state of emergency for a period of 60 days as of 25 January 1987 in the provinces of Lima and Callao.

Notification specifies that the Government of Peru continued to derogate from articles 9, 12, 17 and 21 of the Covenant for the said period of time; the notification specifies that during the state of emergency, the Armed Forces shall maintain responsibility for domestic public order in those regions and that with respect to article 21 of the Covenant, the prefectural authority shall issue the appropriate regulations governing the exercise of the right of assembly, in accordance with the provision of the said article 21 of the Covenant.

2 February 1987

[Dated 2 February 1987]

Notification to the effect that the Government of Peru had extended the state of emergency in the following provinces for a period of 60 days, starting 29 January 1987:

Department of Ayacucho (provinces of Cangallo, Huamanga, Huanta, La Mar, Víctor Fajardo, Huanca Sancos, Vilcashuamán and Sucre);

Department of Huancavelica (provinces of Acobamba, Angaraes, Castro-virreyna, Huancavelica, Tayacaja, Huaytará and Churcampa);

Department of Apurímac (province of Chincheros);

Department of Huánuco (provinces of Huyacabamba, Huamalíes, Dos de Mayo and Ambo).

As a result, articles 9, 12, 17 and 21 of the Covenant will continue to be derogated from in the regions in question for the said period of time.

Both notifications specify that the said extensions of the state of emergency had been declared owing to the continued terrorist acts of violence and sabotage.

4 March 1987

[23 February 1987]

Notification to the effect that the Government of Peru had extended the state of emergency for 60 days as of 13 February 1987 in the provinces of Daniel Alcides Carrión and Pasco (Department of Pasco) and that, as a result, the Government of Peru continued to derogate from articles 9, 12, 17 and 21 (under the same qualifications as before) of the Covenant. The notification specifies that the said extension has been declared owing to the continued terrorist acts of violence and sabotage in those regions.

3 April 1987

[2 April 1987]

Notification to the effect that because of continued acts of violence and sabotage, the Government of Peru had extended the state of emergency in the following provinces for a period of 60 days:

Department of Ayacucho (provinces of Cangallo, Huamanga, Huanta, La Mar, Víctor Fajardo, Huanca Sancos, Vilcashuamán and Sucre);

Department of Apurímac (province of Chincheros); and

Department of Huánuco (province of Ambo and District of Monzón of the province of Huamalíes).

As a result, articles 9, 12, 17 and 21 of the Covenant will continue to be derogated from in the regions in question for the said period of time.

1 June 1987

[26 May 1987]

Notification to the effect that the Government of Peru had extended the state of emergency for a period of 30 days as of 26 May 1987 in the provinces of Lima and Callao.

As a result, the Government of Peru continued to derogate from articles 9, 12, 17 and 21 of the Covenant for the said period of time; the notification specifies that during the state of emergency, the Armed Forces shall maintain responsibility for domestic public order in those regions and that with respect to article 21 of the Covenant, the prefectural authority shall issue the appropriate regulations governing the exercise of the right of assembly, in accordance with the provisions of the said article 21 of the Covenant.

8 June 1987

[26 May 1987]

Notification to the effect that the Government of Peru had extended the state of emergency in the following provinces for a period of 60 days, starting 26 May 1987:

Department of Ayacucho (provinces of Cangallo, Huamanga, Huanta, La Mar, Víctor Fajardo, Huanca Sancos, Vilcashuamán and Sucre);

Department of Huancavelica (provinces of Acobamba, Angaraes, Castrovirreyna, Huancavelica, Tayacaja, Huaytará and Churcampa);

Department of Apurímac (province of Chincheros);

Department of Huánuco (province of Ambo and District of Monzón of the Province of Huamalíes).

As a result, articles 9, 12, 17 and 21 of the Covenant will continue to be derogated from in the regions in question for the said period of time.

18 June 1987

[Dated 8 June 1987]

Notification to the effect that the state of emergency in the provinces of Daniel Alcides Carrión and Pasco (Department of Pasco) had been extended for 60 days as of 8 June 1987.

As a result, the Government of Peru continued to derogate from articles 9, 12, 17 and 21 of the Covenant for the said period of time; the notification specifies that during the state of emergency, the Armed Forces shall continue to exercise political and military control in the provinces in question and that with respect to article 21 of the Covenant, the prefectural authority shall issue the appropriate regulations governing the exercise of the right of assembly, in accordance with the provision of the said article 21.

24 June and 23 July 1987

[Dated 24 June and 20 July 1987]

Notifications to the effect that the state of emergency in the provinces of Lima and Callao had been successively extended for a period of 30 days starting from 20 June 1987 and 20 July 1987.

As a result, the Government of Peru continued to derogate from articles 9, 12, 17 and 21 of the Covenant for the said periods of time; the notifications specify that during the state of emergency, the Armed Forces shall maintain responsibility for domestic public order in those regions and that with respect to article 21 of the Covenant, the prefectural authority shall issue the appropriate regulations governing the exercise of the right of assembly, in accordance with the provisions of the said article 21 of the Covenant.

23 July 1987

[Dated 20 July 1987]

Notification to the effect that the Government of Peru had declared a state of emergency for a period of 60 days, starting from 14 July 1987, in the following areas:

Province of Leoncio Prado and District of Cholón;

Province of Marañón (Department of Huánuco);

Provinces of Mariscal Cáceres and Tocache (Department of San Martín).

The notification specifies that the state of emergency had been declared owing to the continuing acts of terrorism and sabotage in those regions.

As a result, articles 9, 12, 17 and 21 of the Covenant are being derogated from for the said period of time; the notification further specifies that during the state of emergency, the Armed Forces shall continue to exercise political and military control of the areas in question.

4 August 1987

[Dated 25 July 1987]

Notification to the effect that the Government of Peru has declared for a period of 60 days as of 25 July 1987 the state of emergency in the following regions:

Provinces of Cangallo, Huamanga, Huanta, La Mar, Víctor Fajardo, Huanca Sancos, Vilcashuamán and Sucre of the Department of Ayacucho;

Provinces of Acobamba, Angaraes, Castrovirreyna, Huancavelica, Tayacaja, Huaytará and Churcampa of the Department of Huancavelica;

Province of Chincheros of the Department of Apurímac; and

Province of Ambo and the District of Monzón of the province of Huamalíes.

As a result, articles 9, 12, 17 and 21 of the Covenant will be derogated from in the regions for the said period of time.

The notification further states that during the state of emergency, which was adopted due to the continuation of acts of terrorism and sabotage, the Armed Forces shall continue to exercise political and military powers in the regions in question.

13 August 1987

[Dated 7 August 1987]

Notification to the effect that the Government of Peru had declared a state of emergency in the provinces of Daniel Alcides Carrión and Pasco (Department of Pasco) for a period of 60 days as of 7 August 1987.

As a result the prefectural authority shall issue the appropriate regulations governing the exercise of the right of assembly, in accordance with the provision of article 21 of the Covenant and the Armed Forces shall maintain responsibility for domestic public order in those regions.

28 August 1987

[Dated 19 August 1987]

Notification to the effect that the state of emergency in the provinces of Lima and Callao has been extended for a period of 30 days starting from 19 August 1987.

Poland

29 January 1982

"... in connection with the proclamation of martial law by the Council of State of the Polish People's Republic, as based on article 33, paragraph 2, of Poland's Constitution, there has been temporary derogation from or limitation of application of provisions of articles 9, 12, paragraphs 1 and 2, 14, paragraph 5, 19, paragraphs 2, 21 and 22 of the Covenant, to the extent strictly required by the exigencies of the situation ...

"Temporary limitation of certain rights of citizens has been prompted by the supreme national interest. It was caused by the exigencies of averting a civil war, economic anarchy as well as destabilization of State and social structures ...

"The restrictive measures in question are of a temporary nature. They have already been considerably cut back and along with the stabilizing of the situation, will be successively terminated."

22 December 1982

"Based on the law by the Diet (Seym) of the Polish People's Republic of 18 December 1982 concerning special legal regulation in the time of suspension of martial law, derogation from articles 9, 12, paragraphs 1 and 2, 21 and 22 of the Covenant, has been terminated as of 31 December 1982.

"By terms of the same law as well as a result of earlier successive measures, restrictions in the application of provisions of the Covenant which are still derogated from, namely article 14, paragraph 5, and article 19, paragraph 2, have also been considerably reduced.

"For instance, with reference to article 14, paragraph 5, emergency procedures have been lifted in relation to crimes and offences committed in social conflicts out of political motivations, they have only been retained with regard to crimes most dangerous to the State's basic economic interests as well as to life, health and property of its citizens."

25 July 1983

Termination as from 22 July 1983 of derogations.

Sri Lanka

21 May 1984

Proclamation of state of emergency throughout Sri Lanka, and derogation as a consequence from articles 9 (3) and 14 (3) (*b*) of the Covenant as from 18 May 1983.

23 May 1984

The Government of Sri Lanka specified that the emergency regulations and special laws were temporary measures necessitated by the existence of an extraordinary security situation and that it was not intended to continue with them longer that it was absolutely necessary.

United Kingdom of Great Britain and Northern Ireland

17 May 1976

"The Government of the United Kingdom notify other States parties to the present Covenant, in accordance with article 4, of their intention to take and continue measures derogating from their obligations under the Covenant.

"There have been in the United Kingdom in recent years campaigns of organized terrorism related to Northern Irish affairs which have manifested themselves in activities which have included murder, attempted murder, maiming, intimidation and violent civil disturbances and in bombing and fire-raising which have resulted in death, injury and widespread destruction of property. This situation constitutes a public emergency within the meaning of article 4 (1) of the Covenant. The emergency commenced prior to the ratification by United Kingdom of the Covenant and legislation has, from time to time, been promulgated with regard to it.

"The Government of the United Kingdom have found it necessary (and in some cases continue to find it necessary) to take powers, to the extent strictly required by the exigencies of the situation, for the protection of life, for the protection of property and the prevention of outbreaks of public disorder, and including the exercise of powers of arrest and detention and exclusion. In so far as any of these measures is inconsistent with the provisions of articles 9, 10 (2), 10 (3), 12 (1), 14, 17, 19 (2), 21 and 22 of the Covenant, the United Kingdom hereby derogates from its obligations under those provisions."

22 August 1984

Termination forthwith of derogations from articles 9, 10 (2), 10 (3), 12 (1), 14, 17, 19 (2), 21 and 22 of the Covenant.

Uruguay

30 July 1979

[The Government of Uruguay] has the honour to request that the requirement laid down in article 4 (3) of the International Covenant on Civil and Political Rights should be deemed to have been formally fulfilled with regard to the existence and maintenance in Uruguay of a public emergency as referred to in article 4 (1).

This emergency situation, the nature and consequences of which match the description given in article 4, namely that they threaten the life of the nation, is a matter of universal knowledge, and the present communication might thus appear superfluous in so far as the provision of substantive information is concerned.

This issue has been the subject of countless official statements at both the regional and the international level.

None the less, [the] Government wishes both to comply formally with the above-mentioned requirement and to reiterate that the emergency measures which it has taken, and which comply strictly with the requirements of 4 (2), are designed precisely to achieve genuine, effective and lasting protection of human rights, the observance and promotion of which are the essence of our existence as an independent and sovereign nation.

Notwithstanding what has been stated above, the information referred to in article 4 (3) concerning the nature and duration of the emergency measures will be provided in more detailed form when the report referred to in article 40 of the Covenant is submitted, so that the scope and evolution of these measures can be fully understood.

TERRITORIAL APPLICATIONS

Participant	*Date of notification*	*Territories*
Netherlands . . .	11 Dec. 1978	Netherlands Antilles
United Kingdom	20 May 1976	The Bailiwick of Guernsey, the Bailiwick of Jersey, the Isle of Man, Belize, Bermuda, the British Virgin Islands, the Cayman Islands, the Falkland Islands and Dependencies,[14] Gibraltar, the Gilbert Islands, Hong Kong, Montserrat, the Pitcairn Group, St. Helena and Dependencies, the Solomon Islands, the Turks and Caicos Islands and Tuvalu

NOTES

[1] See note 2 in chapter I.

[2] See note 3 in chapter I, for the texts of communications received by the Secretary-General in respect of the signature by Democratic Kampuchea.

[3] With the following declaration: "The said Covenant shall also apply to Berlin (West) with effect from the date on which it enters into force for the Federal Republic of Germany except as far as allied rights and responsibilities are affected."

For communications on this subject addressed to the Secretary-General by various Governments, see note 4 in chapter I.

[4] By a communication received on 6 December 1984, the Government of Australia notified the Secretary-General of its decision to withdraw the following reservations and declarations made upon ratification:

"Articles 2 and 50

"Australia advises that, the people having united as one people in a Federal Commonwealth under the Crown, it has a federal constitutional system. It accepts that the provisions of the Covenant extend to all parts of Australia as a Federal State without any limitations or exceptions. It enters a general reservation that article 2, paragraphs 2 and 3, and article 50 shall be given effect consistently with and subject to the provisions in article 2, paragraph 2.

"Under article 2, paragraph 2, steps to adopt measures necessary to give effect to the rights recognized in the Covenant are to be taken in accordance with each State party's constitutional processes which, in the case of Australia, are the processes of a federation in which legislative, executive and judicial powers to give effect to the rights recognized in the Covenant are distributed among the federal (Commonwealth) authorities and the authorities of the constituent States.

"In particular, in relation to the Australian States the implementation of those provisions of the Covenant over whose subject-matter the federal authorities exercise legislative, executive and judicial jurisdiction will be a matter for those authorities; and the implementation of those provisions of the Covenant over whose subject-matter the authorities of the constituent States exercise legislative, executive and judicial jurisdiction will be a matter for those authorities; and where a provision has both federal and State aspects, its implementation will accordingly be a matter for the respective constitutionally appropriate authorities (for the purpose of implementation, the Northern Territory will be regarded as a constituent State).

"To this end, the Australian Government has been in consultation with the responsible State and Territory Ministers with the object of developing co-operative arrangements to co-ordinate and facilitate the implementation of the Covenant.

"Article 10

"Australia accepts the principle stated in article 10, paragraph 1, and the general principles of the other paragraphs of that article, but makes the reservation that these and other provisions of the Covenant are without prejudice to laws and lawful arrangements, of the type now in force in Australia, for the preservation of custodial discipline in penal establishments. In relation to paragraph 2 (*a*) the principle of segregation is accepted as an objective to be achieved progressively. In relation to paragraphs 2 (*b*) and 3 (second sentence) the obligation to segregate is accepted only to the extent that such segregation is considered by the responsible authorities to be beneficial to the juveniles or adults concerned.

"Article 14

"Australia accepts paragraph 3 (*b*) on the understanding that the reference to adequate facilities does not require provision to prisoners of all the facilities available to a prisoner's legal representative.

"Australia accepts the requirement in paragraph 3 (*d*) that everyone is entitled to be tried in his presence, but reserves the right to exclude an accused person where his conduct makes it impossible for the trial to proceed.

"Australia interprets paragraph 3 (*d*) as consistent with the operation of schemes of legal assistance in which the person assisted is required to make a contribution towards the cost of the defence related to his capacity to pay and determined according to law, or in which assistance is granted in respect of other than indictable offences only after having regard to all relevant matters.

"Australia makes the reservation that the provision of compensation for miscarriage of justice in the circumstances contemplated in article 14, paragraph 6, may be by administrative procedures rather than pursuant to specific legal provision.

"Article 17

"Australia accepts the principles stated in article 17 without prejudice to the right to enact and administer laws which, in so far as they authorize action which impinges on a person's privacy, family, home or correspondence, are necessary in a democratic society in the interests of national security, public safety, the economic well-being of the country, the protection of public health or morals or the protection of the rights and freedoms of others.

"Article 19

"Australia interprets article 19, paragraph 2, as being compatible with the regulation of radio and television broadcasting in the public interest with the object of providing the best possible broadcasting services to the Australian people.

"Article 20

"Australia interprets the rights provided for by articles 19, 21 and 22 as consistent with article 20; accordingly, the Commonwealth and the constituent States, having legislated with respect to the subject-matter of the article in matters of practical concern in the interests of public order (*ordre public*), the right is reserved not to introduce any further legislative provision on these matters.

"Article 25

"The reference in article 25 (*b*), to "universal and equal suffrage", is accepted without prejudice to law which provides that factors such as regional interest may be taken into account in defining electoral divisions, or which establishes franchises for municipal and other local government elections related to the sources of revenue and the functions of such government.

"Convicted Persons

"Australia declares that laws now in force in Australia relating to the rights of persons who have been convicted of serious criminal offences are generally consistent with the requirements of articles 14, 18, 19, 25 and 26 and reserves the right not to seek amendment of such laws.

"Discrimination and Distinction

"The provisions of articles 2 (1), 24 (1), 25 and 26 relating to discrimination and distinction between persons shall be without prejudice to laws designed to achieve for the members of some class or classes of persons equal enjoyment of the rights defined in the

Covenant. Australia accepts article 26 on the basis that the object of the provision is to confirm the right of each person to equal treatment in the application of the law."

[5] In a communication received on 29 March 1985, the Government of Finland notified the Secretary-General of its decision to withdraw the following reservations made upon ratification:

"3. With respect to article 13 of the Covenant, Finland declares that the article does not correspond to the present Finnish legislation regarding an alien's right to be heard or lodge a complaint in respect of a decision concerning his expulsion;

"4. With respect to article 14, paragraph 1, of the Covenant, Finland declares that under Finnish law a sentence can be declared secret if its publication could be an affront to morals or endanger national security;"

The notification indicates that the withdrawal was effected because the relevant provisions of the Finnish legislation have been amended as to correspond fully to articles 13 and 14 (1) of the Covenant.

[6] In this connection, the Secretary-General received on 23 April 1982 from the Government of the Federal Republic of Germany the following declaration with regard to that declaration made by France concerning article 27 of the said Covenant:

The Federal Government refers to the declaration on article 27 made by the French Government and stresses in this context the great importance attaching to the rights guaranteed by article 27. It interprets the French declaration as meaning that the Constitution of the French Republic already fully guarantees the individual rights protected by article 27.

[7] In a communication received on 20 December 1983, the Government of the Netherlands notified the Secretary-General that it was withdrawing its reservation with regard to article 25 (*c*). The text of the reservation reads as follows:

"The Kingdom of the Netherlands does not accept this provision in the case of the Netherlands Antilles."

[8] In a notification received by the Secretary-General on 12 December 1979, the Government of Norway withdrew the reservation formulated simultaneously in respect of article 6 (4).

[9] In a communication received by the Secretary-General on 31 January 1979, the Government of Trinidad and Tobago confirmed that paragraph (vi) constituted an interpretative declaration which did not aim to exclude nor modify the legal effect of the provisions of the Covenant.

[10] See "Entry into force:" at the beginning of this chapter.

[11] A previous declaration received on 6 April 1978 expired on 23 March 1983.

[12] In a communication accompanying the declaration, the Government of the Federal Republic of Germany indicated that it wishes to draw attention to the reservations made upon ratification with respect to articles 19, 21 and 22 in conjunction with articles 2 (1), 14 (3), 14 (5) and 15 (1) of the said Covenant and to the reservation in favour of allied rights and responsibilities contained in the declaration, also made upon ratification, on the application of the Covenant to Berlin (West).

[13] A previous declaration, received 2 April 1976, expired on 28 March 1981.

[14] On 3 October 1983, the Secretary-General received from the Government of Argentina the following objection to the said territorial application:

[The Government of Argentina makes a] formal objection to the [declaration] of territorial extension issued by the United Kingdom with regard to the Malvinas Islands (and dependencies), which that country is illegally occupying and refers to as the "Falkland Islands".

The Argentine Republic rejects and considers null and void the [said declaration] of territorial extension.

In this regard, the Secretary-General received on 28 February 1985 from the Government of the United Kingdom of Great Britain and Northern Ireland, the following declaration:

"The Government of the United Kingdom of Great Britain and Northern Ireland have no doubt as to their right, by notification to the Depositary under the relevant provisions of the above-mentioned Convention to extend the application of the Convention in question to the Falklands Islands or to the Falkland Islands Dependencies, as the case may be.

For this reason alone, the Government of the United Kingdom are unable to regard the Argentine objection as having any legal effect."

Subsequently, upon its ratification, the Government of Argentina made a declaration, the text of which is reproduced in chapter I, note 8.

Chapter III

OPTIONAL PROTOCOL TO THE INTERNATIONAL COVENANT ON CIVIL AND POLITICAL RIGHTS

Adopted by the General Assembly of the United Nations on 16 December 1966

ENTRY INTO FORCE: 23 March 1976, in accordance with article 9.

Participant	Signature	Ratification, accession (a)
Argentina		8 Aug. 1986 *a*
Austria	10 Dec. 1973	
Barbados		5 Jan. 1973 *a*
Bolivia		12 Aug. 1982 *a*
Cameroon		27 June 1984 *a*
Canada		19 May 1976 *a*
Central African Republic		8 May 1981 *a*
China [1,*]		
Colombia	21 Dec. 1966	29 Oct. 1969
Congo		5 Oct. 1983 *a*
Costa Rica	19 Dec. 1966	29 Nov. 1968
Cyprus	19 Dec. 1966	
Denmark	20 Mar. 1968	6 Jan. 1972
Dominican Republic		4 Jan. 1978 *a*
Ecuador	4 Apr. 1968	6 Mar. 1969
El Salvador	21 Sep. 1967	
Finland	11 Dec. 1967	19 Aug. 1975
France		17 Feb. 1984 *a*
Guinea	19 Mar. 1975	
Honduras	19 Dec. 1966	
Iceland		22 Aug. 1979 *a*
Italy	30 Apr. 1976	15 Sep. 1978
Jamaica	19 Dec. 1966	3 Oct. 1975
Luxembourg		18 Aug. 1983 *a*

---

* For notes, see end of chapter.

Participant	Signature	Ratification, accession (a)
Madagascar	17 Sep. 1969	21 June 1971
Mauritius		12 Dec. 1973 *a*
Netherlands	25 June 1969	11 Dec. 1978
Nicaragua		12 Mar. 1980 *a*
Niger		7 Mar. 1986 *a*
Norway	20 Mar. 1968	13 Sep. 1972
Panama	27 July 1976	8 Mar. 1977
Peru	11 Aug. 1977	3 Oct. 1980
Philippines	19 Dec. 1966	
Portugal	1 Aug. 1978	3 May 1983
Saint Vincent and the Grenadines		9 Nov. 1981 *a*
San Marino		18 Oct. 1985 *a*
Senegal	6 July 1970	13 Feb. 1978
Spain		25 Jan. 1985 *a*
Suriname		28 Dec. 1976 *a*
Sweden	29 Sep. 1967	6 Dec. 1971
Trinidad and Tobago		14 Nov. 1980 *a*
Uruguay	21 Feb. 1967	1 Apr. 1970
Venezuela	15 Nov. 1976	10 May 1978
Zaire		1 Nov. 1976 *a*
Zambia		10 Apr. 1984 *a*

DECLARATIONS AND RESERVATIONS

(Unless otherwise indicated, the declarations and reservations were made upon ratification or accession.)

Denmark [2]

"With reference to article 5, paragraph 2 (*a*), the Government of Denmark makes a reservation with respect to the competence of the Human Rights Committee to consider a communication from an individual if the matter has already been considered under other procedures of international investigation."

France

Declaration:

France interprets article 1 of the Protocol as giving the Committee the competence to receive and consider communications from individuals subject to the jurisdiction of the French Republic who claim to be victims of a violation by the Republic of any of the rights set forth in the Covenant which results either from acts, omissions, developments or events occurring after the date on which the Protocol entered into force for the Republic, or from a decision relating to acts, omissions, developments or events after that date.

With regard to article 7, France's accession to the Optional Protocol should not be interpreted as implying any change in its position concerning the resolution referred to in that article.

Reservation:

France makes a reservation to article 5, paragraph 2 (*a*), specifying that the Human Rights Committee shall not have competence to consider a communication from an individual if the same matter is being examined or has already been considered under another procedure of international investigation or settlement.

Iceland [2]

Iceland ... accedes to the said Protocol subject to a reservation, with reference to article 5, paragraph 2, with respect to the competence of the Human Rights Committee to consider a communication from an individual if the matter is being examined or has been examined under another procedure of international investigation or settlement. Other provisions of the Covenant shall be inviolably observed.

Italy [2]

The Italian Republic ratifies the Optional Protocol to the International Covenant on Civil and Political Rights, it being understood that the provisions of article 5, paragraph 2, of the Protocol mean that the Committee provided for in article 28 of the Covenant shall not consider any communication from an individual unless it has ascertained that the same matter is not being and has not been examined under another procedure of international investigation or settlement.

Luxembourg

Declaration:

"The Grand Duchy of Luxembourg accedes to the Optional Protocol to the International Covenant on Civil and Political Rights, on the understanding that the provisions of article 5, paragraph 2, of the Protocol mean that the Committee established by article 28 of the Covenant shall not consider any communication from an individual unless it has ascertained that the same matter is not being examined or has not already been examined under another procedure of international investigation or settlement."

Norway[2]

Subject to the following reservation to article 5, paragraph 2:

". . . The Committee shall not have competence to consider a communication from an individual if the same matter has already been examined under other procedures of international investigation or settlement."

Spain

The Spanish Government accedes to the Optional Protocol to the International Covenant on Civil and Political Rights, on the understanding that the provisions of article 5, paragraph 2, of that Protocol mean that the Human Rights Committee shall not consider any communication from an individual unless it has ascertained that the same matter has not been or is not being examined under another procedure of international investigation or settlement.

Sweden[2]

On the understanding that the provisions of article 5, paragraph 2, of the Protocol signify that the Human Rights Committee provided for in article 28 of the said Covenant shall not consider any communication from an individual unless it has ascertained that the same matter is not being examined or has not been examined under another procedure of international investigation or settlement.

Venezuela

*Same reservation as the one made by Venezuela in respect of article 14 (3)
(d)* of the International Covenant on Civil and Political Rights: see
chapter II.*

TERRITORIAL APPLICATION

Participant	*Date of receipt of notification*	*Territory*
Netherlands . . .	11 Dec. 1978	Netherlands Antilles

NOTES

[1] See note 2 in chapter I.

[2] See under chapter II for the text of the declarations by which these States recognized the competence of the Human Rights Committee established under article 41 of the Covenant.

Chapter IV

INTERNATIONAL CONVENTION ON THE ELIMINATION OF ALL FORMS OF RACIAL DISCRIMINATION

Adopted by the General Assembly of the United Nations on 21 December 1965

ENTRY INTO FORCE: 4 January 1969, in accordance with article 19.

Participant	Signature	Ratification, accession (a), succession (d)
Afghanistan		6 July 1983 *a*
Algeria	9 Dec. 1966	14 Feb. 1972
Argentina	13 July 1967	2 Oct. 1968
Australia	13 Oct. 1966	30 Sep. 1975
Austria	22 July 1969	9 May 1972
Bahamas		5 Aug. 1975 *d*
Bangladesh		11 June 1979 *a*
Barbados		8 Nov. 1972 *a*
Belgium	17 Aug. 1967	7 Aug. 1975
Benin	2 Feb. 1967	
Bhutan	26 Mar. 1973	
Bolivia	7 June 1966	22 Sep. 1970
Botswana		20 Feb. 1974 *a*
Brazil	7 Mar. 1966	27 Mar. 1968
Bulgaria	1 June 1966	8 Aug. 1966
Burkina Faso		18 July 1974 *a*
Burundi	1 Feb. 1967	27 Oct. 1977
Byelorussian SSR	7 Mar. 1966	8 Apr. 1969
Cameroon	12 Dec. 1966	24 June 1971
Canada	24 Aug. 1966	14 Oct. 1970
Cape Verde		3 Oct. 1979 *a*
Central African Republic	7 Mar. 1966	16 Mar. 1971
Chad		17 Aug. 1977 *a*

Participant	Signature	Ratification, accession (a), succession (d)
Chile	3 Oct. 1966	20 Oct. 1971
China [1],*		29 Dec. 1981 *a*
Colombia	23 Mar. 1967	2 Sep. 1981
Costa Rica	14 Mar. 1966	16 Jan. 1967
Côte d'Ivoire		4 Jan. 1973 *a*
Cuba	7 June 1966	15 Feb. 1972
Cyprus	12 Dec. 1966	21 Apr. 1967
Czechoslovakia	7 Oct. 1966	29 Dec. 1966
Democratic Kampuchea	12 Apr. 1966	28 Nov. 1983
Democratic Yemen		18 Oct. 1972 *a*
Denmark	21 June 1966	9 Dec. 1971
Dominican Republic		25 May 1983 *a*
Ecuador		22 Sep. 1966 *a*
Egypt	28 Sep. 1966	1 May 1967
El Salvador		30 Nov. 1979 *a*
Ethiopia		23 June 1976 *a*
Fiji		11 Jan. 1973 *d*
Finland	6 Oct. 1966	14 July 1970
France		28 July 1971 *a*
Gabon	20 Sep. 1966	29 Feb. 1980
Gambia		29 Dec. 1978 *a*
German Democratic Republic .		27 Mar. 1973 *a*
Germany, Federal Republic of [2] .	10 Feb. 1967	16 May 1969
Ghana	8 Sep. 1966	8 Sep. 1966
Greece	7 Mar. 1966	18 June 1970
Grenada	17 Dec. 1981	
Guatemala	8 Sep. 1967	18 Jan. 1983
Guinea	24 Mar. 1966	14 Mar. 1977
Guyana	11 Dec. 1968	15 Feb. 1977
Haiti	30 Oct. 1972	19 Dec. 1972
Holy See	21 Nov. 1966	1 May 1969
Hungary	15 Sep. 1966	4 May 1967
Iceland	14 Nov. 1966	13 Mar. 1967
India	2 Mar. 1967	3 Dec. 1968
Iran (Islamic Republic of)	8 Mar. 1967	29 Aug. 1968
Iraq	18 Feb. 1969	14 Jan. 1970
Ireland	21 Mar. 1968	
Israel	7 Mar. 1966	3 Jan. 1979

* For notes, see end of chapter.

Participant	Signature	Ratification, accession (a), succession (d)
Italy	13 Mar. 1968	5 Jan. 1976
Jamaica	14 Aug. 1966	4 June 1971
Jordan		30 May 1974 *a*
Kuwait		15 Oct. 1968 *a*
Lao People's Democratic Republic		22 Feb. 1974 *a*
Lebanon		12 Nov. 1971 *a*
Lesotho		4 Nov. 1971 *a*
Liberia		5 Nov. 1976 *a*
Libyan Arab Jamahiriya		3 July 1968 *a*
Luxembourg	12 Dec. 1967	1 May 1978
Madagascar	18 Dec. 1967	7 Feb. 1969
Maldives		24 Apr. 1984 *a*
Mali		16 July 1974 *a*
Malta	5 Sep. 1968	27 May 1971
Mauritania	21 Dec. 1966	
Mauritius		30 May 1972 *a*
Mexico	1 Nov. 1966	20 Feb. 1975
Mongolia	3 May 1966	6 Aug. 1969
Morocco	18 Sep. 1967	18 Dec. 1970
Mozambique		18 Apr. 1983 *a*
Namibia (United Nations Council for Namibia)		11 Nov. 1982 *a*
Nepal		30 Jan. 1971 *a*
Netherlands	24 Oct. 1966	10 Dec. 1971
New Zealand	25 Oct. 1966	22 Nov. 1972
Nicaragua		15 Feb. 1978 *a*
Niger	14 Mar. 1966	27 Apr. 1967
Nigeria		16 Oct. 1967 *a*
Norway	21 Nov. 1966	6 Aug. 1970
Pakistan	19 Sep. 1966	21 Sep. 1966
Panama	8 Dec. 1966	16 Aug. 1967
Papua New Guinea		27 Jan. 1982 *a*
Peru	22 July 1966	29 Sep. 1971
Philippines	7 Mar. 1966	15 Sep. 1967
Poland	7 Mar. 1966	5 Dec. 1968
Portugal		24 Aug. 1982 *a*
Qatar		22 July 1976 *a*
Republic of Korea	8 Aug. 1978	5 Dec. 1978
Romania		15 Sep. 1970 *a*

Participant	Signature	Ratification, accession (a), succession (d)
Rwanda		16 Apr. 1975 *a*
Saint Vincent and the Grenadines		9 Nov. 1981 *a*
Senegal	22 July 1968	19 Apr. 1972
Seychelles		7 Mar. 1978 *a*
Sierra Leone	17 Nov. 1966	2 Aug. 1967
Solomon Islands		17 Mar. 1982 *d*
Somalia	26 Jan. 1967	26 Aug. 1975
Spain		13 Sep. 1968 *a*
Sri Lanka		18 Feb. 1982 *a*
Sudan		21 Mar. 1977 *a*
Suriname		15 Mar. 1984 *d*
Swaziland		7 Apr. 1969 *a*
Sweden	5 May 1966	6 Dec. 1971
Syrian Arab Republic	21 Apr. 1969 *a*	
Togo		1 Sep. 1972 *a*
Tonga		16 Feb. 1972 *a*
Trinidad and Tobago	9 June 1967	4 Oct. 1973
Tunisia	12 Apr. 1966	13 Jan. 1967
Turkey	13 Oct. 1972	
Uganda		21 Nov. 1980 *a*
Ukrainian SSR	7 Mar. 1966	7 Mar. 1969
Union of Soviet Socialist Republics	7 Mar. 1966	4 Feb. 1969
United Arab Emirates		20 June 1974 *a*
United Kingdom	11 Oct. 1966	7 Mar. 1969[3]
United Republic of Tanzania		27 Oct. 1972 *a*
United States of America	28 Sep. 1966	
Uruguay	21 Feb. 1967	30 Aug. 1968
Venezuela	21 Apr. 1967	10 Oct. 1967
Viet Nam		9 June 1982 *a*
Yugoslavia	15 Apr. 1966	2 Oct. 1967
Zaire		21 Apr. 1976 *a*
Zambia	11 Oct. 1968	4 Feb. 1972

DECLARATIONS AND RESERVATIONS

(Unless otherwise indicated, the declarations and
reservations were made upon ratification, accession
or succession. For objections thereto and declarations
recognizing the competence of the Committee on the
Elimination of Racial Discrimination, see hereinafter.)

Afghanistan

Reservation:

While acceding to the International Convention on the Elimination of
All Forms of Racial Discrimination, the Democratic Republic of Afghanistan
does not consider itself bound by the provision of article 22 of the Convention
since according to this article, in the event of disagreement between two or
several States parties to the Convention on the interpretation and implementation of provisions of the Convention, the matters could be referred to the
International Court of Justice upon the request of only one side.

The Democratic Republic of Afghanistan, therefore, states that should
any disagreement emerge on the interpretation and implementation of the
Convention, the matter will be referred to the International Court of Justice
only if all concerned parties agree with that procedure.

Declaration:

Furthermore, the Democratic Republic of Afghanistan states that the
provisions of articles 17 and 18 of the International Convention on the
Elimination of All Forms of Racial Discrimination have a discriminatory
nature against some States and therefore are not in conformity with the
principle of universality of international treaties.

Australia

"The Government of Australia ... declares that Australia is not at
present in a position specifically to treat as offences all the matters covered by
article 4 (*a*) of the Convention. Acts of the kind there mentioned are pun-
ishable only to the extent provided by the existing criminal law dealing with
such matters as the maintenance of public order, public mischief, assault, riot,
criminal libel, conspiracy and attempts. It is the intention of the Australian
Government, at the first suitable moment, to seek from Parliament legislation
specifically implementing the terms of article 4 (*a*)."

Austria

"Article 4 of the International Convention on the Elimination of All Forms of Racial Discrimination provides that the measures specifically described in subparagraphs (*a*), (*b*) and (*c*) shall be undertaken with due regard to the principles embodied in the Universal Declaration of Human Rights and the rights expressly set forth in article 5 of the Convention. The Republic of Austria therefore considers that through such measures the right to freedom of opinion and expression and the right to freedom of peaceful assembly and association may not be jeopardized. These rights are laid down in articles 19 and 20 of the Universal Declaration of Human Rights; they were re-affirmed by the General Assembly of the United Nations when it adopted articles 19 and 21 of the International Covenant on Civil and Political Rights and are referred to in article 5 (*d*) (viii) and (ix) of the present Convention."

Bahamas

"First, the Government of the Commonwealth of the Bahamas wishes to state its understanding of article 4 of the International Convention on the Elimination of All Forms of Racial Discrimination. It interprets article 4 as requiring a party to the Convention to adopt further legislative measures in the fields covered by subparagraphs (*a*), (*b*) and (*c*) of that article only in so far as it may consider with due regard to the principles embodied in the Universal Declaration set out in article 5 of the Convention (in particular the right to freedom of opinion and expression and the right of freedom of peaceful assembly and association) that some legislative addition to, or variation of existing law and practice in these fields is necessary for the attainment of the ends specified in article 4. Lastly, the Constitution of the Commonwealth of the Bahamas entrenches and guarantees to every person in the Commonwealth of the Bahamas the fundamental rights and freedoms of the individual irrespective of his race or place of origin. The Constitution prescribes judicial process to be observed in the event of the violation of any of these rights whether by the State or by a private individual. Acceptance of this Convention by the Commonwealth of the Bahamas does not imply the acceptance of obligations going beyond the constitutional limits nor the acceptance of any obligations to introduce judicial process beyond those prescribed under the Constitution."

Barbados

"The Constitution of Barbados entrenches and guarantees to every person in Barbados the fundamental rights and freedoms of the individual irrespective of his race or place of origin. The Constitution prescribes judicial processes to be observed in the event of the violation of any of these rights whether by the State or by a private individual. Accession to the Convention does not imply the acceptance of obligations going beyond the constitutional limits nor the acceptance of any obligations to introduce judicial processes beyond those provided in the Constitution.

"The Government of Barbados interprets article 4 of the said Convention as requiring a party to the Convention to enact measures in the fields covered by subparagraph (*a*), (*b*) and (*c*) of that article only where it is considered that the need arises to enact such legislation."

Belgium

In order to meet the requirements of article 4 of the International Convention of the Elimination of All Forms of Racial Discrimination, the Kingdom of Belgium will take care to adapt its legislation to the obligations it has assumed in becoming a party to the said Convention.

The Kingdom of Belgium nevertheless wishes to emphasize the importance which it attaches to the fact that article 4 of the Convention provides that the measures laid down in subparagraphs (*a*), (*b*), and (*c*) should be adopted with due regard to the principles embodied in the Universal Declaration of Human Rights and the rights expressly set forth in article 5 of the Convention. The Kingdom of Belgium therefore considers that the obligations imposed by article 4 must be reconciled with the right to freedom of opinion and expression and the right to freedom of peaceful assembly and association. Those rights are proclaimed in articles 19 and 20 of the Universal Declaration of Human Rights and have been reaffirmed in articles 19 and 21 of the International Covenant on Civil and Political Rights. They have also been stated in article 5, subparagraph (*d*) (viii) and (ix) of the said Convention.

The Kingdom of Belgium also wishes to emphasize the importance which it attaches to respect for the rights set forth in the Convention for the Protection of Human Rights and Fundamental Freedoms, especially in articles 10 and 11 dealing respectively with freedom of opinion and expression and freedom of peaceful assembly and association.

Bulgaria

The Government of the People's Republic of Bulgaria considers that the provisions of article 17, paragraph 1, and article 18, paragraph 1, of the International Convention on the Elimination of All Forms of Racial Discrimination, the effect of which is to prevent sovereign States from becoming parties to the Convention, are of a discriminatory nature. The Convention, in accordance with the principle of the sovereign equality of States, should be open for accession by all States without any discrimination whatsoever.

The People's Republic of Bulgaria does not consider itself bound by the provision of article 22 of the International Convention on the Elimination of All Forms of Racial Discrimination, which provides for the compulsory jurisdiction of the International Court of Justice in the settlement of disputes with respect to the interpretation or application of the Convention. The People's Republic of Bulgaria maintains its position that no dispute between two or more States can be referred to the International Court of Justice without the consent in each particular case of all the States parties to the dispute.

Byelorussian Soviet Socialist Republic

The Byelorussian Soviet Socialist Republic states that the provision in article 17, paragraph 1, of the International Convention on the Elimination of All Forms of Racial Discrimination whereby a number of States are deprived of the opportunity to become parties to the Convention is of a discriminatory nature, and hold that, in accordance with the principle of the sovereign equality of States, the Convention should be open to participation by all interested States without discrimination or restriction of any kind.

The Byelorussian Soviet Socialist Republic does not consider itself bound by the provision of article 22 of the Convention, under which any dispute between two or more States parties with respect to the interpretation or application of the Convention is, at the request of any of the parties to the dispute, to be referred to the International Court of Justice for decision, and states that, in each individual case, the consent of all parties to such a dispute is necessary for referral of the dispute to the International Court.

China

Reservation:

The People's Republic of China has reservation on the provision of article 22 of the Convention and will not be bound by it. (The reservation was circulated by the Secretary-General on 13 January 1982.)[4]

Declaration:

The signing and ratification of the said Convention by the Taiwan authorities in the name of China are illegal and null and void.

Cuba

Upon signature:

The Government of the Republic of Cuba will make such reservations as it may deem appropriate if and when the Convention is ratified.

Upon ratification:
Reservation:

The Revolutionary Government of the Republic of Cuba does not accept the provision of article 22 of the Convention to the effect that disputes between two or more States parties shall be referred to the International Court of Justice, since it considers that such disputes should be settled exclusively by the procedures expressly provided for in the Convention or by negotiation through the diplomatic channel between the disputants.

Statement:

This Convention, intended to eliminate all forms of racial discrimination, should not, as it expressly does in articles 17 and 18, exclude States not Members of the United Nations, members of the specialized agencies or parties to the Statute of the International Court of Justice from making an effective contribution under the Convention, since these articles constitute in themselves a form of discrimination that is at variance with the principles set out in the Convention; the Revolutionary Government of the Republic of Cuba accordingly ratifies the Convention, but with the qualification just indicated.

Czechoslovakia

"The Czechoslovak Socialist Republic considers that the provision of article 17, paragraph 1, is not in keeping with the aims and objectives of the Convention since it fails to ensure that all States without any distinction and discrimination be given the opportunity to become parties to the Convention.

"The Czechoslovak Socialist Republic does not consider itself bound by the provision of article 22 and maintains that any dispute between two or more parties over the interpretation or application of the Convention, which is not settled by negotiation or by procedures expressly provided for in the Convention, can be referred to the International Court of Justice only at the request of all the parties to the dispute, if they did not agree to another means of settlement."

Democratic Yemen[5]

"The accession of the People's Democratic Republic of Yemen to this Convention shall in no way signify recognition of Israel or entry into a relationship with it regarding any matter regulated by the said Convention.

"The People's Democratic Republic of Yemen does not consider itself bound by the provision of article 22 of the Convention, under which any dispute between two or more States parties with respect to the interpretation or application of the Convention is, at the request of any of the parties to the dispute, to be referred to the International Court of Justice for decision, and states that, in each individual case, the consent of all parties to such a dispute is necessary for referral of the dispute to the International Court of Justice.

"The People's Democratic Republic of Yemen states that the provisions of article 17, paragraph 1, and article 18, paragraph 1, of the International Convention on the Elimination of All Forms of Racial Discrimination whereby a number of States are deprived of the opportunity to become parties to the Convention is of a discriminatory nature, and holds that, in accordance with the principle of the sovereign equality of States, the Convention should be opened to participation by all interested States without discrimination or restriction of any kind."

Denmark[6]

Egypt

"The United Arab Republic does not consider itself bound by the provision of article 22 of the Convention, under which any dispute between two or more States parties with respect to the interpretation or application of the Convention is, at the request of any of the parties to the dispute, to be referred to the International Court of Justice for decision, and it states that, in each individual case, the consent of all parties to such a dispute is necessary for referring the dispute to the International Court of Justice.

"... "[7, 8]

Fiji

The reservation and declarations formulated by the Government of the United Kingdom on behalf of Fiji are affirmed but have been redrafted in the following terms:

"To the extent, if any, that any law relating to elections in Fiji may not fulfil the obligations referred to in article 5 (*c*), that any law relating to land in Fiji which prohibits or restricts the alienation of land by the indigenous inhabitants may not fulfil the obligations referred to in article 5 (*d*) (v), or that the school system of Fiji may not fulfil the obligations referred to in articles 2, 3, or 5 (*e*) (v), the Government of Fiji reserves the right not to implement the aforementioned provisions of the Convention.

"The Government of Fiji wishes to state its understanding of certain articles in the Convention. It interprets article 4 as requiring a party to the Convention to adopt further legislative measures in the fields covered by subparagraphs (*a*), (*b*) and (*c*) of that article only in so far as it may consider with due regard to the principles embodied in the Universal Declaration of Human Rights and the rights expressly set forth in article 5 of the Convention (in particular the right to freedom of opinion and expression and the right to freedom of peaceful assembly and association) that some legislative addition to or variation of existing law and practice in those fields is necessary for the attainment of the end specified in the earlier part of article 4. Further, the Government of Fiji interprets the requirement in article 6 concerning 'reparation or satisfaction' as being fulfilled if one or other of these forms of redress, is made available and interprets 'satisfaction' as including any form of redress effective to bring the discriminatory conduct to an end. In addition it interprets article 20 and the other related provisions of Part III of the Convention as meaning that if a reservation is not accepted the State making the reservation does not become a party to the Convention.

"The Government of Fiji maintains the view that article 15 is discriminatory in that it establishes a procedure for the receipt of petitions relating to dependent territories whilst making no comparable provision for States without such territories."

France[9]

With regard to article 4, France wishes to make it clear that it interprets the reference made therein to the principles of the Universal Declaration of Human Rights and to the rights set forth in article 5 of the Convention as releasing the States parties from the obligation to enact anti-discrimination legislation which is incompatible with the freedoms of opinion and expression and of peaceful assembly and association guaranteed by those texts.

With regard to article 6, France declares that the question of remedy through tribunals is, as far as France is concerned, governed by the rules of ordinary law.

With regard to article 15, France's accession to the Convention may not be interpreted as implying any change in its position regarding the resolution mentioned in that provision.

German Democratic Republic

The German Democratic Republic does not consider itself bound by article 22 of the Convention, under which any dispute between two or more States parties with respect to the interpretation or application of the Convention is, at the request of any of the parties to the dispute, to be referred to the International Court of Justice for decision, and declares that, in each individual case, the consent of all parties to such a dispute is necessary for referral of the dispute to the International Court of Justice.

The German Democratic Republic deems it necessary to state that article 17, paragraph 1, of the Convention deprives a number of States of the opportunity to become parties to the Convention. As the Convention regulates matters affecting the interests of all States, it should be open to participation by all States whose policies are guided by the purposes and principles of the Charter of the United Nations.

Guyana

"The Government of the Republic of Guyana do not interpret the provisions of this Convention as imposing upon them any obligation going beyond the limits set by the Constitution of Guyana or imposing upon them any obligation requiring the introduction of judicial processes going beyond those provided under the same Constitution."

Hungary

"The Hungarian People's Republic considers that the provisions of article 17, paragraph 1, and of article 18, paragraph 1, of the Convention, barring accession to the Convention by all States, are of a discriminating nature and contrary to international law. The Hungarian People's Republic maintains its general position that multilateral treaties of a universal character should, in conformity with the principles of sovereign equality of States, be open for accession by all States without any discrimination whatever.

"The Hungarian People's Republic does not consider itself bound by article 22 of the Convention providing that any dispute between two or more States parties with respect to the interpretation or application of the Convention shall, at the request of any of the parties to the dispute, be referred to the International Court of Justice for decision. The Hungarian People's Republic takes the view that such disputes shall be referred to the International Court of Justice only by agreement of all parties concerned."

India [10]

"The Government of India declare that for reference of any dispute to the International Court of Justice for decision in terms of article 22 of the International Convention on the Elimination of All Forms of Racial Discrimination, the consent of all parties to the dispute is necessary in each individual case."

Iraq [8]

Upon signature:

"The Ministry for Foreign Affairs of the Republic of Iraq hereby declares that signature for and on behalf of the Republic of Iraq of the International Convention on the Elimination of All Forms of Racial Discrimination, which was adopted by the General Assembly of the United Nations on 21 December 1965, as well as approval by the Arab States of the said Convention and entry into it by their respective Governments, shall in no way signify recognition of Israel or lead to entry by the Arab States into such dealings with Israel as may be regulated by the said Convention.

"Furthermore, the Government of the Republic of Iraq does not consider itself bound by the provision of article 22 of the aforementioned Convention and affirms its reservation that it does not accept the compulsory jurisdiction of the International Court of Justice provided for in the said article."

Upon ratification:

1. The acceptance and ratification of the Convention by Iraq shall in no way signify recognition of Israel or be conducive to entry by Iraq into such dealings with Israel as are regulated by the Convention; [11]

2. Iraq does not accept the provision of article 22 of the Convention, concerning the compulsory jurisdiction of the International Court of Justice. The Republic of Iraq does not consider itself to be bound by the provision of article 22 of the Convention and deems it necessary that in all cases the approval of all parties to the dispute be secured before the case is referred to the International Court of Justice.

Israel

"The State of Israel does not consider itself bound by the provision of article 22 of the said Convention."

Italy

Declaration made upon signature and confirmed upon ratification:

(*a*) The positive measures, provided for in article 4 of the Convention and specifically described in subparagraphs (*a*) and (*b*) of that article, designed to eradicate all incitements to, or acts of, discrimination, are to be interpreted, as that article provides, "with due regard to the principles embodied in the Universal Declaration of Human Rights and the rights expressly set forth in article 5" of the Convention. Consequently, the obligations deriving from the aforementioned article 4 are not to jeopardize the right to freedom of opinion and expression and the right to freedom of peaceful assembly and association, which are laid down in articles 19 and 20 of the Universal Declaration of Human Rights, were reaffirmed by the General Assembly of the United Nations when it adopted articles 19 and 21 of the International Covenant on Civil and Political Rights, and are referred to in article 5 (*d*) (viii) and (ix) of the Convention. In fact, the Italian Government, in conformity with the obligations resulting from Articles 55 (*c*) and 56 of the Charter of the United Nations, remains faithful to the principle laid down in article 29 (2) of the Universal Declaration, which provides that "in the exercise of his rights and freedoms, everyone shall be subject only to such limitations as are determined by law solely for the purpose of securing due recognition and respect for the rights and freedoms of others and of meeting the just requirements of morality, public order and the general welfare in a democratic society".

(*b*) Effective remedies against acts of racial discrimination which violate his individual rights and fundamental freedoms will be assured to everyone, in conformity with article 6 of the Convention, by the ordinary courts within the framework of their respective jurisdiction. Claims for reparation for any damage suffered as a result of acts of racial discrimination must be brought against the persons responsible for the malicious or criminal acts which caused such damage.

Jamaica

"The Constitution of Jamaica entrenches and guarantees to every person in Jamaica the fundamental rights and freedoms of the individual irrespective of his race or place of origin. The Constitution prescribes judicial processes to be observed in the event of the violation of any of these rights whether by the State or by a private individual. Ratification of the Convention by Jamaica does not imply the acceptance of obligations going beyond the constitutional limits nor the acceptance of any obligation to introduce judicial processes beyond those prescribed under the Constitution."

Kuwait[8]

"In acceding to the said Convention, the Government of the State of Kuwait takes the view that its accession does not in any way imply recognition of Israel, nor does it oblige it to apply the provisions of the Convention in respect of the said country.

"The Government of the State of Kuwait does not consider itself bound by the provision of article 22 of the Convention, under which any dispute between two or more States parties with respect to the interpretation or application of the Convention is, at the request of any party to the dispute, to be referred to the International Court of Justice for decision, and it states that, in each individual case, the consent of all parties to such a dispute is necessary for referring the dispute to the International Court of Justice."

Lebanon

The Republic of Lebanon does not consider itself bound by the provision of article 22 of the Convention, under which any dispute between two or more States parties with respect to the interpretation or application of the Convention is, at the request of any party to the dispute, to be referred to the International Court of Justice for decision, and it states that, in each individual case, the consent of all States parties to such a dispute is necessary for referring the dispute to the International Court of Justice.

Libyan Arab Jamahiriya[8]

"(*a*) The Kingdom of Libya does not consider itself bound by the provision of article 22 of the Convention, under which any dispute between two or more States parties with respect to the interpretation or application of the Convention is, at the request of any of the parties to the dispute, to be referred to the International Court of Justice for decision, and it states that, in each individual case, the consent of all parties to such a dispute is necessary for referring the dispute to the International Court of Justice.

"(*b*) It is understood that the accession to this Convention does not mean in any way a recognition of Israel by the Government of the Kindgom of Libya. Furthermore, no treaty relations will arise between the Kingdom of Libya and Israel."

Madagascar

The Government of the Malagasy Republic does not consider itself bound by the provision of article 22 of the Convention, under which any dispute between two or more States parties with respect to the interpretation or application of the Convention is, at the request of any of the parties to the dispute, to be referred to the International Court of Justice for decision, and states that, in each individual case, the consent of all parties to such a dispute is necessary for referral of the dispute to the International Court.

Malta

Declaration made upon signature and confirmed upon ratification:

"The Government of Malta wishes to state its understanding of certain articles in the Convention.

"It interprets article 4 as requiring a party to the Convention to adopt further measures in the fields covered by subparagraphs (*a*), (*b*) and (*c*) of that article should it consider, with due regard to the principles embodied in the Universal Declaration of Human Rights and the rights set forth in article 5 of the Convention, that the need arises to enact '*ad hoc*' legislation, in addition to or variation of existing law and practice to bring to an end any act of racial discrimination.

"Further, the Government of Malta interprets the requirements in article 6 concerning 'reparation or satisfaction' as being fulfilled if one or other of these forms of redress is made available and interprets 'satisfaction' as including any form of redress effective to bring the discriminatory conduct to an end."

Mongolia

The Mongolian People's Republic states that the provision in article 17, paragraph 1, of the Convention whereby a number of States are deprived of the opportunity to become parties to the Convention is of a discriminatory nature, and it holds that, in accordance with the principle of the sovereign equality of States, the International Convention on the Elimination of All Forms of Racial Discrimination should be open to participation by all interested States without discrimination or restriction of any kind.

The Mongolian People's Republic does not consider itself bound by the provision of article 22 of the Convention, under which any dispute between two or more States parties with respect to the interpretation or application of the Convention is, at the request of any of the parties to the dispute, to be referred to the International Court of Justice for decision, and it states that, in each individual case, the consent of all parties to such a dispute is necessary for referral of the dispute to the International Court.

Morocco

The Kingdom of Morocco does not consider itself bound by the provision of article 22 of the Convention, under which any dispute between two or more States parties with respect to the interpretation or application of the Convention is, at the request of any of the parties to the dispute, to be referred to the International Court of Justice for decision. The Kingdom of Morocco states that, in each individual case, the consent of all parties to such a dispute is necessary for referring the dispute to the International Court of Justice.

Mozambique

Reservation:

The People's Republic of Mozambique does not consider itself to be bound by the provision of article 22 and wishes to restate that for the submission of any dispute to the International Court of Justice for decision in terms of the said article, the consent of all parties to such a dispute is necessary in each individual case.

Nepal

"The Constitution of Nepal contains provisions for the protection of individual rights, including the right to freedom of speech and expression, the right to form unions and associations not motivated by party politics and the right to freedom of professing his/her own religion; and nothing in the Convention shall be deemed to require or to authorize legislation or other action by Nepal incompatible with the provisions of the Constitution of Nepal.

"His Majesty's Government interprets article 4 of the said Convention as requiring a party to the Convention to adopt further legislative measures in the fields covered by subparagraphs (*a*), (*b*) and (*c*) of that article only in so far as His Majesty's Government may consider, with due regard to the principles embodied in the Universal Declaration of Human Rights, that some legislative addition to, or variation of, existing law and practice in those fields is necessary for the attainment of the end specified in the earlier part of article 4. His Majesty's Government interprets the requirement in article 6 concerning 'reparation or satisfaction' as being fulfilled if one or other of these forms of redress is made available; and further interprets 'satisfaction' as including any form of redress effective to bring the discriminatory conduct to an end.

"His Majesty's Government does not consider itself bound by the provision of article 22 of the Convention under which any dispute between two or more States parties with respect to the interpretation or application of the Convention is, at the request of any of the parties to the dispute, to be referred to the International Court of Justice for decision."

Papua New Guinea

Reservation:

"The Government of Papua New Guinea interprets article 4 of the Convention as requiring a party to the Convention to adopt further legislative measures in the areas covered by subparagraphs (*a*), (*b*) and (*c*) of that article only in so far as it may consider with due regard to the principles contained in the Universal Declaration set out in article 5 of the Convention that some legislative addition to, or variation of existing law and practice, is necessary to give effect to the provisions of article 4. In addition, the Constitution of Papua New Guinea guarantees certain fundamental rights and freedoms to all persons irrespective of their race or place of origin. The Constitution also provides for judicial protection of these rights and freedoms. Acceptance of this Convention does not therefore indicate the acceptance of obligations by the Government of Papua New Guinea which go beyond those provided by the Constitution, nor does it indicate the acceptance of any obligation to introduce judicial process beyond that provided by the Constitution." [The reservation was circulated by the Secretary-General on 22 February 1982.][4]

Poland

The Polish People's Republic does not consider itself bound by the provision of article 22 of the Convention.

The Polish People's Republic considers that the provisions of article 17, paragraph 1, and article 18, paragraph 1, of the International Convention on the Elimination of All Forms of Racial Discrimination, which make it impossible for many States to become parties to the said Convention, are of a discriminatory nature and are incompatible with the object and purpose of that Convention.

The Polish People's Republic considers that, in accordance with the principle of the sovereign equality of States, the said Convention should be open for participation by all States without any discrimination or restrictions whatsoever.

Romania

The Socialist Republic of Romania declares that it does not consider itself bound by the provision of article 22 of the International Convention on the Elimination of All Forms of Racial Discrimination, whereby any dispute between two or more States parties with respect to the interpretation or application of the Convention which is not settled by negotiation or by the procedures expressly provided for in the Convention shall, at the request of any of the parties to the dispute, be referred to the International Court of Justice.

The Socialist Republic of Romania considers that such disputes may be referred to the International Court of Justice only with the consent of all parties to the dispute in each individual case.

The Council of State of the Socialist Republic of Romania declares that the provisions of articles 17 and 18 of the International Convention on the Elimination of All Forms of Racial Discrimination are not in accordance with the principle that multilateral treaties, the aims and objectives of which concern the world community as a whole, should be open to participation by all States.

Rwanda

The Rwandese Republic does not consider itself as bound by article 22 of the Convention.

Spain

With a reservation in respect of the whole of article 22 (jurisdiction of the International Court of Justice).

Syrian Arab Republic[8]

1. The accession of the Syrian Arab Republic to this Convention shall in no way signify recognition of Israel or entry into a relationship with it regarding any matter regulated by the said Convention.

2. The Syrian Arab Republic does not consider itself bound by the provision of article 22 of the Convention, under which any dispute between two or more States parties with respect to the interpretation or application of the Convention is, at the request of any of the parties to the dispute, to be referred to the International Court of Justice for decision. The Syrian Arab Republic states that, in each individual case, the consent of all parties to such a dispute is necessary for referring the dispute to the International Court of Justice.

Tonga[12]

Reservation:

"To the extent, [. . .], that any law relating to land in Tonga which prohibits or restricts the alienation of land by the indigenous inhabitants may not fulfil the obligations referred to in article 5 (*d*) (v), [. . .], the Kingdom of Tonga reserves the right not to apply the Convention to Tonga.

Declaration:

"Secondly, the Kingdom of Tonga wishes to state its understanding of certain articles in the Convention. It interprets article 4 as requiring a party to the Convention to adopt further legislative measures in the fields covered by subparagraphs (*a*), (*b*) and (*c*) of that article only in so far as it may consider with due regard to the principles embodied in the Universal Declaration of Human Rights and the rights expressly set forth in article 5 of the Convention (in particular the right to freedom of opinion and expression and the right to freedom of peaceful assembly and association) that some legislative addition to or variation of existing law and practice in those fields is necessary for the attainment of the end specified in the earlier part of article 4. Further, the Kingdom of Tonga interprets the requirement in article 6 concerning 'reparation or satisfaction' as being fulfilled if one or other of these forms of redress is made available and interprets 'satisfaction' as including any form of redress effective to bring the discriminatory conduct to an end. In addition it interprets article 20 and the other related provisions of Part III of the Convention as meaning that if a reservation is not accepted the State making the reservation does not become a party to the Convention.

"Lastly, the Kingdom of Tonga maintains its position in regard to article 15. In its view this article is discriminatory in that it establishes a procedure for the receipt of petitions relating to dependent territories while making no comparable provision for States without such territories. Moreover, the article purports to establish a procedure applicable to the dependent territories of States whether or not those States have become parties to the Convention. His Majesty's Government have decided that the Kingdom of Tonga should accede to the Convention, these objections notwithstanding because of the importance they attach to the Convention as a whole."

Ukrainian Soviet Socialist Republic

The Ukrainian Soviet Socialist Republic states that the provision of article 17, paragraph 1, of the International Convention on the Elimination of All Forms of Racial Discrimination whereby a number of States are deprived of the opportunity to become parties to the Convention is of a discriminatory nature, and hold that, in accordance with the principle of the sovereign equality of States, the Convention should be open to participation by all interested States without discrimination or restriction of any kind.

The Ukrainian Soviet Socialist Republic does not consider itself bound by the provision of article 22 of the Convention, under which any dispute between two or more States parties with respect to the interpretation or application of the Convention is, at the request of any of the parties to the dispute, to be referred to the International Court of Justice for decision, and states that, in each individual case, the consent of all parties to such a dispute is necessary for referral of the dispute to the International Court.

Union of Soviet Socialist Republics

The Union of Soviet Socialist Republics states that the provision of article 17, paragraph 1, of the International Convention on the Elimination of All Forms of Racial Discrimination whereby a number of States are deprived of the opportunity to become parties to the Convention is of a discriminatory nature, and hold that, in accordance with the principle of the sovereign equality of States, the Convention should be open to participation by all interested States without discrimination or restriction of any kind.

The Union of Soviet Socialist Republics does not consider itself bound by the provision of article 22 of the Convention, under which any dispute between two or more States parties with respect to the interpretation or application of the Convention is, at the request of any of the parties to the dispute, to be referred to the International Court of Justice for decision, and states that, in each individual case, the consent of all parties to such a dispute is necessary for referral of the dispute to the International Court.

United Arab Emirates[8]

"The accession of the United Arab Emirates to this Convention shall in no way amount to recognition of nor the establishment of any treaty relations with Israel."

United Kingdom of Great Britain and Northern Ireland

Upon signature:

Subject to the following reservation and interpretative statements:

"First, in the present circumstances deriving from the usurpation of power in Rhodesia by the illegal régime, the United Kingdom must sign subject to a reservation of the right not to apply the Convention to Rhodesia unless and until the United Kingdom informs the Secretary-General of the United Nations that it is in a position to ensure that the obligations imposed by the Convention in respect of that territory can be fully implemented.

"Secondly, the United Kingdom wishes to state its understanding of certain articles in the Convention. It interprets article 4 as requiring a party to the Convention to adopt further legislative measures in the fields covered by subparagraphs (*a*), (*b*) and (*c*) of that article only in so far as it may consider with due regard to the principles embodied in the Universal Declaration of Human Rights and the rights expressly set forth in article 5 of the Convention (in particular the right to freedom of opinion and expression and the right to freedom of peaceful assembly and association) that some legislative addition to or variation of existing law and practice in those fields is necessary for the attainment of the end specified in the earlier part of article 4. Further, the United Kingdom interprets the requirement in article 6 concerning "reparation or satisfaction" as being fulfilled if one or other of these forms of redress is made available and interprets "satisfaction" as including any form of redress effective to bring the discriminatory conduct to an end. In addition it interprets article 20 and the other related provisions of Part III of the Convention as meaning that if a reservation is not accepted the State making the reservation does not become a party to the Convention.

"Lastly, the United Kingdom maintains its position in regard to article 15. In its view this article is discriminatory in that it establishes a procedure for the receipt of petitions relating to dependent territories while making no comparable provision for States without such territories. Moreover, the article purports to establish a procedure applicable to the dependent territories of States whether or not those States have become parties to the Convention. Her Majesty's Government have decided that the United Kingdom should sign the Convention, these objections notwithstanding, because of the importance they attach to the Convention as a whole."

Upon ratification:

"First, the reservation and interpretative statements made by the United Kingdom at the time of signature of the Convention are maintained.

"Secondly, the United Kingdom does not regard the Commonwealth Immigrants Acts, 1962 and 1968, or their application, as involving any racial discrimination within the meaning of article 1, paragraph 1, or any other provision of the Convention, and fully reserves its right to continue to apply those Acts.

"Lastly, to the extent if any, that any law relating to election in Fiji may not fulfil the obligations referred to in article 5 (*c*), that any law relating to land in Fiji which prohibits or restricts the alienation of land by the indigenous inhabitants may not fulfil the obligations referred to in article 5 (*d*) (*v*), or that the school system of Fiji may not fulfil the obligations referred to in articles 2, 3 or 5 (*e*) (*v*), the United Kingdom reserves the right not to apply the Convention to Fiji.".

United States of America

"The Constitution of the United States contains provisions for the protection of individual rights, such as the right of free speech, and nothing in the Convention shall be deemed to require or to authorize legislation or other action by the United States of America incompatible with the provisions of the Constitution of the United States of America."

Viet Nam

Declaration:

(1) The Government of the Socialist Republic of Viet Nam declares that the provisions of article 17 (1) and of article 18 (1) of the Convention whereby a number of States are deprived of the opportunity of becoming parties to the said Convention are of a discriminatory nature and it considers that, in accordance with the principle of the sovereign equality of States, the Convention should be open to participation by all States without discrimination or restriction of any kind. (The reservation was circulated by the Secretary-General on 10 August 1982.)[4]

Reservation:

(2) The Government of the Socialist Republic of Viet Nam does not consider itself bound by the provision of article 22 of the Convention and holds that, for any dispute with regard to the interpretation or application of the Convention to be brought before the International Court of Justice, the consent of all parties to the dispute is necessary.

OBJECTIONS

(Unless otherwise indicated, the objections were made
upon ratification, accession or succession.)

Byelorussian Soviet Socialist Republic

29 December 1983

The ratification of the above-mentioned International Convention by the so-called "Government of Democratic Kampuchea" — the Pol Pot clique of hangmen overthrown by the Kampuchean people — is completely unlawful and has no legal force. Only the representatives authorized by the State Council of the People's Republic of Kampuchea can act in the name of Kampuchea. There is only one State of Kampuchea in the world — the People's Republic of Kampuchea, which has been recognized by a large number of countries. All power in this State is entirely in the hands of its only lawful Government, the Government of the People's Republic of Kampuchea, which has the exclusive right to act in the name of Kampuchea in the international arena, including the right to ratify international agreements prepared within the United Nations.

Nor should one fail to observe that the farce involving the ratification of the above-mentioned International Convention by a clique representing no one mocks the norms of law and morality and is a direct insult to the memory of millions of Kampuchean victims of the genocide committed against the Kampuchean people by the Pol Pot Sary régime. The entire international community is familiar with the bloody crimes of that puppet clique.

Czechoslovakia

12 March 1984

"The Government of the Czechoslovak Socialist Republic as a party to the International Convention on the Elimination of All Forms of Racial Discrimination, opened for signature in New York on 7 March 1966, does not recognize any legal effects of the instrument of ratification of the Convention deposited with the Secretary-General of the United Nations on 28 November 1983 by the so-called Government of 'Democratic Kampuchea'.

"The Czechoslovak Socialist Republic recognizes the Government of the People's Republic of Kampuchea as the sole representative of the Kampuchean people which alone is entitled to represent and defend the interests of the People's Republic of Kampuchea in bilateral or multilateral international relations and to act as a party to international treaties and agreements.

"For the above-stated reasons, the Czechoslovak Socialist Republic does not recognize any right of the Government of the so-called 'Democratic Kampuchea' to act and to assume international obligations in the name of the Kampuchean people."

Ethiopia

25 January 1984

"The Provisional Military Government of Socialist Ethiopia would like to reiterate that the Government of the People's Republic of Kampuchea is the sole legitimate representative of the people of Kampuchea and as such it alone has the authority to act on behalf of Kampuchea.

"'The Provisional Military Government of Socialist Ethiopia, therefore, considers the ratification of the so-called 'Government of Democratic Kampuchea' to be null and void."

France

15 May 1984

The Government of the French Republic, which does not recognize the Coalition Government of Democratic Kampuchea, declares that the instrument of ratification by the Coalition Government of Democratic Kampuchea of the [International] Convention on the Elimination of All Forms of Racial Discrimination, opened for signature at New York on 7 March 1966, is without effect.

German Democratic Republic

26 April 1984

"The German Democratic Republic does not recognize the so-called coalition Government of Democratic Kampuchea and therefore regards its instrument of ratification concerning the International Convention on the Elimination of All Forms of Racial Discrimination of [7 March 1966] as being without legal force. The only legitimate representative of the people of Kampuchea is the Government of the People's Republic of Kampuchea. It has the exclusive right to act in the name of Kampuchea in the international arena, including the right to sign and to ratify international agreements."

Mongolia

7 June 1984

"The Government of the Mongolian People's Republic considers that only the People's Revolutionary Council of Kampuchea as the sole authentic and lawful representative of the Kampuchean people has the right to assume international obligations on behalf of the Kampuchean people. Therefore the Government of the Mongolian People's Republic considers that the ratification of the International Convention on the Elimination of All Forms of Racial Discrimination by the so-called Democratic Kampuchea, a régime that ceased to exist as a result of the people's revolution in Kampuchea, is null and void."

Ukrainian Soviet Socialist Republic

17 January 1984

The ratification of the above-mentioned International Convention by the Pol Pot-Ieng Sary clique, which it guilty of the annihilation of millions of

Kampucheans and which was overthrown in 1979 by the Kampuchean people, is thoroughly illegal and has no juridical force. There is only one Kampuchean State in the world, namely, the People's Republic of Kampuchea. All authority in this State is vested wholly in its sole legitimate Government, the Government of the People's Republic of Kampuchea. This Government alone has the exclusive right to speak on behalf of Kampuchea at the international level, while the supreme organ of State power, the State Council of the People's Republic of Kampuchea has the exclusive right to ratify international agreements drawn up within the framework of the United Nations.

Union of Soviet Socialist Republics

28 December 1983

The ratification of the above-mentioned International Convention by the so-called "Government of Democratic Kampuchea"—the Pol Pot-Ieng Sary clique of hangmen overthrown by the Kampuchean people—is completely unlawful and has no legal force. Only the representatives authorized by the State Council of the People's Republic of Kampuchea can act in the name of Kampuchea. There is only one State of Kampuchea in the world—the People's Republic of Kampuchea—which has been recognized by a large number of countries. All power in this State is entirely in the hands of its only lawful Government, the Government of the People's Republic of Kampuchea, which has the exclusive right to ratify international agreements prepared within the United Nations.

Nor should one fail to observe that the farce involving the ratification of the above-mentioned International Convention by a clique representing no one mocks the norms of law and morality and is a direct insult to the memory of millions of Kampuchean victims of the genocide committed against the Kampuchean People by the Pol Pot-Ieng Sary régime.

Viet Nam

29 February 1984

"The Government of the Socialist Republic of Viet Nam considers that only the Government of the People's Republic of Kampuchea, which is the sole genuine and legitimate representative of the Kampuchean People, is empowered to act in their behalf to sign, ratify or accede to international conventions.

"The Government of the Socialist Republic of Viet Nam rejects as null and void the ratification of the above-mentioned International Convention by the so-called 'Democratic Kampuchea'—a genocidal régime overthrown by the Kampuchean people since 7 January 1979.

"Furthermore, the ratification of the Convention by a genocidal régime, which massacred more than 3 million Kampuchean people in gross violation of fundamental standards of morality and international laws on human rights, simply plays down the significance of the Convention and jeopardizes the prestige of the United Nations."

DECLARATIONS RECOGNIZING THE COMPETENCE OF THE COMMITTEE ON THE ELIMINATION OF RACIAL DISCRIMINATION IN ACCORDANCE WITH ARTICLE 14 OF THE CONVENTION[13]

(Unless otherwise indicated the declaration was
made upon ratification, accession or succession.)

Costa Rica

8 January 1974

Costa Rica recognizes the competence of the Committee on the Elimination of Racial Discrimination established under article 8 of the International Convention on the Elimination of All Forms of Racial Discrimination, in accordance with article 14 of the Convention, to receive and consider communications from individuals or groups of individuals within its jurisdiction claiming to be victims of a violation by the State of any of the rights set forth in the Convention.

Denmark

11 October 1985

. . . Denmark recognizes the competence of the Committee on the Elimination of Racial Discrimination to receive and consider communications from individuals or groups of individuals within Danish jurisdiction claiming to be victims of a violation by Denmark of any of the rights set forth in the Convention, with the reservation that the Committee shall not consider any communication unless it has ascertained that the same matter has not been, and is not being, examined under another procedure of international investigation or settlement.

Ecuador

18 March 1977

The State of Ecuador, by virtue of article 14 of the International Convention on the Elimination of All Forms of Racial Discrimination, recognizes the competence of the Committee on the Elimination of Racial Discrimination to receive and consider communications from individuals or groups of individuals within its jurisdiction claiming to be victims of a violation of the rights set forth in the above-mentioned Convention.

France

16 August 1982

[The Government of the French Republic declares], in accordance with article 14 of the International Convention on the Elimination of All Forms of Racial Discrimination opened for signature on 7 March 1966, [that it] recognizes the competence of the Committee on the Elimination of Racial Discrimination to receive and consider communications from individuals or groups of individuals within French jurisdiction that either by reason of acts or omissions, events or deeds occurring after 15 August 1982, or by reason of a decision concerning the acts or omissions, events or deeds after the said date, would complain of being victims of a violation, by the French Republic, of one of the rights mentioned in the Convention.

Iceland

10 August 1981

"In accordance with article 14 of the International Convention on the Elimination of All Forms of Racial Discrimination which was opened for signature in New York on 7 March 1966 that Iceland recognizes the competence of the Committee on the Elimination of Racial Discrimination to receive and consider communications from individuals or groups of individuals within the jurisdiction of Iceland claiming to be victims of a violation by Iceland of any of the rights set forth in the Convention, with the reservation that the Committee shall not consider any communication from an individual or group of individuals unless the Committee has ascertained that the same matter is not being examined or has not been examined under another procedure of international investigation or settlement."

Italy

5 May 1978

With reference to article 14, paragraph 1, of the International Convention on the Elimination of All Forms of Racial Discrimination, opened for signature at New York on 7 March 1966, the Government of the Italian Republic recognizes the competence of the Committee on the Elimination of Racial Discrimination, established by the aforementioned Convention, to receive and consider communications from individuals or groups of individuals within Italian jurisdiction claiming to be victims of a violation by Italy of any of the rights set forth in the Convention.

The Government of the Italian Republic recognizes that competence on the understanding that the Committee on the Elimination of Racial Discrimination shall not consider any communication without ascertaining that the same matter is not being considered or has not already been considered by another international body of investigation or settlement.

Netherlands

In accordance with article 14, paragraph 1, of the International Convention on the Elimination of All Forms of Racial Discrimination concluded at New York on 7 March 1966, the Kingdom of the Netherlands recognizes, for the Kingdom in Europe, Surinam and the Netherlands Antilles, the competence of the Committee for the Elimination of Racial Discrimination to receive and consider communications from individuals or groups of individuals within its jurisdiction claiming to be victims of a violation, by the Kingdom of the Netherlands, of any of the rights set forth in the abovementioned Convention.

Norway

23 January 1976

"The Norwegian Government recognizes the competence of the Committee on the Elimination of Racial Discrimination to receive and consider communications from individuals or groups of individuals within the jurisdiction of Norway claiming to be victims of a violation by Norway of any of the rights set forth in the International Convention on the Elimination of All Forms of Racial Discrimination of 21 December 1965 according to article 14 of the said Convention, with the reservation that the Committee shall not consider any communication from an individual or group of individuals unless the Committee has ascertained that the same matter is not being examined or has not been examined under another procedure of international investigation or settlement."

Peru

27 November 1984

[The Government of the Republic of Peru declares] that, in accordance with its policy of full respect for human rights and fundamental freedoms, without distinction as to race, sex, language or religion, and with the aim of strengthening the international instruments on the subject, Peru recognizes the competence of the Committee on the Elimination of Racial Discrimination to receive and consider communications from individuals or groups of individuals within its jurisdiction, who claim to be victims of violations of any of the rights set forth in the International Convention on the Elimination of All Forms of Racial Discrimination, in conformity with the provisions of article 14 of the Convention.

Senegal

3 December 1982

... In accordance with [article 14], the Government of Senegal declares that it recognizes the competence of the Committee (on the Elimination of Racial Discrimination) to receive and consider communications from individuals within its jurisdiction claiming to be victims of a violation by Senegal of any of the rights set forth in the International Convention on the Elimination of All Forms of Racial Discrimination.

Sweden

"... Sweden recognizes the competence of the Committee on the Elimination of Racial Discrimination to receive and consider communications from individuals or groups of individuals within the jurisdiction of Sweden claiming to be victims of a violation by Sweden of any of the rights set forth in the Convention, with the reservation that the Committee shall not consider any communication from an individual or a group of individuals unless the Committee has ascertained that the same matter is not being examined or has not been examined under another procedure of international investigation or settlement."

Uruguay

11 September 1972

The Government of Uruguay recognizes the competence of the Committee on the Elimination of Racial Discrimination, under article 14 of the Convention.

NOTES

[1] The Convention had previously been signed and ratified on behalf of the Republic of China on 31 March 1966 and 10 December 1970 respectively. See note concerning signatures, ratifications, accessions, etc. on behalf of China (note 2 in chapter I).

With reference to the above-mentioned signature and/or ratification, communications have been received by the Secretary-General from the Governments of Bulgaria (12 March 1971), Mongolia (11 January 1971), the Byelorussian Soviet Socialist Republic (9 June 1971), the Ukrainian Soviet Socialist Republic (21 April 1971) and the Union of Soviet Socialist Republics (18 January 1971) stating that they considered the said signature and/or ratification as null and void, since the so-called "Government of China" had no right to speak or assume obligations on behalf of China, there being only one Chinese State, the People's Republic of China, and one Government entitled to represent it, the Government of the People's Republic of China.

In letters addressed to the Secretary-General in regard to the above-mentioned communications, the Permanent Representative of China to the United Nations stated that the Republic of China, a sovereign State and Member of the United Nations, had attended the twentieth regular session of the United Nations General Assembly, contributed to the formulation of the Convention concerned, signed the Convention and duly deposited the instrument of ratification thereof, and that "any statements and reservations relating to the above-mentioned Convention that are incompatible with or derogatory to the legitimate position of the Government of the Republic of China shall in no way affect the rights and obligations of the Republic of China under this Convention".

Finally, upon depositary its instrument of accession, the Government of the People's Republic of China made the following declaration: The signing and ratification of the said Convention by the Taiwan authorities in the name of China are illegal and null and void.

[2] In a note accompanying the instrument of ratification, the Government of the Federal Republic of Germany declared that the Convention "shall also apply to Land Berlin with effect from the date on which it enters into force for the Federal Republic of Germany".

With reference to the above-mentioned declaration, the Secretary-General received communications from the Governments of Bulgaria (16 September 1969), Czechoslovakia (3 November 1969), Mongolia (7 January 1970), Poland (20 June 1969), the Ukrainian Soviet Socialist Republic (10 November 1969) and the Union of Soviet Socialist Republics (4 August 1969). In the said communications, they state, in essence, that they consider the above-mentioned declaration as having no legal force on the ground that West Berlin is not, and never has been, a State territory of the Federal Republic of Germany and that, consequently, the Government of the Federal Republic of Germany is in no way competent to assume any obligations in respect of West Berlin or to extend to it the application of international agreements.

On 27 December 1973, the Government of the German Democratic Republic made in respect of the above-mentioned declaration a declaration stating in essence that Berlin (West) is no constituent part of the Federal Republic of Germany and must not be governed by it. For this reason the statement of the Government of the Federal Republic of Germany, according to which this convention also applies to the 'Land Berlin', is in contradiction to the Quadripartite Agreement and cannot produce any validity.

Subsequently, the Secretary-General received from the Governments of the Federal Republic of Germany (15 July 1974 and 19 September 1975), France, the United Kingdom and the United States of America (17 June 1974 and 8 July 1975), the Ukrainian Soviet Socialist Republic (19 September 1974) and the Union of Soviet Socialist Republics (12 September 1974 and 8 December 1975), declarations identical in essence, *mutatis mutandis*, to the corresponding ones reproduced in note 4 in chapter I.

[3] With respect to the Associated States (Antigua, Dominica, Grenada, Saint Christopher-Nevis-Anguilla and Saint Lucia) and Territories under the territorial sovereignty of the United Kingdom, as well as the State of Brunei, the Kingdom of Tonga and the British Solomon Islands Protectorate.

[4] None of the States concerned having objected to the reservation by the end of a period of 90 days after the date when it was circulated by the Secretary-General, the said reservation is deemed to have been permitted in accordance with the provision of article 20 (1).

[5] In a communication received by the Secretary-General on 12 February 1973 the Permanent Representative of Israel to the United Nations stated: "The Government of Israel has noted the political character of a reservation made by the Government of the People's Democratic Republic of Yemen on that occasion. In the view of the Government of Israel, this Convention is not the proper place for making such political pronouncements. Moreover, that declaration cannot in any way affect the obligations of the People's Democratic Republic of Yemen already existing under general international law or under particular treaties. The Government of Israel will, in so far as concerns the substance of the matter, adopt towards the Government of the People's Democratic Republic of Yemen, an attitude of complete reciprocity."

[6] In a communication received on 4 October 1972, the Government of Denmark notified the Secretary-General that it withdrew the reservation made with regard to the implementation on the Faroe Islands of the Convention. For the text of the reservation see United Nations, *Treaty Series*, vol. 820, p. 457.

The legislation by which the Convention has been implemented on the Faroe Islands entered into force by 1 November 1972, from which date the withdrawal of the above reservation became effective.

[7] In a notification received on 18 January 1980, the Government of Egypt informed the Secretary-General that it had decided to withdraw the declaration relating to Israel. For the text of the declaration see United Nations, *Treaty Series*, vol. 660, p. 318. The notification indicates 25 January 1980 as the effective date of the withdrawal.

[8] In a communication received by the Secretary-General on 10 July 1969, the Government of Israel declared that it "has noted the political character of the declaration made by the Government of Iraq on signing the above Convention.

In the view of the Government of Israel, the Convention is not the proper place for making such political pronouncements. The Government of Israel will, in so far as concerns the substance of the matter, adopt towards the Government of Iraq an attitude of complete reciprocity. Moreover, it is the view of the Government of Israel that no legal relevance can be attached to those Iraqi statements which purport to represent the views of the other States".

Except for the omission of the last sentence, identical communications in essence, *mutatis mutandis*, were received by the Secretary-General from the Government of Israel as follows: on 29 December 1966 in respect of the declaration made on signature of the Convention by the Government of the United Arab Republic; on 16 August 1968 in respect of the declaration made on accession by the Government of Libya; on 12 December 1968 in respect of the declaration made on accession by the Government of Kuwait; on 9 July 1969 in respect of the declaration made on accession by the Government of Syria, and on 25 September 1974 in respect of the declaration made upon accession by the United Arab Emirates.

[9] In a communication received subsequently, the Government of France indicated that the first paragraph of the declaration did not purport to limit the obligations under the Convention in respect of the French Government, but only to record the latter's interpretation of article 4 of the Convention.

[10] In a communication received on 24 February 1969, the Government of Pakistan notified the Secretary-General that it "has decided not to accept the reservation made by the Government of India in her instrument of ratification".

[11] On 21 April 1970, the Secretary-General received the following notification from the Government of Israel: "With regard to the political declaration in the guise of a reservation made on the occasion of the ratification of the above treaty, the Government of Israel wishes to refer to its objection circulated by the Secretary-General in his letter [. . .] [see note 8] and to maintain that objection".

[12] By a notification received on 28 October 1977, the Government of Tonga informed the Secretary-General that it had decided to withdraw only those reservations made upon accession relating to article 5 (*c*) in so far as it relates to elections, and reservations relating to articles 2, 3 and 5 (*e*) (*v*), in so far as these articles relate to education and training. For the text of the original reservation see United Nations, *Treaty Series*, vol. 829, p. 371.

[13] The first ten declarations recognizing the competence of the Committee on the Elimination of Racial Discrimination took effect on 3 December 1982, date of the deposit of the tenth declaration, according to article 14, paragraph 1 of the Convention.

Chapter V

INTERNATIONAL CONVENTION ON THE SUPPRESSION AND PUNISHMENT OF THE CRIME OF *APARTHEID*

Adopted by the General Assembly of the United Nations on 30 November 1973

ENTRY INTO FORCE: 18 July 1976, in accordance with article XV, paragraph 1.

Participant	Signature	Ratification, accession (a)
Afghanistan		6 July 1983 a
Algeria	23 Jan. 1974	26 May 1982
Antigua and Barbuda		7 Oct. 1982 a
Argentina	6 June 1975	7 Nov. 1985
Bahamas		31 Mar. 1981 a
Bangladesh		5 Feb. 1985 a
Barbados		7 Feb. 1979 a
Benin	7 Oct. 1974	30 Dec. 1974
Bolivia		6 Oct. 1983 a
Bulgaria	27 June 1974	18 July 1974
Burkina Faso	3 Feb. 1976	24 Oct. 1978
Burundi		12 July 1978 a
Byelorussian SSR	4 Mar. 1974	2 Dec. 1975
Cameroon		1 Nov. 1976 a
Cape Verde		12 June 1979 a
Central African Republic		8 May 1981 a
Chad	23 Oct. 1974	23 Oct. 1974
China		18 Apr. 1983 a
Congo		5 Oct. 1983 a
Costa Rica		15 Oct. 1986 a
Cuba		1 Feb. 1977 a
Czechoslovakia	29 Aug. 1975	25 Mar. 1976

Participant	Signature	Ratification, accession (a)
Democratic Kampuchea[1],* . . .		28 July 1981 a
Democratic Yemen	31 July 1974	
Ecuador	12 Mar. 1975	12 May 1975
Egypt		13 June 1977 a
El Salvador		30 Nov. 1979 a
Ethiopia		19 Sep. 1978 a
Gabon		29 Feb. 1980 a
Gambia		29 Dec. 1978 a
German Democratic Republic .	2 May 1974	12 Aug. 1974
Ghana		1 Aug. 1978 a
Guinea	1 Mar. 1974	3 Mar. 1975
Guyana		30 Sep. 1977 a
Haiti		19 Dec. 1977 a
Hungary	26 Apr. 1974	20 June 1974
India		22 Sep. 1977 a
Iran (Islamic Republic of)		17 Apr. 1985 a
Iraq	1 July 1975	9 July 1975
Jamaica	30 Mar. 1976	18 Feb. 1977
Jordan	5 June 1974	
Kenya	2 Oct. 1974	
Kuwait		23 Feb. 1977 a
Lao People's Democratic Republic		5 Oct. 1981 a
Lesotho		4 Nov. 1983 a
Liberia		5 Nov. 1976 a
Libyan Arab Jamahiriya		8 July 1976 a
Madagascar		26 May 1977 a
Maldives		24 Apr. 1984 a
Mali		19 Aug. 1977 a
Mexico		4 Mar. 1980 a
Mongolia	17 May 1974	8 Aug. 1975
Mozambique		18 Apr. 1983 a
Namibia (United Nations Council for Namibia)		11 Nov. 1982 a
Nepal		12 July 1977 a
Nicaragua		28 Mar. 1980 a
Niger		28 June 1978 a
Nigeria	26 June 1974	31 Mar. 1977

---

* For notes, see end of chapter.

Participant	Signature	Ratification, accession (a)
Oman	3 Apr. 1974	
Pakistan		27 Feb. 1986 *a*
Panama	7 May 1976	16 Mar. 1977
Peru		1 Nov. 1978 *a*
Philippines	2 May 1974	26 Jan. 1978
Poland	7 June 1974	15 Mar. 1976
Qatar	18 Mar. 1975	19 Mar. 1975
Romania	6 Sep. 1974	15 Aug. 1978
Rwanda	15 Oct. 1974	23 Jan. 1981
Saint Vincent and the Grenadines		9 Nov. 1981 *a*
Sao Tome and Principe		5 Oct. 1979 *a*
Senegal		18 Feb. 1977 *a*
Seychelles		13 Feb. 1978 *a*
Somalia	2 Aug. 1974	28 Jan. 1975
Sri Lanka		18 Feb. 1982 *a*
Sudan	10 Oct. 1974	21 Mar. 1977
Suriname		3 June 1980 *a*
Syrian Arab Republic	17 Jan. 1974	18 June 1976
Togo		24 May 1984 *a*
Trinidad and Tobago	7 Apr. 1975	26 Oct. 1979
Tunisia		21 Jan. 1977 *a*
Uganda	11 Mar. 1975	10 June 1986
Ukrainian SSR	20 Feb. 1974	10 Nov. 1975
Union of Soviet Socialist Republics	12 Feb. 1974	26 Nov. 1975
United Arab Emirates	9 Sep. 1975	15 Oct. 1975
United Republic of Tanzania		11 June 1976 *a*
Venezuela		28 Jan. 1983 *a*
Viet Nam		9 June 1981 *a*
Yemen		17 Aug. 1987 *a*
Yugoslavia	17 Dec. 1974	1 July 1975
Zaire		11 July 1978 *a*
Zambia		14 Feb. 1983 *a*

DECLARATIONS AND RESERVATIONS

(Unless otherwise indicated, the declarations and
reservations were made upon ratification or accession.
For objections thereto, see hereinafter.)

Argentina

Declaration:

It is the understanding of the Argentine Republic that article XII of the
Convention should be interpreted to mean that its express consent shall be
required in order for any dispute to which it is a party and which has not been
settled by negotiation to be brought before the International Court of Justice.

Egypt[2]

India

"The Government of the Republic of India accede to the said convention
with effect from 17 August 1977."

Iraq

Ratification by the Republic of Iraq of the above Convention shall in no
way imply recognition of Israel, or be conducive to the establishment of such
relations therewith as may be provided for in the Convention.

Kuwait

"It is understood that the accession of the State of Kuwait [...] does not
mean in any way recognition of Israel by the State of Kuwait."

Mozambique

The People's Republic of Mozambique interprets article XII of the Convention as to mean that the submission of any dispute concerning the inter-

pretation and application of the Convention to the International Court of Justice shall be at the previous consent and request of all the parties to the dispute.

Nepal

"The Constitution of Nepal contains provisions for the protection of individual rights, including the right to freedom of speech and expression, the right to form unions and associations not motivated by party politics and the right to freedom of professing his/her own religion; and nothing in the Convention shall be deemed to require or to authorize legislation or other action by Nepal incompatible with the provisions of the Constitution of Nepal.

"His Majesty's Government interprets article IV of the said Convention as requiring a party to the Convention to adopt further legislative measures in the fields covered by subparagraphs (a) and (b) of that article only in so far as His Majesty's Government may consider, with due regard to the principles embodied in the Universal Declaration of Human Rights, that some legislative addition to, or variation of, existing law and practice in those fields is necessary for the attainment of the end specified in the earlier part of article IV.

"His Majesty's Government does not consider itself bound by the provision of article XII of the Convention under which any dispute between two or more States parties with respect to the interpretation or application of the Convention is, at the request of any of the parties to the dispute, to be referred to the International Court of Justice for decision."

United Arab Emirates

"The ratification of the United Arab Emirates to this Convention shall in no way amount to recognition of nor the establishment of any treaty relations with Israel."

Venezuela

"With a reservation excluding the provision of article XII of the Convention."

OBJECTIONS

(Unless otherwise indicated, the objection was made
upon ratification or accession.)

Israel

12 May 1977

"The instrument deposited by the Government of Kuwait contains a statement of a political character in respect to Israel. In the view of the Government of Israel, this is not the proper place for making such political pronouncements, which are, moreover, in flagrant contradiction to the principles, objects and purposes of the Organization. That pronouncement by the Government of Kuwait cannot in any way affect whatever obligations are binding upon Kuwait under general international law or under particular treaties.

"The Government of Israel will, in so far as concerns the substance of the matter, adopt towards the Government of Kuwait an attitude of complete reciprocity."

NOTES

[1] The Secretary-General received on 10 September 1981 from the Government of Viet Nam the following objection with regard to the accession of Democratic Kampuchea:

> "The accession to the above-mentioned International Convention on behalf of the so-called 'Government of Kampuchea' by the genocidal clique of Pol Pot-Ieng Sary-Khieu Samphan, which was overthrown on 7 January 1979 by the Kampuchean people, is completely illegal and has no legal value. Only the Government of the People's Republic of Kampuchea, which is actually in power in Kampuchea, is empowered to represent the Kampuchea people and to sign and accede to international agreements and conventions.

> "As a party to that Convention, the Socialist Republic of Viet Nam is of the opinion that the accession of the so-called 'Government of Democratic Kampuchea' constitutes not only a gross violation of the standards of law and international morality, but also one of the most cynical affronts to the three million Kampucheans who were the victims of the most despicable crime of contemporary history, committed by the Pol Pot régime which is spurned by the whole of mankind."

Thereafter, similar communications objecting to the signature by Democratic Kampuchea were received by the Secretary-General on 14 September 1981 from the Government of the German Democratic Republic, on 12 November 1981 fom the Union of Soviet Socialist Republics, on 19 November 1981 from the Government of the Byelorussian Soviet Socialist Republic, on 3 December 1981 from the Government of Hungary, on 5 January 1982 from the Government of Bulgaria, on 13 January 1982 fom the Government of Mongolia, and on 17 May 1982 from the Government of Czechoslovakia.

[2] In a notification received on 18 January 1980, the Government of Egypt informed the Secretary-General that it had decided to withdraw the declaration relating to Israel. For the text of the declaration, see United Nations, *Treaty Series,* vol. 1045, p. 397. The notification indicates 25 January 1980 as the effective date of the withdrawal.

With respect to the above declaration, the Secretary-General had received, on 30 August 1977, the following declaration from the Government of Israel:

"The instrument deposited by the Government of Egypt contains a statement of a political character in respect to Israel. In the view of the Government of Israel, this is not the proper place for making such political pronouncements, which are, moreover, in flagrant contradiction to the principles, objects and purposes of the Organization. That pronouncement by the Government of Egypt cannot in any way affect whatever obligations are binding upon Egypt under general international law or under particular treaties.

"The Government of Israel will, in so far as concerns the substance of the matter, adopt towards the Government of Egypt an attitude of complete reciprocity."

Chapter VI

INTERNATIONAL CONVENTION AGAINST *APARTHEID* IN SPORTS

Adopted by the General Assembly of the United Nations on 10 December 1985

Not yet in force.

Participant	Signature	Ratification, accession (a), acceptance (A), approval (AA)
Algeria	16 May 1986	
Antigua and Barbuda	28 May 1986	
Bahamas	20 May 1986	13 Nov. 1986
Barbados	16 May 1986	2 Oct. 1986
Benin	16 May 1986	
Bolivia	16 May 1986	
Bulgaria	10 June 1986	18 Aug. 1987
Burkina Faso	16 May 1986	
Burundi	16 May 1986	
Byelorussian SSR	16 May 1986	1 July 1987
Cape Verde	16 May 1986	
Central African Republic	16 May 1986	
Colombia	31 July 1986	
Cuba	16 May 1986	
Cyprus	9 July 1987	
Czechoslovakia	25 Feb. 1987	29 July 1987
Democratic Yemen	16 May 1986	
Ecuador	16 May 1986	
Egypt	16 May 1986	
Equatorial Guinea		27 Mar. 1987 *a*
Ethiopia	16 May 1986	22 July 1987
Gabon	16 May 1986	
German Democratic Republic	16 May 1986	15 Sep. 1986
Ghana	16 May 1986	

Participant	Signature	Ratification, accession (a), acceptance (A), approval (AA)
Guinea	16 May 1986	
Guinea-Bissau	16 May 1986	
Guyana	1 Oct. 1986	1 Oct. 1986
Haiti	16 May 1986	
Hungary	25 June 1986	
Indonesia	16 May 1986	
Iran (Islamic Republic of) ...	16 May 1986	
Jamaica	16 May 1986	2 Oct. 1986
Jordan	16 May 1986	26 Aug. 1987
Kenya	16 May 1986	
Lebanon	7 Nov. 1986	
Liberia	22 May 1986	
Libyan Arab Jamahiriya	16 May 1986	
Madagascar	16 May 1986	
Malaysia	16 May 1986	
Maldives	3 Oct. 1986	
Mexico	16 May 1986	18 June 1987
Mongolia	16 May 1986	
Morocco	16 May 1986	
Nepal	24 June 1986	
Nicaragua	16 May 1986	
Niger	27 May 1986	2 Sep. 1986
Nigeria	16 May 1986	20 May 1987
Panama	16 May 1986	
Peru	30 May 1986	
Philippines	16 May 1986	27 July 1987
Poland	16 May 1986	
Rwanda	16 May 1986	
Saint Christopher and Nevis ..	16 May 1986	
Saint Lucia	29 May 1987	
Senegal	16 May 1986	15 Oct. 1986
Sierra Leone	16 May 1986	
Somalia	4 June 1986	
Sudan	16 May 1986	
Syrian Arab Republic	16 May 1986	
Togo	29 May 1986	23 Apr. 1987
Trinidad and Tobago	21 May 1986	
Tunisia	16 May 1986	
Uganda	16 May 1986	29 Aug. 1986

Participant	Signature	Ratification, accession (a), acceptance (A), approval (AA)
Ukrainian SSR	16 May 1986	19 June 1987
Union of Soviet Socialist Republics	16 May 1986	11 June 1987
United Republic of Tanzania . .	16 May 1986	
Uruguay	28 May 1986	
Venezuela	16 May 1986	
Yugoslavia	16 May 1986	
Zaire	16 May 1986	
Zimbabwe	16 May 1986	14 July 1987

Chapter VII

CONVENTION ON THE ELIMINATION OF ALL FORMS OF DISCRIMINATION AGAINST WOMEN

Adopted by the General Assembly of the United Nations on 18 December 1979

ENTRY INTO FORCE: 3 September 1981, in accordance with
article 27 (1).

Participant	Signature	Ratification, accession (a)
Afghanistan	14 Aug. 1980	
Angola		17 Sep. 1986 *a*
Argentina	17 July 1980	15 July 1985
Australia	17 July 1980	28 July 1983
Austria	17 July 1980	31 Mar. 1982
Bangladesh		6 Nov. 1984 *a*
Barbados	24 July 1980	16 Oct. 1980
Belgium	17 July 1980	10 July 1985
Benin	11 Nov. 1981	
Bhutan	17 July 1980	31 Aug. 1981
Bolivia	30 May 1980	
Brazil	31 Mar. 1981	1 Feb. 1984
Bulgaria	17 July 1980	8 Feb. 1982
Burundi	17 July 1980	
Byelorussian SSR	17 July 1980	4 Feb. 1981
Cameroon	6 June 1983	
Canada	17 July 1980	10 Dec. 1981
Cape Verde		5 Dec. 1980 *a*
Chile	17 July 1980	
China	17 July 1980	4 Nov. 1980
Colombia	17 July 1980	19 Jan. 1982
Congo	29 July 1980	26 July 1982
Costa Rica	17 July 1980	4 Apr. 1986
Côte d'Ivoire	17 July 1980	

Participant	Signature	Ratification, accession (a)
Cuba	6 Mar. 1980	17 July 1980
Cyprus		23 July 1985 *a*
Czechoslovakia	17 July 1980	16 Feb. 1982
Democratic Kampuchea[1,*] . . .	17 Oct. 1980	
Democratic Yemen		30 May 1984 *a*
Denmark	17 July 1980	21 Apr. 1983
Dominica	15 Sep. 1980	15 Sep. 1980
Dominican Republic	17 July 1980	2 Sep. 1982
Ecuador	17 July 1980	9 Nov. 1981
Egypt	16 July 1980	18 Sep. 1981
El Salvador	14 Nov. 1980	19 Aug. 1981
Equatorial Guinea		23 Oct. 1984 *a*
Ethiopia	8 July 1980	10 Sep. 1981
Finland	17 July 1980	4 Sep. 1986
France	17 July 1980	14 Dec. 1983
Gabon	17 July 1980	21 Jan. 1983
Gambia	29 July 1980	
German Democratic Republic .	25 June 1980	9 July 1980
Germany, Federal Republic of .	17 July 1980	10 July 1985[2]
Ghana	17 July 1980	2 Jan. 1986
Greece	2 Mar. 1982	7 June 1983
Grenada	17 July 1980	
Guatemala	8 June 1981	12 Aug. 1982
Guinea	17 July 1980[3]	9 Aug. 1982
Guinea-Bissau	17 July 1980	23 Aug. 1985
Guyana	17 July 1980	17 July 1980
Haiti	17 July 1980	20 July 1981
Honduras	11 June 1980	3 Mar. 1983
Hungary	6 June 1980	22 Dec. 1980
Iceland	24 July 1980	18 June 1985
India	30 July 1980	
Indonesia	29 July 1980	13 Sep. 1984
Iraq		13 Aug. 1986 *a*
Ireland		23 Dec. 1985 *a*
Israel	17 July 1980	
Italy	17 July 1980	10 June 1985
Jamaica	17 July 1980	19 Oct. 1984
Japan	17 July 1980	25 June 1985

---

* For notes, see end of chapter.

Participant	Signature	Ratification, accession (a)
Jordan	3 Dec. 1980	
Kenya		9 Mar. 1984 *a*
Lao People's Democratic Republic	17 July 1980	14 Aug. 1981
Lesotho	17 July 1980	
Liberia		17 July 1984 *a*
Luxembourg	17 July 1980	
Madagascar	17 July 1980	
Malawi		12 Mar. 1987 *a*
Mali	5 Feb. 1985	10 Sep. 1985
Mauritius		9 July 1984 *a*
Mexico	17 July 1980	23 Mar. 1981
Mongolia	17 July 1980	20 July 1981
Netherlands	17 July 1980	
New Zealand	17 July 1980	10 Jan. 1985 [4]
Nicaragua	17 July 1980	27 Oct. 1981
Nigeria	23 Apr. 1984	13 June 1985
Norway	17 July 1980	21 May 1981
Panama	26 June 1980	29 Oct. 1981
Paraguay		6 Apr. 1987 *a*
Peru	23 July 1981	13 Sep. 1982
Philippines	15 July 1980	5 Aug. 1981
Poland	29 May 1980	30 July 1980
Portugal	24 Apr. 1980	30 July 1980
Republic of Korea	25 May 1983	27 Dec. 1984
Romania	4 Sep. 1980	7 Jan. 1982
Rwanda	1 May 1980	2 Mar. 1981
Saint Christopher and Nevis		25 Apr. 1985 *a*
Saint Lucia		8 Oct. 1982 *a*
Saint Vincent and the Grenadines		4 Aug. 1981 *a*
Senegal	29 July 1980	5 Feb. 1985
Spain	17 July 1980	5 Jan. 1984
Sri Lanka	17 July 1980	5 Oct. 1981
Sweden	7 Mar. 1980	2 July 1980
Switzerland	23 Jan. 1987	
Thailand		9 Aug. 1985 *a*
Togo		26 Sep. 1983 *a*
Trinidad and Tobago	27 June 1985	
Tunisia	24 July 1980	20 Sep. 1985

Participant	Signature	Ratification, accession (a)
Turkey		20 Dec. 1985 *a*
Uganda	30 July 1980	22 July 1985
Ukrainian SSR	17 July 1980	12 Mar. 1981
Union of Soviet Socialist Republics	17 July 1980	23 Jan. 1981
United Kingdom	22 July 1981	7 Apr. 1986[5]
United Republic of Tanzania . .	17 July 1980	20 Aug. 1985
United States of America	17 July 1980	
Uruguay	30 Mar. 1981	9 Oct. 1981
Venezuela	17 July 1980	2 May 1983
Viet Nam	29 July 1980	17 Feb. 1982
Yugoslavia	17 July 1980	26 Feb. 1982
Zaire	17 July 1980	17 Oct. 1986
Zambia	17 July 1980	21 June 1985

DECLARATIONS AND RESERVATIONS

(Unless otherwise indicated, the declarations and
reservations were made upon ratification or accession.)

Argentina

Reservation:

The Government of Argentina declares that it does not consider itself
bound by article 29, paragraph 1, of the Convention on the Elimination of All
Forms of Discrimination against Women.

Australia

Reservations:

"The Government of Australia states that maternity leave with pay is
provided in respect of most women employed by the Commonwealth
Government and the Governments of New South Wales and Victoria.
Unpaid maternity leave is provided in respect of all other women employed
in the State of New South Wales and elsewhere to women employed under
Federal and some State industrial awards. Social Security benefits subject to
income tests are available to women who are sole parents.

"The Government of Australia advises that it is not at present in a position to take the measures required by article 11 (2) to introduce maternity leave with pay or with comparable social benefits throughout Australia.

"The Government of Australia advises that it does not accept the application of the Convention in so far as it would require alteration of Defence Force policy which excludes women from combat and combat-related duties. The Government of Australia is reviewing this policy so as more closely to define "combat" and "combat-related duties".

Declaration:

"Australia has a Federal Constitutional System in which Legislative, Executive and Judicial Powers are shared or distributed between the Commonwealth and the Constituent States. The implementation of the Treaty throughout Australia will be effected by the Commonwealth State and Territory Authorities having regard to their respective constitutional powers and arrangements concerning their exercise."

Austria

Reservation:

"Austria reserves its right to apply the provision of article 7 (*b*), as far as service in the armed forces is concerned, and the provision of article 11, as far as night work of women and special protection of working women is concerned, within the limits established by national legislation."

Bangladesh

"The Government of the People's Republic of Bangladesh does not consider as binding upon itself the provisions of articles 2, 13 (*a*) and 16 (1) (*c*) and (*f*) as they conflict with Shariah law based on Holy Koran and Sunna."

Belgium

Reservations:

Article 7
The application of article 7 shall not affect the validity of the provisions of the Constitution as laid down in article 60, which reserves for men the

exercise of royal powers, and in article 58, which reserves for the sons of the King or, where there are none, for Belgian princes of the branch of the royal family in line to the throne, the function of *ex officio* senators as from the age of 18 years, with entitlement to vote as from the age of 25 years.

Article 15, paragraphs 2 and 3

The application of article 15, paragraphs 2 and 3, shall not affect the validity of the interim provisions enacted for couples married before the entry into force of the Act of 14 July 1976 concerning the reciprocal rights and duties of husbands and wives and their marriage contracts, in cases where, in accordance with the option available to them under the Act, they have declared that they are maintaining *in toto* their prior marriage contracts.

Brazil

Reservation made upon signature and confirmed upon ratification:

"The Government of the Federative Republic of Brazil hereby expresses its reservations to article 15, paragraph 4, and to article 16, paragraph 1 (*a*), (*c*), (*g*) and (*h*), of the Convention on the Elimination of All Forms of Discrimination against Women.

"Furthermore, Brazil does not consider itself bound by article 29, paragraph 1, of the above-mentioned Convention."

Bulgaria

Reservation made upon signature and confirmed upon ratification:

The People's Republic of Bulgaria does not consider itself bound by the provision of article 29, paragraph 1, of the Convention.

Byelorussian Soviet Socialist Republic

Reservation made upon signature and confirmed upon ratification:

Pursuant to article 29, paragraph 2, of the Convention, the Byelorussian Soviet Socialist Republic does not consider itself bound by the provision of article 29, paragraph 1, of the Convention, to the effect that any dispute between two or more States parties concerning the interpretation or application of the Convention which is not settled by negotiation shall, at the request of one of them, be submitted to arbitration or referred to the International

Court of Justice, and declares that for the submission of such a dispute to arbitration or its referral to the International Court of Justice the consent of all parties to the dispute must be obtained in each individual case.

Canada

Statement:

"The Government of Canada states that the competent legislative authorities within Canada have addressed the concept of equal pay referred to in article 11 (1) (*d*) by legislation which requires the establishment of rates of remuneration without discrimination on the basis of sex. The competent legislative authorities within Canada will continue to implement the object and purpose of article 11 (1) (*d*) and to that end have developed, and where appropriate will continue to develop, additional legislative and other measures."

Chile

Upon signature:

Declaration:

The Government of Chile has signed this Convention on the Elimination of All Forms of Discrimination against Women, mindful of the important step which this document represents, not only in terms of the elimination of all forms of discrimination against women, but also in terms of their full and permanent integration into society in conditions of equality.

The Government is obliged to state, however, that some of the provisions of the Convention are not entirely compatible with current Chilean legislation.

At the same time, it reports the establishment of a Commission for the Study and Reform of the Civil Code, which now has before it various proposals to amend, *inter alia,* those provisions which are not fully consistent with the terms of the Convention.

China

Declaration made upon signature and confirmed upon ratification:

The People's Republic of China does not consider itself bound by article 29, paragraph 1, of the Convention.

Cuba

Reservation:

The Government of the Republic of Cuba makes a specific reservation concerning the provisions of article 29 of the Convention inasmuch as it holds that any disputes that may arise between States parties should be resolved through direct negotiations through the diplomatic channel.

Cyprus

Reservation:

"... The Government of the Republic of Cyprus wishes to enter a reservation concerning the granting to women of equal rights with men with respect to the nationality of their children, mentioned in article 9, paragraph 2, of the Convention. This reservation is to be withdrawn upon amendment of the relevant law."

Czechoslovakia

Reservation made upon signature and confirmed upon ratification:

"The Czechoslovak Socialist Republic, in accordance with article 29, paragraph 2, of the Convention on the Elimination of All Forms of Discrimination against Women, does not consider itself to be bound under its article 29, paragraph 1. In the opinion of the Czechoslovak Socialist Republic any dispute concerning the interpretation or implementation of this Convention, should be solved by direct negotiation between the parties to the dispute or in another manner to be agreed upon by the parties to the dispute."

Democratic Yemen

The Government of the People's Democatic Republic of Yemen declares that it does not consider itself bound by article 29, paragraph 1, of the said Convention, relating to the settlement of disputes which may arise concerning the application or interpretation of the Convention.

Egypt

Reservations made upon signature and confirmed upon ratification:

In respect of article 9:

Reservation to the text of article 9, paragraph 2, concerning the granting to women of equal rights with men with respect to the nationality of their children, without prejudice to the acquisition by a child born of a marriage of the nationality of his father. This is in order to prevent a child's acquisition of two nationalities where his parents are of different nationalities, since this may be prejudicial to his future. It is clear that the child's acquisition of his father's nationality is the procedure most suitable for the child and that this does not infringe upon the principle of equality between men and women, since it is customary for a woman to agree, upon marrying an alien, that her children shall be of the father's nationality.

In respect of article 16:

Reservation to the text of article 16 concerning the equality of men and women in all matters relating to marriage and family relations during the marriage and upon its dissolution, without prejudice to the Islamic Shariah's provisions whereby women are accorded rights equivalent to those of their spouses so as to ensure a just balance between them. This is out of respect for the sacrosanct nature of the firm religious beliefs which govern marital relations in Egypt and which may not be called in question and in view of the fact that one of the most important bases of these relations is an equivalency of rights and duties so as to ensure complementarity which guarantees true equality between the spouses. The provisions of the Shariah lay down that the husband shall pay bridal money to the wife and maintain her fully and shall also make a payment to her upon divorce, whereas the wife retains full rights over her property and is not obliged to spend anything on her keep. The Shariah therefore restricts the wife's rights to divorce by making it contingent on a judge's ruling, whereas no such restriction is laid down in the case of the husband.

In respect of article 29:

The Egyptian delegation also maintains the reservation contained in article 29, paragraph 2, concerning the right of a State signatory to the Convention to declare that it does not consider itself bound by paragraph 1 of that article concerning the submission to an arbitral body of any dispute which may arise between States concerning the interpretation or application of the Convention. This is in order to avoid being bound by the system of arbitration in this field.

Reservation made upon ratification:

General reservation on article 2:

The Arab Republic of Egypt is willing to comply with the content of this article, provided that such compliance does not run counter to the Islamic Shariah.

El Salvador

Upon signature:

. . . Upon ratification of the Convention, the Government of El Salvador will make the reservation provided for in article 29.

Upon ratification:

Reservation:

With reservation as to the application of the provision of article 29, paragraph 1.

Ethiopia

Reservation:

In ratifying the said Convention, Socialist Ethiopia does not consider itself bound by article 29, paragraph 1, of the Convention.

France

Upon signature:

Declarations and reservation:

. . . 6

5. The Government of the French Republic declares that article 9 of the Convention must not be interpreted as precluding the application of the second paragraph of article 96 of the code of French nationality.

. . . 6

[The remaining declarations and the reservations were all confirmed in substance upon ratification.]

Upon ratification:

Declarations:

The Government of the French Republic declares that the preamble to the Convention—in particular the eleventh preambular paragraph—contains debatable elements which are definitely out of place in this text.

The Government of the French Republic declares that the term "family education" in article 5 (b) of the Convention must be interpreted as meaning public education concerning the family and that, in any event, article 5 will be applied subject to respect for article 17 of the International Covenant on Civil and Political Rights and article 8 of the Convention for the Protection of Human Rights and Fundamental Freedoms.

The Government of the French Republic declares that no provision of the Convention must be interpreted as prevailing over provisions of French legislation which are more favourable to women than to men:

Reservations:

Articles 5 (b) *and 16, 1* (d)

1. The Government of the French Republic declares that article 5 (*b*) and article 16, paragraph 1 (*d*), must not be interpreted as implying joint exercise of parental authority in situations in which French legislation allows of such exercise by only one parent.

2. The Government of the French Republic declares that article 16, paragraph 1 (*d*), of the Convention must not preclude the application of article 383 of the Civil Code.

Article 7

. . .[6]

Article 14

1. The Government of the French Republic declares that article 14, paragraph 2 (*c*), should be interpreted as guaranteeing that women who fulfil the conditions relating to family or employment required by French legislation for personal participation shall acquire their own rights within the framework of social security.

2. The Government of the French Republic declares that article 14, paragraph 2 (*h*), of the Convention should not be interpreted as implying the actual provision, free of charge, of the services mentioned in that paragraph.

Articles 15, 2 and 3, and 16 1 (c), (d) *and* (h)[6]

Article 16 1 (g)

The Government of the French Republic enters a reservation concerning the right to choose a family name mentioned in article 16, paragraph 1 (*g*), of the Convention.

Article 29

The Government of the French Republic declares, in pursuance of article 29, paragraph 2, of the Convention, that it will not be bound by the provision of article 29, paragraph 1.

German Democratic Republic

Declaration made upon signature and renewed upon ratification:

Pursuant to article 29, paragraph 2, of the Convention, the German Democratic Republic declares that it does not consider itself bound by article 29, paragraph 1.

Germany, Federal Republic of

Declaration:

The right of peoples to self-determination, as enshrined in the Charter of the United Nations and in the International Covenants of 19 December 1966, applies to all peoples and not only to those living "under alien and colonial domination and foreign occupation". All peoples thus have the inalienable right freely to determine their political status and freely to pursue their economic, social and cultural development. The Federal Republic of Germany would be unable to recognize as legally valid an interpretation of the right to self-determination which contradicts the unequivocal wording of the Charter of the United Nations and of the two International Covenants on Civil and Political Rights and on Economic, Social and Cultural Rights of 16 December 1966. It will interpret the eleventh paragraph of the preamble accordingly.

Reservation:

Article 7 (*b*) will not be applied to the extent that it contradicts the second sentence of Article 12 a (4) of the Basic Law of the Federal Republic of Germany. Pursuant to this provision of the Constitution, women may on no account render service involving the use of arms.

Hungary

Reservation made upon signature and confirmed upon ratification:

"The Hungarian People's Republic declares that it does not consider itself bound by the terms of article 29, paragraph 1, of the Convention."

India

Upon signature:

Declarations:

"(i) With regard to articles 5 (*a*) and 16 (1) of the Convention on the Elimination of All Forms of Discrimination against Women, the Government of the Republic of India declares that it shall abide by and ensure these provisions in conformity with its policy of non-interference in the personal affairs of any Community without its initiative and consent.

"(ii) With regard to article 16 (2) of the Convention on the Elimination of All Forms of Discrimination against Women, the Government of the Republic of India declares that though in principle it fully supports the principle of compulsory registration of marriages, it is not practical in a vast country like India with its variety of customs, religions and level of literacy."

Reservation:

"With regard to article 29 of the Convention on the Elimination of All Forms of Discrimination against Women, the Government of the Republic of India declares that it does not consider itself bound by paragraph 1 of this article."

Indonesia

The Government of the Republic of Indonesia does not consider itself bound by the provision of article 29, paragraph 1, of this Convention and takes the position that any dispute relating to the interpretation or application of the Convention may only be submitted to arbitration or to the International Court of Justice with the agreement of all the parties to the dispute.

Iraq[7]

Reservations:

1. Approval of and accession to this Convention shall not mean that the Republic of Iraq is bound by the provisions of article 2, paragraphs (*f*) and (*g*), of article 9, paragraphs 1 and 2, nor of article 16 of the Convention, the reservation to this last-mentioned article shall be without prejudice to the provisions of the Islamic Shariah according women rights equivalent to the rights of their spouses so as to ensure a just balance between them. Iraq also enters a reservation to article 29, paragraph 1, of this Convention with regard to the principle of international arbitration in connection with the interpretation or application of this Convention.

2. This approval in no way implies recognition of or entry into any relations with Israel.

Ireland

Reservations:

    . . .[8]

Article 13 (b) *and* (c)

The question of supplementing the guarantee of equality contained in the Irish Constitution with special legislation governing access to financial credit and other services and recreational activities, where these are provided by private persons, organizations or enterprises is under consideration. For the time being Ireland reserves the right to regard its existing law and measures in this area as appropriate for the attainment in Ireland of the objectives of the Convention.

Article 15

With regard to paragraph 3 of this article, Ireland reserves the right not to supplement the existing provisions in Irish law which accord women a legal capacity identical to that of men with further legislation governing the validity of any contract or other private instrument freely entered into by a woman.

    . . .[8]

Article 16 (1) (d) *and* (f)

Ireland is of the view that the attainment in Ireland of the objectives of the Convention does not necessitate the extension to men of rights identical to those accorded by law to women in respect of the guardianship, adoption and custody of children born out of wedlock and reserves the right to implement the Convention subject to that understanding.

Articles 11 (1) and 13 (a)

Ireland reserves the right to regard the Anti-Discrimination (Pay) Act 1974 and the Employment Equality Act 1977 and other measures taken in implementation of the European Economic Community standards concerning employment opportunities and pay as sufficient implementation of articles 11 (1) (*b*), (*c*) and (*d*).

Ireland reserves the right for the time being to maintain provisions of Irish legislation in the area of social security which are more favourable to women than men.

. . .[8]

Italy

Upon signature:

Reservation:

Italy reserves the right to exercise, when depositing the instrument of ratification, the option provided for in article 19 of the Vienna Convention on the Law of Treaties of 23 May 1969.

Jamaica

"The Government of Jamaica does not consider itself bound by the provision of article 9, paragraph 2, of the Convention."

"The Government of Jamaica declares that it does not consider itself bound by the provision of article 29, paragraph 1, of the Convention."

Jordan

Upon signature:

1. Reservation with respect to article 9, paragraph 2;

2. Reservation with respect to article 15, paragraph 4 (a wife's residence with her husband);

3. A reservation to the wording of article 16, paragraph (1) (*c*), relating to the rights arising upon the dissolution of marriage with regard to maintenance and compensation;

4. A reservation to the wording of article 16, paragraph (1) (*d*) and (*g*).

Malawi

"Owing to the deep-rooted nature of some traditional customs and practices of Malawians, the Government of the Republic of Malawi shall not, for the time being, consider itself bound by such of the provisions of the Convention as require immediate eradication of such traditional customs and practices."

"While the Government of the Republic of Malawi accepts the principles of article 29, paragraph 2, of the Convention this acceptance should nonetheless be read in conjunction with [its] declaration of 12 December 1966, concerning the recognition, by the Government of the Republic of Malawi, as compulsory the jurisdiction of the International Court of Justice under Article 36, paragraph 2, of the Statute of the Court."

Mauritius

"The Government of Mauritius does not consider itself bound by article 11, paragraph 1, subparagraphs (*b*) and (*d*), and article 16, paragraph 1, subparagraph (*g*).

"The Government of Mauritius does not consider itself bound by article 29, paragraph 1, of the Convention, in pursuance of article 29, paragraph 2."

Mexico

Upon signature:

Declaration:

In signing *ad referendum* the Convention on the Elimination of All Forms of Discrimination against Women, which the General Assembly opened for signature by States on 18 December 1979, the Government of the United Mexican States wishes to place on record that it is doing so on the understanding that the provisions of the said Convention, which agree in all essentials with the provisions of Mexican legislation, will be applied in Mexico in accordance with the modalities and procedures prescribed by Mexican legislation and that the granting of material benefits in pursuance of the Convention will be as generous as the resources available to the Mexican State permit.

Mongolia

Reservation made upon signature and confirmed upon ratification:

The Mongolian People's Republic does not consider itself bound by the provision of article 29, paragraph 1, of this Convention and states that for submission of any dispute concerning the interpretation or application of the Convention to arbitration or to the International Court of Justice, the consent of all the parties involved in the given dispute is necessary.

New Zealand

Reservations:

"The Government of New Zealand, the Government of the Cook Islands and the Government of Niue reserve the right not to apply the provision of article 11 (2) (*b*).

"The Government of New Zealand, the Government of the Cook Islands and the Government of Niue reserve the right not to apply the provisions of the Convention in so far as they are inconsistent with policies relating to recruitment into or service in

"(*a*) the Armed Forces which reflect either directly or indirectly the fact that members of such forces are required to serve on armed forces aircraft or vessels and in situations involving armed combat or

"(*b*) the law enforcement forces which reflect either directly or indirectly the fact that members of such forces are required to serve in situations involving violence or threat of violence.

"The Government of New Zealand, the Government of the Cook Islands and the Government of Niue reserve the right, to the extent the Convention is inconsistent with the provisions of the Convention concerning the Employment of Women on Underground Work in Mines of all Kinds (ILO Convention No. 45) which was ratified by the Government of New Zealand on 29 March 1938, to apply the provisions of the latter.

"The Government of the Cook Islands reserves the right not to apply article 2 (*f*) and article 5 (*a*) to the extent that the customs governing the inheritance of certain Cook Islands chiefly titles may be inconsistent with those provisions."

Poland

Reservation:

The People's Republic of Poland does not consider itself bound by article 29, paragraph 1, of the Convention.

Republic of Korea

Upon signature:

Reservations:

"1. The Government of the Republic of Korea does not consider itself bound by the provisions of article 9 of the Convention on the Elimination of All Forms of Discrimination against Women of 1979.

"2. Bearing in mind the fundamental principles as embodied in the said Convention, the Government of the Republic of Korea has recently established the Korea women's welfare and social activities. A committee under the chairmanship of the Prime Minister will shortly be set up to consider and co-ordinate overall policies on women.

"3. The Government of the Republic of Korea will make continued efforts to take further measures in line with the provisions stipulated in the Convention."

Upon ratification

The Government of the Republic of Korea, having examined the said Convention, hereby ratifies the Convention considering itself not bound by the provisions of article 9 and article 16, paragraph 1, subparagraphs (*c*), (*d*), (*f*) and (*g*) of the Convention.

Romania

Reservation made upon signature and upon ratification:

The Socialist Republic of Romania states that it does not consider itself to be bound by the provision of article 29, paragraph 1, of the Convention, whereby any dispute between two or more States parties concerning the interpretation or application of the Convention which is not settled by negotiation shall, at the request of one of them, be submitted to arbitration.

The Socialist Republic of Romania believes that such disputes shall be submitted to arbitration only with the consent of all States parties to the dispute, for each specific case.

Spain

Declaration:

The ratification of the Convention by Spain shall not affect the constitutional provisions concerning succession to the Spanish crown.

Thailand

Declaration:

The Royal Thai Government wishes to express its understanding that the purposes of the Convention are to eliminate discrimination against women and to accord to every person, men and women alike, equality before the law, and are in accordance with the principles prescribed by the Constitution of the Kingdom of Thailand.

Reservations:

1. In all matters which concern national security, maintenance of public order and service or employment in the military or paramilitary forces, the Royal Thai Government reserves its right to apply the provisions of the Convention on the Elimination of All Forms of Discrimination against Women, in particular articles 7 and 10, only within the limits established by national laws, regulations and practices.

2. With regard to article 9, paragraph 2, and article 11, paragraph 1 (b), as far as night work of women and special protection of working women are concerned, the Royal Thai Government considers that the application of the said provisions shall be subject to the limits and criteria established by national law, regulations and practices.

3. The Royal Thai Government does not consider itself bound by the provisions of article 15, paragraph 3, article 16 and article 29, paragraph 1, of the Convention.

Trinidad and Tobago

Reservation made upon signature:

"The Republic of Trinidad and Tobago declares that it does not consider itself bound by article 29 of the said Convention, relating to the settlement of disputes which may arise concerning the application or interpretation of the Convention."

Tunisia

Reservations:

1. *General declaration:*

The Tunisian Government declares that it shall not take any organization or legislative decision in conformity with the requirements of this Convention where such a decision would conflict with the provisions of chapter I of the Tunisian Constitution.

2. *Reservation concerning article 9, paragraph 2:*

The Tunisian Government expresses its reservation with regard to the provision in article 9, paragraph 2, of the Convention, which must not conflict with the provisions of chapter VI of the Tunisian Nationality Code.

3. *Reservation concerning article 16, paragraph 1* (c), (d), (f), (g) *and* (h):

The Tunisian Government considers itself not bound by article 16, paragraph 1 (*c*), (*d*) and (*f*), of the Convention and declares that paragraph 1 (*g*) and (*h*) of that article must not conflict with the provisions of the Personal Status Code concerning the granting of family names to children and the acquisition of property through inheritance.

4. *Reservation concerning article 29, paragraph 1:*

The Tunisian Government declares, in conformity with the requirements of article 29, paragraph 2, of the Convention, that it shall not be bound by the provision of paragraph 1 of that article which specifies that any dispute between two or more States parties concerning the interpretation or application of the present Convention which is not settled by negotiation shall be referred to the International Court of Justice at the request of any one of those parties.

The Tunisian Government considers that such disputes should be submitted for arbitration or consideration by the International Court of Justice only with the consent of all parties to the dispute.

5. *Declaration concerning article 15, paragraph 4:*

In accordance with the provisions of the Vienna Convention on the Law of Treaties, dated 23 May 1969, the Tunisian Government emphasizes that the requirements of article 15, paragraph 4, of the Convention on the Elimination of All Forms of Discrimination against Women, and particularly that part relating to the right of women to choose their residence and domicile, must not be interpreted in a manner which conflicts with the provisions of the Personal Status Code on this subject, as set forth in chapters 23 and 61 of the Code.

Turkey

Reservations:

Reservations of the Government of the Republic of Turkey with regard to the articles of the Convention dealing with family relations which are not completely compatible with the provisions of the Turkish Civil Code, in particular, article 15, paragraphs 2 and 4, and article 16, paragraph 1 (*c*), (*d*), (*f*) and (*g*), as well as with respect to article 29, paragraph 1. In pursuance of article 29, paragraph 2, of the Convention, the Government of the Republic of Turkey declares that it does not consider itself bound by paragraph 1 of this article.

Declaration:

"Article 9, paragraph 1, of the Convention is not in conflict with the provisions of article 5, paragraph 1, and articles 15 and 17 of the Turkish Law on Nationality, relating to the acquisition of citizenship, since the intent of those provisions regulating acquisition of citizenship through marriage is to prevent statelessness."

Ukrainian Soviet Socialist Republic

Reservation made upon signature and confirmed upon ratification:

Pursuant to article 29, paragraph 2, of the Convention the Ukrainian Soviet Socialist Republic does not consider itself bound by the provision of article 29, paragraph 1, of the Convention, according to which any dispute between two or more States parties with respect to the interpretation or application of this Convention, which is not settled by negotiation, shall, upon the request of any one of the parties, be referred to arbitration or to the International Court of Justice, and declares that the referral of any such dispute to arbitration or to the International Court of Justice shall in each case require the consent of all parties to the dispute.

Union of Soviet Socialist Republics

Reservation made upon signature and confirmed upon ratification:

In accordance with article 29, paragraph 2, of the Convention, the Union of Soviet Socialist Republics declares that it does not consider itself bound by the provision of article 29, paragraph 1, of the Convention, which provides that any dispute between two or more States parties concerning the interpretation or application of the present Convention which is not settled by negotiation shall, at the request of one of them, be submitted to arbitration or to the International Court of Justice, and that for such dispute to be submitted to arbitration or to the International Court of Justice in every case there must be agreement between all the parties involved in the dispute.

United Kingdom of Great Britain and Northern Ireland

Upon signature:

"The Government of the United Kingdom of Great Britain and Northern Ireland declare that it is their intention to make certain reservations and declarations upon ratification of the Convention."

Upon ratification:

A. *On behalf of the United Kingdom of Great Britain and Northern Ireland:*

(*a*) The United Kingdom understands the main purpose of the Convention, in the light of the definition contained in article 1, to be the reduction, in accordance with its terms, of discrimination against women, and does not therefore regard the Convention as imposing any requirement to repeal or modify any existing laws, regulations, customs or practices which provide for women to be treated more favourably than men, whether temporarily or in the longer term; the United Kingdom's undertakings under article 4, paragraph 1, and other provisions of the Convention are to be construed accordingly.

(*b*) The United Kingdom reserves the right to regard the provisions of the Sex Discrimination Act 1975, the Employment Protection (Consolidation) Act 1978, the Employment Act 1980, the Sex Discrimination (Northern Ireland) Order 1976, the Industrial Relations (No. 2) (Northern Ireland)

Order 1976, the Industrial Relations (Northern Ireland) Order 1982, the Equal Pay Act 1970 (as amended) and the Equal Pay Act (Northern Ireland) 1970 (as amended), including the exceptions and exemptions contained in any of these Acts and Orders, as constituting appropriate measures for the practical realization of the objectives of the Convention in the social and economic circumstances of the United Kingdom, and to continue to apply these provisions accordingly; this reservation will apply equally to any future legislation which may modify or replace the above Acts and Orders on the understanding that the terms of such legislation will be compatible with the United Kingdom's obligations under the Convention.

(*c*) In the light of the definition contained in article 1, the United Kingdom's ratification is subject to the understanding that none of its obligations under the Convention shall be treated as extending to the succession to, or possession and enjoyment of, the Throne, the peerage, titles of honour, social precedence or armorial bearings, or as extending to the affairs of religious denominations or orders or to the admission into or service in the Armed Forces of the Crown.

(*d*) The United Kingdom reserves the right to continue to apply such immigration legislation governing entry into, stay in, and departure from, the United Kingdom as it may deem necessary from time to time and, accordingly, its acceptance of article 15 (4) and of the other provisions of the Convention is subject to the provisions of any such legislation as regards persons not at the time having the right under the law of the United Kingdom to enter and remain in the United Kingdom.

Article 1

With reference to the provisions of the Sex Discrimination Act 1975 and other applicable legislation, the United Kingdom's acceptance of article 1 is subject to the reservation that the phrase "irrespective of their marital status" shall not be taken to render discriminatory any difference of treatment accorded to single persons as against married persons, so long as there is equality of treatment as between married men and married women and as between single men and single women.

Article 2

In the light of the substantial progress already achieved in the United Kingdom in promoting the progressive elimination of discrimination against women, the United Kingdom reserves the right, without prejudice to the other reservations made by the United Kingdom, to give effect to paragraphs (*f*) and (*g*) by keeping under review such of its laws and regulations as may still embody significant differences in treatment between men and women with a view to making changes to those laws and regulations when to do so would be compatible with essential and over-riding considerations of economic policy.

In relation to forms of discrimination more precisely prohibited by other provisions of the Convention, the obligations under this article must (in the case of the United Kingdom) be read in conjunction with the other reservations and declarations made in respect of those provisions including the declarations and reservations of the United Kingdom contained in paragraphs (*a*) to (*d*) above.

With regard to paragraphs (*f*) and (*g*) of this article the United Kingdom reserves the right to continue to apply its law relating to sexual offences and prostitution; this reservation will apply equally to any future law which may modify or replace it.

Article 9

The British Nationality Act 1981, which was brought into force with effect from January 1983, is based on principles which do not allow of any discrimination against women within the meaning of article 1 as regards acquisition, change or retention of their nationality or as regards the nationality of their children. The United Kingdom's acceptance of article 9 shall not, however, be taken to invalidate the continuation of certain temporary or transitional provisions which will continue in force beyond that date.

The United Kingdom reserves the right to take such steps as may be necessary to comply with its obligations under article 2 of the First Protocol to the Convention for the Protection of Human Rights and Fundamental Freedoms signed at Paris on 20 March 1952 and its obligations under article 13, paragraph 3, of the International Covenant on Economic, Social and Cultural Rights opened for signature at New York on 16 December 1966, to the extent that the said provisions preserve the freedom of parental choice in respect of the education of children; and reserves also the right not to take any measures which may conflict with its obligation under article 13, paragraph 4, of the said Covenant not to interfere with the liberty of individuals and bodies to establish and direct educational institutions, subject to the observation of certain principles and standards.

Moreover, the United Kingdom can only accept the obligations under article 10, paragraph (*c*), within the limits of the statutory powers of central Government, in the light of the fact that the teaching curriculum, the provision of text-books and teaching methods are reserved for local control and are not subject to central Government direction; moreover, the acceptance of the objective of encouraging co-education is without prejudice to the right of the United Kingdom also to encourage other types of education.

Article 11

The United Kingdom interprets the "right to work" referred to in paragraph 1 (*a*) as a reference to the "right to work" as defined in other human rights instruments to which the United Kingdom is a party, notably article 6 of the International Covenant on Economic, Social and Cultural Rights of 16 December 1966.

The United Kingdom interprets article 11, paragraph 1, in the light of the provision of article 4, paragraph 2, as not precluding prohibitions, restrictions or conditions on the employment of women in certain areas, or on the work done by them, where this is considered necessary or desirable to protect the health and safety of women or the human fœtus, including such prohibitions, restrictions or conditions imposed in consequence of other international obligations of the United Kingdom; the United Kingdom declares that, in the event of a conflict between obligations under the present Convention and its obligations under the Convention concerning the Employment of Women on Underground Work in Mines of all Kinds (ILO Convention No. 45), the provisions of the last mentioned Convention shall prevail.

The United Kingdom reserves the right to apply all United Kingdom legislation and the rules of pension schemes affecting retirement pensions, survivors' benefits and other benefits in relation to death or retirement (including retirement on grounds of redundancy), whether or not derived from a Social Security scheme.

This reservation will apply equally to any future legislation which may modify or replace such legislation, or the rules of pension schemes, on the understanding that the terms of such legislation will be compatible with the United Kingdom's obligations under the Convention.

The United Kingdom reserves the right to apply the following provisions of United Kingdom legislation concerning the benefits specified:

(*a*) Social Security benefits for persons engaged in caring for a severely disabled person under section 37 of the Social Security Act 1975 and section 37 of the Social Security (Northern Ireland) Act 1975;

(*b*) increases of benefits for adult dependants under sections 44 to 47, 49 and 66 of the Social Security Act 1975 and under Sections 44 to 47, 49 and 66 of the Social Security (Northern Ireland) Act 1975;

(*c*) retirement pensions and survivors' benefits under the Social Security Acts 1975 to 1982 and the Social Security (Northern Ireland) Acts 1975 to 1982;

(*d*) family income supplements under the Family Income Supplements Act 1970 and the Family Income Supplements Act (Northern Ireland) 1971.

This reservation will apply equally to any future legislation which may modify or replace any of the provisions specified in subparagraphs (*a*) to (*d*) above, on the understanding that the terms of such legislation will be compatible with the United Kingdom's obligations under the Convention.

The United Kingdom reserves the right to apply any non-discriminatory requirement for a qualifying period of employment or insurance for the application of the provisions contained in article 11 (2).

Article 13

The United Kingdom reserves the right, notwithstanding the obligations undertaken in article 13, or any other relevant article of the Convention, to continue to apply the income tax and capital gains tax legislation which:

(i) deems for income tax purposes the income of a married woman living with her husband in a year, or part of a year, of assessment to be her husband's income and not to be her income (subject to the right of the husband and the wife to elect jointly that the wife's earned income shall be charged to income tax as if she were a single woman with no other income); and

(ii) requires tax in respect of such income and of chargeable gains accruing to such a married woman to be assessed on her husband (subject to the right of either of them to apply for separate assessment) and consequently (if no such application is made) restricts to her husband the right to appeal against any such assessment and to be heard or to be represented at the hearing of any such appeal; and

(iii) entitles a man who has his wife living with him, or whose wife is wholly maintained by him, during the year of assessment to a deduction from his total income of an amount larger than that to which an individual in any other case is entitled and entitles an individual whose total income includes any earned income of his wife to have that deduction increased by the amount of that earned income or by an amount specified in the legislation whichever is the less.

Article 15

In relation to article 15, paragraph 2, the United Kingdom understands the term "legal capacity" as referring merely to the existence of a separate and distinct legal personality.

In relation to article 15, paragraph 3, the United Kingdom understands the intention of this provision to be that only those terms or elements of a contract or other private instrument which are discriminatory in the sense described are to be deemed null and void, but not necessarily the contract or instrument as a whole.

Article 16

As regards article 16, paragraph 1 (*f*), the United Kingdom does not regard the reference to the paramountcy of the interests of the children as being directly relevant to the elimination of discrimination against women, and declares in this connection that the legislation of the United Kingdom regulating adoption, while giving a principal position to the promotion of the children's welfare, does not give to the child's interests the same paramount place as in issues concerning custody over children.

The United Kingdom's acceptance of article 16, paragraph 1, shall not be treated as either limiting the freedom of a person to dispose of his property as he wishes or as giving a person a right to property the subject of such a limitation.

B. *On behalf of the Isle of Man, the British Virgin Islands, the Falkland Islands, South Georgia and the South Sandwich Islands, and the Turks and Caicos Islands:*

[*Same reservations as those made on behalf of the United Kingdom under paragraph A* (a), (c), *and* (d) *except that in the case of* (d) *it applies to the territories and their laws.*]

Article 1

[*Same reservation as that made in respect of the United Kingdom except with regard to the absence of a reference to United Kingdom legislation.*]

Article 2

[*Same reservations as those made in respect of the United Kingdom except that reference is made to the laws of the territories, and not the laws of the United Kingdom.*]

Article 9

[*Same reservations as those made in respect of the United Kingdom.*]

Article 11

[*Same reservations as those made in respect of the United Kingdom except that a reference is made to the laws of the territories, and not to the laws of the United Kingdom.*]

Also, as far as the territories are concerned, the specific benefits listed and which may be applied under the provisions of these territories' legislation are as follows:

(*a*) Social Security benefits for persons engaged in caring for a severely disabled person;

(*b*) increases of benefit for adult dependants;

(*c*) retirement pensions and survivors' benefits;

(*d*) family income supplements.

This reservation will apply equally to any future legislation which may modify or replace any of the provisions specified in subparagraphs (*a*) to (*d*) above, on the understanding that the terms of such legislation will be compatible with the United Kingdom's obligations under the Convention.

The United Kingdom reserves the right to apply any non-discriminatory requirement for a qualifying period of employment or insurance for the application of the provisions contained in article 11 (2).

Articles 13, 15 and 16

[Same reservations as those made on behalf of the United Kingdom.]

Venezuela

Made upon ratification confirming in substance the reservation made upon signature:

Reservation:

Venezuela makes a formal reservation with regard to article 29, paragraph 1, of the Convention, since it does not accept arbitration or the jurisdiction of the International Court of Justice for the settlement of disputes concerning the interpretation or application of this Convention.

Viet Nam

Reservation:

In implementing this Convention, the Socialist Republic of Viet Nam will not be bound by the provision of article 29, paragraph 1.

OBJECTIONS

(Unless otherwise indicated, the objections were
received upon ratification, accession, acceptance,
approval or definitive signature.)

German Democratic Republic

22 April 1987

With regard to the application to Berlin (West) of the Convention on the Elimination of All Forms of Discrimination against Women the German

Democratic Republic notes, in accordance with the Quadripartite Agreement of 3 September 1971, that Berlin (West) is not a constituent part of the Federal Republic of Germany and is not to be governed by it. The Federal Republic of Germany's declaration that the said Convention was to be extended to Berlin (West) is contradictoy to the Quadripartite Agreement which provides that agreements concerning matters of the security and status of Berlin (West) must not be extended to the latter by the Federal Republic of Germany. Consequently, the Federal Republic of Germany's declaration can have no legal effect.

Germany, Federal Republic of

10 July 1985

The Federal Republic of Germany considers that the reservations made by Egypt regarding article 2, article 9, paragraph 2, and article 16, by Bangladesh regarding article 2, article 13 (*a*) and article 16, paragraph 1 (*c*) and (*f*), by Brazil regarding article 15, paragraph 4, and article 16, paragraph 1 (*a*), (*c*), (*g*) and (*h*), by Jamaica regarding article 9, paragraph 2, by the Republic of Korea regarding article 9 and article 16, paragraph 1 (*c*), (*d*), (*f*) and (*g*), and by Mauritius regarding article 11, paragraph 1 (*b*) and (*d*), and article 16, paragraph 1 (*g*), are incompatible with the object and purpose of the Convention (article 28, paragraph 2) and therefore objects to them. In relation to the Federal Republic of Germany, they may not be invoked in support of a legal practice which does not pay due regard to the legal status afforded to women and children in the Federal Republic of Germany in conformity with the above-mentioned articles of the Convention.

This objection shall not preclude the entry into force of the Convention as between Egypt, Bangladesh, Brazil, Jamaica, the Republic of Korea, Mauritius and the Federal Republic of Germany.

Objections, identical in essence, *mutatis mutandis,* were also formulated by the Government of the Federal Republic of Germany in regard to reservations made by various States, as follows:

(i) 15 October 1986: In respect of reservations formulated by the Government of Thailand concerning article 9, paragraph 2, article 10, article 11, paragraph 1 (*b*), article 15, paragraph 3 and article 16; (The Federal Republic of Germany also holds the view that the reservation made by Thailand regarding article 7 of the Convention is likewise incompatible with the object and purpose of the Convention for all matters which concern national security it reserves in a general and thus unspecific manner the right of the Royal Thai Government to apply the provisions only within the limits established by national laws, regulations and practices).

(ii) 15 October 1986: In respect of reservations and some declarations formulated by the Government of Tunisia concerning article 9, paragraph 2, and article 16, as well as the declaration concerning article 15, paragraph 4.

The Government of the Federal Republic of Germany rejects as incompatible with the object and purpose of the Convention on the Elimination of All Forms of Discrimination against Women the reservations made by Turkey with regard to such articles of the Convention dealing with family relations as are not completely compatible with the provisions of the Turkish Civil Code, in particular article 15, paragraphs 2 and 4, and article 16, paragraph 1 (*c*), (*d*), (*f*) and (*g*).

This declaration is not to be interpreted as preventing the entry into force of the Convention between the Federal Republic of Germany and Turkey.

3 March 1987

The Government of the Federal Republic of Germany rejects as incompatible with the object and purpose of the Convention on the Elimination of All Forms of Discrimination against Women the reservations made by Iraq with regard to article 2, paragraphs (*f*) and (*g*), article 9 and article 16 of the Convention.

In relation to the Federal Republic of Germany they may not be invoked in support of a legal practice which does not pay due regard to the legal status accorded to women and children in the Federal Republic of Germany in conformity with the above-mentioned articles of the Convention.

This declaration is not to be interpreted as preventing the entry into force of the Convention between the Federal Republic of Germany and Iraq.

Mexico

11 January 1985

The Government of the United Mexican States has studied the content of the reservations made by Mauritius to article 11, paragraph 1 (*b*) and (*d*), and article 16, paragraph 1 (*g*), of the Convention and has concluded that they should be considered invalid in the light of article 28, paragraph 2, of the Convention, because they are incompatible with its object and purpose.

Indeed, these reservations, if implemented, would inevitably result in discrimination against women on the basis of sex, which is contrary to all the articles of the Convention. The principles of equal rights of men and women and non-discrimination on the basis of sex, which are embodied in the second preambular paragraph and Article 1, paragraph 3, of the Charter of the United

Nations, to which Mauritius is a signatory, and in articles 2 and 16 of the Universal Declaration of Human Rights of 1948, were previously accepted by the Government of Mauritius when it acceded, on 12 December 1973, to the International Covenant on Civil and Political Rights and the International Covenant on Economic, Social and Cultural Rights. The above principles were stated in article 2, paragraph 1, and article 3 of the former Covenant and in article 2, paragraph 2, and article 3 of the latter. Consequently, it is inconsistent with these contractual obligations previously assumed by Mauritius for its Government now to claim that it has reservations, on the same subject, about the 1979 Convention.

The objection of the Government of the United Mexican States to the reservations in question should not be interpreted as an impediment to the entry into force of the 1979 Convention between the United Mexican States and Mauritius.

Objections, identical in essence, *mutatis mutandis,* were also formulated by the Government of Mexico in regard to reservations made by various States, as follows:

(i) 21 February 1985: In respect of reservations by Bangladesh concerning article 2, article 13 (*a*) and article 16, paragraph 1 (*c*) and (*f*). (Bangladesh not being a party to the Convention, its participation in the said Convention was not invoked by Mexico in its objection.)

(ii) 21 February 1985: In respect of the reservation by Jamaica concerning article 9 (2).

(iii) 22 May 1985: In respect of reservations by New Zealand (those which are also applicable to the Cook Islands) concerning article 2 (*f*) and article 5 (*a*).

(iv) 6 June 1985: In respect of reservations by the Republic of Korea concerning article 9 and article 16, paragraph 1 (*c*), (*d*), (*f*) and (*g*).

(v) 29 January 1986: In respect of the reservation made by Cyprus to article 9, paragraph 2.

(vi) 7 May 1986: In respect of the reservations made by Turkey to article 15, paragraphs 2 and 4, and article 16, paragraph 1 (*c*), (*d*), (*f*) and (*g*).

(vii) 16 July 1986: In respect of reservations made by Egypt to articles 9 and 16.

(viii) 16 October 1986: In respect of reservations by Thailand concerning article 9, paragraph 2, article 15, paragraph 3, and article 16.

(ix) 4 December 1986: In respect of reservations by Iraq concerning article 2, paragraphs (*f*) and (*g*), article 9, paragraphs 1 and 2, and article 16.

(x) 5 August 1987: The Government of the United Mexican States hopes that the process of eradication of traditional customs and practices referred to in the first reservation of the Republic of Malawi will not be so protracted as to impair fulfilment of the purpose and intent of the Convention.

In the case of the objections contained in paragraphs (iii) and (v), Mexico stated that the principles of the equal rights of men and women and of non-discrimination on the basis of sex are embodied in the second preambular paragraph and Article 1, paragraph 3, of the Charter of the United Nations, and in articles 2 and 16 of the Universal Declaration of Human Rights of 1948, and that they were previously accepted by the Governments of New Zealand and Cyprus respectively when they ratified the International Covenant on Civil and Political Rights and the International Covenant on Economic, Social and Cultural Rights of 1966.

Sweden

17 March 1986

[*Same objection,* mutatis mutandis, *as that made by Mexico with regard to reservations made by the following States:*

Thailand: on 9 August 1985 regarding article 9, paragraph 2, article 15, paragraph 3, and article 16,

Tunisia: on 20 September 1985 regarding article 9, paragraph 2, article 15, paragraph 4, and article 16, paragraph 1 (*c*), (*d*), (*f*), (*g*) and (*h*),

Bangladesh: on 6 November 1984 regarding article 2, article 13 (*a*), and article 16, paragraph 1 (*c*) and (*f*),

Brazil: on 1 February 1984 regarding article 15, paragraph 4, and article 16, paragraph 1 (*a*), (*c*), (*g*) and (*h*),

Egypt: on 18 September 1981 regarding article 2, article 9, paragraph 2, and article 16,

Mauritius: on 9 July 1984 regarding article 11, paragraph 1 (*b*) and (*d*), and article 16, paragraph 1(*g*),

Jamaica: on 19 October 1984 regarding article 9, paragraph 2,

Republic of Korea: on 27 December 1984 regarding article 9 and article 16, paragraph 1 (*c*), (*d*), (*f*) and (*g*),

New Zealand: on 10 January 1985, in respect of the Cook Islands regarding article 2, paragraph (*f*), and article 5, paragraph (*a*).

The Government of Sweden added the following comments:

"In this context the Government of Sweden wishes to take this opportunity to make the observation that the reason why reservations incompatible with the object and purpose of a treaty are not acceptable is precisely that otherwise they would render a basic international obligation of a contractual nature meaningless. Incompatible reservations, made in respect of the Convention on the Elimination of All Forms of Discrimination against Women, do not only cast doubts on the commitment of the reserving States to the objects and purpose of this Convention, but moreover, contribute to undermine the basis of international contractual law. It is in the common interest of States that treaties to which they have chosen to become parties also are respected, as to object and purpose, by other parties."

12 March 1987

"The Government of Sweden has examined the contents of the reservations made by Iraq to article 2, paragraphs (*f*) and (*g*), article 9, paragraph 1, and article 16 of the Convention and has come to the conclusion that they are incompatible with the object and purpose of the Convention (article 28, paragraph 2). The Government of Sweden therefore objects to them.

"If the reservations were to apply they would inevitably have the effect of discriminating against women on the grounds of sex, which is contrary to everything the Convention stands for. It should also be borne in mind that the principles of the equal rights of men and women and of non-discrimination on the grounds of sex are set forth in the Charter of the United Nations as one of its purposes, in the Universal Declaration of Human Rights of 1948, and in the International Covenants on Economic, Social and Cultural Rights and on Civil and Political Rights, both of 1966, to which Iraq is a party.

"In this context the Government of Sweden wishes to take this opportunity to make the observation that the reason why reservations incompatible with the object and purpose of a treaty are not acceptable is precisely that otherwise they would render a basic international obligation of a contractual nature meaningless. Incompatible reservations, made in respect of the Convention on the Elimination of All Forms of Discrimination against Women, do not only cast doubts on the commitment of the reserving States to the object and purpose of this Convention, but moreover, contribute to undermine the basis of international contractual law. It is in the common interest of States that treaties to which they have chosen to become parties also are respected, as to object and purpose, by other parties."

NOTES

[1] The Secretary-General received several objections to the signature of the above Convention by Democratic Kampuchea. These objections are identical in matter, *mutatis mutandis,* as those reproduced in note 3 in chapter I. Following is the list of States who have notified their objection with the date of receipt of the notifications:

German Democratic Republic	11 Dec. 1980
Hungary	19 Jan. 1981
Bulgaria	29 Jan. 1981
Union of Soviet Socialist Republics	13 Feb. 1981
Byelorussian Soviet Socialist Republic	18 Feb. 1981
Czechoslovakia	10 Mar. 1981

[2] In a note accompanying the instrument, the Government of the Federal Republic of Germany declared that the Convention shall also apply to Berlin (West) with effect from the date on which it enters into force for the Federal Republic of Germany.

In this regard, the Secretary-General received on 15 April 1986 from the Government of the Union of Soviet Socialist Republics, the following objection:

The declaration made by the Government of the Federal Republic of Germany upon ratification of the Convention on the Elimination of All Forms of Discrimination against Women, adopted on 18 December 1979, regarding the extension of the said Convention to West Berlin directly contradicts the Quadripartite Agreement of 3 September 1971. This Agreement, as is known, clearly established that international agreements entered into by the Federal Republic of Germany may be extended to West Berlin only provided that such agreements do not affect matters of security and status. The said Convention, by virtue of its content, directly affects such matters.

In particular, it governs matters relating to the adoption of legislation, including amendments to national constitutions, by States parties, to their use of sanctions or other coercive measures, and to the provision by means of the competent national courts or other State institutions of effective legal protection for citizens.

The rights and duties referred to in the Convention are a manifestation of State sovereignty. Such rights and duties cannot be exercised by a State in a territory which does not fall within its jurisdiction.

In view of the foregoing, the Soviet Union considers the declaration made by the Government of the Federal Republic of Germany regarding the extension of the Convention on the Elimination of All Forms of Discrimination against Women to West Berlin to be unlawful and not legally valid.

Accordingly, the declaration and reservation made by the Government of the Federal Republic of Germany upon ratification are unlawful and not legally valid with respect to West Berlin.

On 20 March 1987, the Secretary-General received the following communication from the Governments of France, the United Kingdom and the United States of America:

"In a communication to the Government of the Union of Soviet Socialist Republics, which is an integral part (annex IV A) of the Quadripartite Agreement of 3 September 1971, the Governments of France, the United Kingdom and the United States, without prejudice to the maintenance of their rights and responsibilities relating to the representation abroad of the interests of the Western Sectors of Berlin, confirmed that, provided that matters of security and status are not affected and provided that the extension is specified in each case, international agreements and arrangements entered into by the Federal Republic of Germany may be extended to the Western Sectors of Berlin in accordance with established procedures.

"The Government of the Union of Soviet Socialist Republics, in a communication to the Governments of the three Powers which is similarly an integral part (annex IV B) of the Quadripartite Agreement, affirmed that it would raise no objections to such extension.

"The established procedures referred to above, which were endorsed in the Quadripartite Agreement, are designed, *inter alia*, to afford the authorities of the three Powers the opportunity to ensure that international agreements and arrangements entered into by the Federal Republic of Germany which are to be extended to the Western Sectors of Berlin are extended in such a way that matters of security and status are not affected.

"When authorizing the extension of the Convention on the Elimination of All Forms of Discrimination against Women to the Western Sectors of Berlin, the authorities of the three Powers took such steps as were necessary to ensure that matters of security and status were not affected. Accordingly, the Berlin declaration made by the Federal Republic of Germany in accordance with established procedures is valid and the Convention will apply to the Western Sectors of Berlin, subject to allied rights and responsibilities."

[3] An instrument of accession had been deposited on 14 March 1980 with the Secretary-General. The signature was affixed on 17 July 1980 and was accompanied by the following declaration:

"... The People's Revolutionary Republic of Guinea wishes to sign the Convention ... with the understanding that this procedure annuls the procedure of accession previously followed by Guinea with respect to the Convention."

[4] The instrument of ratification indicates that in accordance with the special relationships which exist between New Zealand and the Cook Islands and between New Zealand and Niue, there have been consultations regarding the Convention between the Government of New Zealand and the Government of the Cook Islands and between the Government of New Zealand and the Government of Niue; that the Government of the Cook Islands, which has exclusive competence to implement treaties in the Cook Islands, has requested that the Convention should extend to the Cook Islands; that the Government of Niue which has exclusive competence to implement treaties in Niue, has requested that the Convention should extend to Niue. The said instrument specifies that accordingly the Convention shall apply also to the Cook Islands and Niue.

[5] The instrument of ratification specifies that the said Convention is ratified in respect of the United Kingdom of Great Britain and Northern Ireland, the Isle of Man, British Virgin Islands, Falkland Islands, South Georgia and the South Sandwich Islands, and Turks and Caicos Islands.

[6] In a notification received on 26 March 1984, the Government of France informed the Secretary-General of its decision to withdraw the reservation to article 7 of the Convention made upon ratification. The reservation had read as follows:

"The Government of the French Republic declares that article 7 must not preclude the application of the second paragraph of article LO 128 of the electoral code. The notification specifies that the withdrawal was effected because Organic Law No. 83-1096 of 20 December 1983 has abrogated article LO 128 of the electoral code relating to temporary disqualifications of persons who have obtained French nationality."

Subsequently, in a notification received on 21 July 1986, the Government of France informed the Secretary-General that it decided to withdraw its reservation relating to article 15, paragraphs 2 and 3, and article 16, paragraph 1 (*c*), (*d*) and (*h*), of the Convention, made upon ratification. The text of the reservation had read as follows:

Article 15 (2) and (3) and article 16, paragraph 1 (c) *and* (h).

"The Government of the French Republic declares that article 15, paragraphs 2 and 3, and article 16, paragraph 1 (*c*) and (*h*), of the Convention must not preclude the application of the provisions of Book Three, Part V, chapter II of the Civil Code."

Article 16, paragraph 1 (d)

"The Government of the French Republic declares that article 16, paragraph 1 (*d*) of the Convention must not preclude the application of article 383 of the Civil Code."

The notification specified that the withdrawal was effected because the existing discriminatory provisions, against women, in the rules governing property rights arising out of matrimonial relationship and in those concerning the legal administration of the property of children were abrogated by Act No. 85-1372 of 23 December 1985 concerning equality of spouses in respect of property rights arising out of a matrimonial relationship and equality of parents in respect of the property of minor children, which entered into force on 1 July 1986.

[7] On 12 December 1986, the Secretary-General received from the Government of Israel the following objection:

"... In the view of the Government of the State of Israel, such declaration which is explicitly of a political character is incompatible with the purposes and objectives of the Convention and cannot in any way affect whatever obligations are binding upon Iraq under general international law or under particular conventions.

"The Government of the State of Israel will, in so far as concerns the substance of the matter, adopt towards Iraq an attitude of complete reciprocity."

[8] On 19 December 1986, the Government of Ireland notified the Secretary-General of its withdrawal of the following reservations made upon accession:

Article 9 (1)

"Pending the proposed amendment to the law relating to citizenship, which is at an advanced stage, Ireland reserves the right to retain the provisions in its existing law concerning the acquisition of citizenship on marriage.

Article 15

"With regard to paragraph 4 of this article, Ireland observes the equal rights of women relating to the movement of persons and the freedom to choose their residence; pending the proposed amendment of the law of domicile, which is at an advanced stage, it reserves the right to retain its existing law.

Articles 11 (1) and 13 (a)

"... and pending the coming into force of the Social Welfare (Amendment) (No. 2) Act, 1985, to apply special conditions to the entitlement of married women to certain social security schemes."

Chapter VIII

CONVENTION ON THE PREVENTION AND PUNISHMENT OF THE CRIME OF GENOCIDE

Adopted by the General Assembly of the United Nations on 9 December 1948

ENTRY INTO FORCE: 12 January 1951, in accordance with article XIII.

Participant	Signature	Ratification, accession (a), succession (d)
Afghanistan		22 Mar. 1956 *a*
Albania		12 May 1955 *a*
Algeria		31 Oct. 1963 *a*
Argentina		5 June 1956 *a*
Australia	11 Dec. 1948	8 July 1949
Austria		19 Mar. 1958 *a*
Bahamas		5 Aug. 1975 *d*
Barbados		14 Jan. 1980 *a*
Belgium	12 Dec. 1949	5 Sep. 1951
Bolivia	11 Dec. 1948	
Brazil	11 Dec. 1948	15 Apr. 1952
Bulgaria		21 July 1950 *a*
Burkina Faso		14 Sep. 1965 *a*
Burma	30 Dec. 1949	14 Mar. 1956
Byelorussian SSR	16 Dec. 1949	11 Aug. 1954
Canada	28 Nov. 1949	3 Sep. 1952
Chile	11 Dec. 1948	3 June 1953
China [1], *	20 July 1949	18 Apr. 1983
Colombia	12 Aug. 1949	27 Oct. 1959
Costa Rica		14 Oct. 1950 *a*
Cuba	28 Dec. 1949	4 Mar. 1953
Cyprus		29 Mar. 1982 *a*

---

* For notes, see end of chapter.

Participant	Signature	Ratification, accession (a), succession (d)
Czechoslovakia	28 Dec. 1949	21 Dec. 1950
Democratic Kampuchea		14 Oct. 1950 a
Democratic Yemen		9 Feb. 1987 a
Denmark	28 Sep. 1949	15 June 1951
Dominican Republic	11 Dec. 1948	
Ecuador	11 Dec. 1948	21 Dec. 1949
Egypt	12 Dec. 1948	8 Feb. 1952
El Salvador	27 Apr. 1949	28 Sep. 1950
Ethiopia	11 Dec. 1948	1 July 1949
Fiji		11 Jan. 1973 d
Finland		18 Dec. 1959 a
France	11 Dec. 1948	14 Oct. 1950
Gabon		21 Jan. 1983 a
Gambia		29 Dec. 1978 a
German Democratic Republic .		27 Mar. 1973 a
Germany, Federal Republic of [2]		24 Nov. 1954 a
Ghana		24 Dec. 1958 a
Greece	29 Dec. 1949	8 Dec. 1954
Guatemala	22 June 1949	13 Jan. 1950
Haiti	11 Dec. 1948	14 Oct. 1950
Honduras	22 Apr. 1949	5 Mar. 1952
Hungary		7 Jan. 1952 a
Iceland	14 May 1949	29 Aug. 1949
India	29 Nov. 1949	27 Aug. 1959
Iran (Islamic Republic of)	8 Dec. 1949	14 Aug. 1956
Iraq		20 Jan. 1959 a
Ireland		22 June 1976 a
Israel	17 Aug. 1949	9 Mar. 1950
Italy		4 June 1952 a
Jamaica		23 Sep. 1968 a
Jordan		3 Apr. 1950 a
Lao People's Democratic Republic		8 Dec. 1950 a
Lebanon	30 Dec. 1949	17 Dec. 1953
Lesotho		29 Nov. 1974 a
Liberia	11 Dec. 1948	9 June 1950
Luxembourg		7 Oct. 1981 a
Maldives		24 Apr. 1984 a
Mali		16 July 1974 a
Mexico	14 Dec. 1948	22 July 1952

Participant	Signature	Ratification, accession (a), succession (d)
Monaco		30 Mar. 1950 *a*
Mongolia		5 Jan. 1967 *a*
Morocco		24 Jan. 1958 *a*
Mozambique		18 Apr. 1983 *a*
Nepal		17 Jan. 1969 *a*
Netherlands		20 June 1966 *a*
New Zealand	25 Nov. 1949	28 Dec. 1978
Nicaragua		29 Jan. 1952 *a*
Norway	11 Dec. 1948	22 July 1949
Pakistan	11 Dec. 1948	12 Oct. 1957
Panama	11 Dec. 1948	11 Jan. 1950
Papua New Guinea		27 Jan. 1982 *a*
Paraguay	11 Dec. 1948	
Peru	11 Dec. 1948	24 Feb. 1960
Philippines	11 Dec. 1948	7 July 1950
Poland		14 Nov. 1950 *a*
Republic of Korea		14 Oct. 1950 *a*
Romania		2 Nov. 1950 *a*
Rwanda		16 Apr. 1975 *a*
Saint Vincent and the Grenadines		9 Nov. 1981 *a*
Saudi Arabia		13 July 1950 *a*
Senegal		4 Aug. 1983 *a*
Spain		13 Sep. 1968 *a*
Sri Lanka		12 Oct. 1950 *a*
Sweden	30 Dec. 1949	27 May 1952
Syrian Arab Republic		25 June 1955 *a*
Togo		24 May 1984 *a*
Tonga		16 Feb. 1972 *a*
Tunisia		29 Nov. 1956 *a*
Turkey		31 July 1950 *a*
Ukrainian SSR	16 Dec. 1949	15 Nov. 1954
Union of Soviet Socialist Republics	16 Dec. 1949	3 May 1954
United Kingdom		30 Jan. 1970 *a*
United Republic of Tanzania . .		5 Apr. 1984 *a*
United States of America	11 Dec. 1948	
Uruguay	11 Dec. 1948	11 July 1967
Venezuela		12 July 1960 *a*
Viet Nam [3]		9 June 1981 *a*[4]

		Ratification, *accession* (a),
Participant	*Signature*	*succession* (d)
Yugoslavia	11 Dec. 1948	29 Aug. 1950
Zaire		31 May 1962 *d*

DECLARATIONS AND RESERVATIONS

(Unless otherwise indicated, the declarations and
reservations were made upon ratification, accession or
succession. For objections thereto and territorial
applications see hereinafter.)

Albania

As regards article IX: The People's Republic of Albania does not consider
as binding upon itself the provision of article IX which provides that disputes
between the Contracting parties with regard to the interpretation, application
and implementation of the Convention shall be referred for examination to
the International Court of Justice at the request of any party to the dispute.
The People's Republic of Albania declares that, as regards the International
Court's jurisdiction in respect of disputes concerning the interpretation,
application and implementation of the Convention, the People's Republic of
Albania will, as hitherto, maintain the position that in each particular case the
agreement of all parties to the dispute is essential for the submission of any
particular dispute to the International Court for decision.

As regards article XII: The People's Republic of Albania declares that it
is not in agreement with article XII of the Convention and considers that all
the provisions of the Convention should extend to Non-Self-Governing
Territories, including Trust Territories.

Algeria

The People's Democratic Republic of Algeria does not consider itself
bound by article IX of the Convention, which confers on the International
Court of Justice jurisdiction in all disputes relating to the said Convention.

The People's Democratic Republic of Algeria declares that no provision
of article VI of the said Convention shall be interpreted as depriving its

tribunals of jurisdiction in cases of genocide or other acts enumerated in article III which have been committed in its territory or as conferring such jurisdiction on foreign tribunals.

International tribunals may, as an exceptional measure, be recognized as having jurisdiction, in cases in which the Algerian Government has given its express approval.

The People's Democratic Republic of Algeria declares that it does not accept the terms of article XII of the Convention and considers that all the provisions of the said Convention should apply to Non-Self-Governing Territories, including Trust Territories.

Argentina

Ad *article IX:* The Argentine Government reserves the right not to submit to the procedure laid down in this article any dispute relating directly or indirectly to the territories referred to in its reservation to article XII.

Ad *article XII:* If any other Contracting party extends the application of the Convention to territories under the sovereignty of the Argentine Republic, this extension shall in no way affect the rights of the Republic.

Bulgaria

As regards article IX: The People's Republic of Bulgaria does not consider as binding upon itself the provision of article IX which provides that disputes between the Contracting parties with regard to the interpretation, application and implementation of the present Convention shall be referred for examination to the International Court of Justice at the request of any party to the dispute, and declares that, as regards the International Court's jurisdiction in respect of disputes concerning the interpretation, application and implementation of the Convention, the People's Republic of Bulgaria will, as hitherto, maintain the position that in each particular case the agreement of all parties to the dispute is essential for the submission of any particular dispute to the International Court for decision.

As regards article XII: The People's Republic for Bulgaria declares that it is not in agreement with article XII of the Convention and considers that all the provisions of the Convention should extend to Non-Self-Governing Territories, including Trust Territories.

Burma

"(1) With reference to article VI, the Union of Burma makes the reservation that nothing contained in the said article shall be construed as depriving the courts and tribunals of the Union of jurisdiction or as giving foreign courts and tribunals jurisdiction over any cases of genocide or any of the other acts enumerated in article III committed within the Union territory.

"(2) With reference to article VIII, the Union of Burma makes the reservation that the said article shall not apply to the Union."

Byelorussian Soviet Socialist Republic

As regards article IX: The Byelorussian SSR does not consider as binding upon itself the provision of article IX which provides that disputes between the Contracting parties with regard to the interpretation, application and implementation of the present Convention shall be referred for examination to the International Court of Justice at the request of any party to the dispute, and declares that, as regards the International Court's jurisdiction in respect of disputes concerning the interpretation, application and implementation of the Convention, the Byelorussian SSR will, as hitherto, maintain the position that in each particular case the agreement of all parties to the dispute is essential for the submission of any particular dispute to the International Court for decision.

As regards article XII: The Byelorussian SSR declares that it is not in agreement with article XII of the Convention and considers that all the provisions of the Convention should extend to Non-Self-Governing Territories, including Trust Territories.

China

Declaration:

1. The ratification to the said Convention by the Taiwan local authorities on 19 July 1951 in the name of China is illegal and therefore null and void.

Reservation:

2. The People's Republic of China does not consider itself bound by article IX of the said Convention.

Czechoslovakia

"As regards article IX: Czechoslovakia does not consider as binding upon itself the provision of article IX which provides that disputes between the Contracting parties with regard to the interpretation, application and implementation of the present Convention shall be referred for examination to the International Court of Justice at the request of any party to the dispute, and declares that, as regards the International Court's jurisdiction in respect of disputes concerning the interpretation, application and implementation of the Convention, Czechoslovakia will, as hitherto, maintain the position that in each particular case the agreement of all parties to the dispute is essential for the submission of any particular dispute to the International Court for decision.

"As regards article XII: Czechoslovakia declares that it is not in agreement with article XII of the Convention and considers that all the provisions of the Convention should extend to Non-Self-Governing Territories, including Trust Territories."

Democratic Yemen

As regards article IX: In acceding to this Convention, the People's Democratic Republic of Yemen does not consider itself bound by article IX of the Convention, which provides that disputes between the Contracting parties relating to the interpretation, application or fulfilment of the Convention shall be submitted to the International Court of Justice at the request of any of the parties to the dispute. It declares that the competence of the International Court of Justice with respect to disputes concerning the interpretation, application or fulfilment of the Convention shall in each case be subject to the express consent of all parties to the dispute.

Finland

". . . Subject to the provisions of article 47, paragraph 2, of the Constitution Act, 1919, concerning the impeachment of the President of the Republic of Finland."

German Democratic Republic

As regards article IX: The German Democratic Republic does not consider itself bound by the provision of article IX of the Convention, which provides that disputes between the Contracting parties relating to the interpretation, application or fulfilment of the Convention are, at the request of any of the parties to the dispute, to be submitted to the International Court of Justice, and declares that, as regards the jurisdiction of the International Court of Justice in respect of disputes relating to the interpretation, application or fulfilment of the Convention, the German Democratic Republic takes the position that, in each individual case, the consent of all parties to the dispute is necessary for the submission of a given dispute to the International Court of Justice for decision.

As regards article XII: The German Democratic Republic declares that it cannot accept the provision of article XII of the Convention and considers that the Convention should also extend to Non-Self-Governing Territories, including Trust Territories.

The German Democratic Republic deems it necessary to state that article XI of the Convention deprives a number of States of the opportunity to become parties to the Convention. As the Convention regulates matters affecting the interests of all States, it should be open to participation by all States whose policies are guided by the purposes and principles of the Charter of the United Nations.

Hungary

The Hungarian People's Republic reserves its rights with regard to the provision of article IX of the Convention which grants wide jurisdiction to the International Court of Justice at The Hague, and with regard to the provision of article XII which does not define the obligations of countries having colonies with regard to questions of colonial exploitation and to acts which might be described as genocide.

India

"With reference to article IX of the Convention, the Government of India declares that, for the submission of any dispute to terms of this article to the jurisdiction of the International Court of Justice, the consent of all the parties to the dispute is required in each case."

Mongolia

The Government of the Mongolian People's Republic deems it necessary to state that the Mongolian People's Republic does not consider itself bound by the provision of article IX which stipulates that disputes between the Contracting parties relating to the interpretation, application or implementation of the present Convention shall be submitted to the International Court of Justice at the request of any of the parties to the dispute and declares that the Mongolian People's Republic will maintain the position that in each particular case the consent of all contending parties is essential for the submission of any particular dispute to the International Court of Justice.

The Government of the Mongolian People's Republic declares that it is not in a position to agree with article XII of the Convention and considers that the provision of the said article should be extended to Non-Self-Governing Territories, including Trust Territories.

The Government of the Mongolian People's Republic deems it appropriate to draw attention to the discriminatory character of article XI of the Convention, under the terms of which a number of States are precluded from acceding to the Convention and declares that the Convention deals with matters which affect the interests of all States and it should, therefore, be open for accession by all States.

Morocco

With reference to article VI, the Government of His Majesty the King considers that Moroccan courts and tribunals alone have jurisdiction with respect to acts of genocide committed within the territory of the Kingdom of Morocco.

The competence of international courts may be admitted exceptionally in cases with respect to which the Moroccan Government has given its specific agreement.

With reference to article IX, the Moroccan Government states that no dispute relating to the interpretation, application or fulfilment of the present Convention can be brought before the International Court of Justice, without the prior agreement of the parties to the dispute.

Philippines

"1. With reference to article IV of the Convention, the Philippine Government cannot sanction any situation which would subject its Head of State, who is not a ruler, to conditions less favourable than those accorded to other Heads of State, whether constitutionally responsible rulers or not. The

Philippine Government does not consider said article, therefore, as overriding the existing immunities from judicial processes guaranteed to certain public officials by the Constitution of the Philippines.

"2. With reference to article VII of the Convention, the Philippine Government does not undertake to give effect to said article until the Congress of the Philippines has enacted the necessary legislation defining and punishing the crime of genocide, which legislation, under the Constitution of the Philippines, cannot have any retroactive effect.

"3. With reference to articles VI and IX of the Convention, the Philippine Government takes the position that nothing contained in said articles shall be construed as depriving Philippine courts of jurisdiction over all cases of genocide committed within Philippine territory save only in those cases where the Philippine Government consents to have the decision of the Philippine courts reviewed by either of the international tribunals referred to in said articles. With further reference to article IX of the Convention, the Philippine Government does not consider said article to extend the concept of State responsibility beyond that recognized by the generally accepted principles of international law."

Poland

As regards article IX: Poland does not regard itself as bound by the provision of this article since the agreement of all the parties to a dispute is a necessary condition in each specific case for submission to the International Court of Justice.

As regards article XII: Poland does not accept the provision of this article, considering that the Convention should apply to Non-Self-Governing Territories, including Trust Territories.

Romania

As regards article IX: The People's Republic of Romania does not consider itself bound by the provision of article IX, which provides that disputes between the Contracting parties relating to the interpretation, application or fulfilment of the Convention shall be submitted to the International Court of Justice at the request of any of the parties to the dispute, and declares that as regards the jurisdiction of the Court in disputes relating to the interpretation, application or fulfilment of the Convention, the People's Republic of Romania will adhere to the view which it has held up to the present, that in each particular case, the agreement of all the parties to a dispute is required before it can be referred to the International Court of Justice for settlement.

As regards article XII: The People's Republic of Romania declares that it is not in agreement with article XII of the Convention, and considers that all the provisions of the Convention should apply to the Non-Self-Governing Territories including the Trust Territories.

Rwanda

The Rwandese Republic does not consider itself as bound by article IX of the Convention.

Spain

With a reservation in respect of the whole of article IX (jurisdiction of the International Court of Justice).

Ukrainian Soviet Socialist Republic

As regards article IX: The Ukrainian SSR does not consider as binding upon itself the provision of article IX which provides that disputes between the Contracting parties with regard to the interpretation, application and implementation of the present Convention shall be referred for examination to the International Court of Justice at the request of any party to the dispute, and declares that, as regards the International Court's jurisdiction in respect of disputes concerning the interpretation, application and implementation of the Convention, the Ukrainian SSR will, as hitherto, maintain the position that in each particularly case the agreement of all parties to the dispute is essential for the submission of any particular dispute to the International Court for decision.

As regards article XII: The Ukrainian SSR declares that it is not in agreement with article XII of the Convention and considers that all the provisions of the Convention should extend to Non-Self-Governing Territories, including Trust Territories.

Union of Soviet Socialist Republics

As regards article IX: The Soviet Union does not consider as binding upon itself the provision of article IX which provides that disputes between the Contracting parties with regard to the interpretation, application and implementation of the present Convention shall be referred for examination to the International Court of Justice at the request of any party to the dispute, and declares that, as regards the International Court's jurisdiction in respect of disputes concerning the interpretation, application and implementation of the Convention, the Soviet Union will, as hitherto, maintain the position that in each particular case the agreement of all parties to the dispute is essential for the submission of any particular dispute to the International Court for decision.

As regards article XII: The Union of Soviet Socialist Republics declares that it is not in agreement with article XII of the Convention and considers that all the provisions of the Convention should extend to Non-Self-Governing Territories, including Trust Territories.

Venezuela

With reference to article VI, notice is given that any proceedings to which Venezuela may be a party before an international penal tribunal would be invalid without Venezuela's prior express acceptance of the jurisdiction of such international tribunal.

With reference to article VII, notice is given that the laws in force in Venezuela do not permit the extradition of Venezuelan nationals.

With reference to article IX, the reservation is made that the submission of a dispute to the International Court of Justice shall be regarded as valid only when it takes place with Venezuela's approval, signified by the express conclusion of a prior agreement in each case.

Viet Nam

1. The Socialist Republic of Viet Nam does not consider itself bound by article IX of the Convention which provides for the jurisdiction of the International Court of Justice in solving disputes between the Contracting parties relating to the interpretation, application or fulfilment of the Convention at the request of any of the parties to disputes. The Socialist Republic of Viet

Nam is of the view that, regarding the jurisdiction of the International Court of Justice in solving disputes referred to in article IX of the Convention, the consent of all parties to a dispute, except the criminals, is absolutely necessary for the submission of that dispute to the International Court of Justice for decision.

2. The Socialist Republic of Viet Nam does not accept article XII of the Convention and considers that all provisions of the Convention should also extend to Non-Self-Governing Territories, including Trust Territories.

3. The Socialist Republic of Viet Nam considers that article XI is of a discriminatory nature, depriving a number of States of the opportunity to become parties to the Convention, and holds that the Convention should be open for accession by all States.

OBJECTIONS

(Unless otherwise indicated, the objections were made
upon ratification, accession or succession)

Australia

"The Australian Government does not accept any of the reservations contained in the instrument of accession of the People's Republic of Bulgaria, or in the instrument of ratification of the Republic of the Philippines."

15 November 1950

"The Australian Government does not accept any of the reservations made at the time of signature of the Convention by the Byelorussian Soviet Socialist Republic, Czechoslovakia, the Ukrainian Soviet Socialist Republic and the Union of Soviet Socialist Republics."

19 January 1951

"The Australian Government does not accept the reservations contained in the instruments of accession of the Governments of Poland and Romania."

Belgium

The Government of Belgium does not accept the reservations made by Bulgaria, the Byelorussian Soviet Socialist Republic, Czechoslovakia,

Poland, Romania, the Ukrainian Soviet Socialist Republic and the Union of Soviet Socialist Republics.

Brazil

The Government of Brazil objects to the reservations made to the Convention by Bulgaria, the Byelorussian Soviet Socialist Republic, Czechoslovakia, the Philippines, Poland, Romania, the Ukrainian Soviet Socialist Republic and the Union of Soviet Socialist Republics. The Brazilian Government considers the said reservations as incompatible with the object and purpose of the Convention.

The position taken by the Government of Brazil is founded on the Advisory Opinion of the International Court of Justice of 28 May 1951 [5] and on the resolution adopted by the sixth session of the General Assembly on 12 January 1952 on reservations to multilateral conventions. [6]

The Brazilian Government reserves the right to draw any such legal consequences as it may deem fit from its formal objection to the above-mentioned reservations.

China

15 November 1954

"The Government of China ... objects to all the identical reservations made at the time of signature or ratification or accession to the Convention by Bulgaria, the Byelorussian Soviet Socialist Republic, Czechoslovakia, Hungary, Poland, Romania, the Ukrainian Soviet Socialist Republic and the Union of Soviet Socialist Republics. The Chinese Government considers the above-mentioned reservations as incompatible with the object and purpose of the Convention and therefore, by virtue of the Advisory Opinion of the International Court of Justice of 28 May 1951, [5] would not regard the above-mentioned States as being parties to the Convention."

13 September 1955

[Same communication, *mutatis mutandis,* in respect of the reservations made by Albania.]

25 July 1956

[Same communication, *mutatis mutandis,* in respect of the reservations made by Burma.]

Cuba[7]

Ecuador

31 March 1950

The Government of Ecuador is not in agreement with the reservations made to articles IX and XII of the Convention by the Governments of the Byelorussian Soviet Socialist Republic, Czechoslovakia, the Ukrainian Soviet Socialist Republic and the Union of Soviet Socialist Republics and, therefore, they do not apply to Ecuador which accepted without any modifications the integral text of the Convention.

21 August 1950

[Same communication, *mutatis mutandis,* in respect of the reservations made by Bulgaria.]

9 January 1951

The Government of Ecuador does not accept the reservations made by the Governments of Poland and Romania to articles IX and XII of the Convention.

Greece

We further declare that we have not accepted and do not accept any reservation which has already been made or which may hereafter be made by the countries signatory to this instrument or by countries which have acceded or may hereafter accede thereto.

Netherlands

"The Government of the Kingdom of the Netherlands declares that it considers the reservations made by Albania, Algeria, Bulgaria, the Byelorussian Soviet Socialist Republic, Czechoslovakia, Hungary, India, Morocco, Poland, Romania, the Ukrainian Soviet Socialist Republic and the Union of Soviet Socialist Republics in respect of article IX of the Convention on the Prevention and Punishment of the Crime of Genocide, opened for signature at Paris on 9 December 1948, to be incompatible with the object and purpose of the Convention. The Government of the Kingdom of the Netherlands therefore does not deem any State which has made or which will make such reservation a party to the Convention."

Norway

10 April 1952

"The Norwegian Government does not accept the reservations made to the Convention by the Government of the Philippines at the time of ratification."

Sri Lanka

6 February 1951

"The Government of Ceylon does not accept the reservations made by Romania to the Convention."

United Kingdom of Great Britain and Northern Ireland

"The Government of the United Kingdom of Great Britain and Northern Ireland do not accept the reservations to articles IV, VII, VIII, IX and XII of the Convention made by Albania, Algeria, Argentina, Bulgaria, Burma, the Byelorussian Soviet Socialist Republic, Czechoslovakia, Hungary, India, Mongolia, Morocco, the Philippines, Poland, Romania, Spain, the Ukrainian Soviet Socialist Republic, the Union of Soviet Socialist Republics and Venezuela."

21 November 1975

"The Government of the United Kingdom have consistently stated that they are unable to accept reservation in respect of article IX of the said Convention; in their view this is not the kind of reservation which intending parties to the Convention have the right to make.

"Accordingly, the Government of the United Kingdom do not accept the reservation entered by the Republic of Rwanda against article IX of the Convention. They also wish to place on record that they take the same view of the similar reservation made by the German Democratic Republic as notified by the circular letter [. . .] of 25 April 1973."

26 August 1983

With regard to a declaration and reservation made by Viet Nam and China concerning article IX:

"The Government of the United Kingdom have consistently stated that they are unable to accept reservation to this article. Likewise, in conformity with the attitude adopted by them in previous cases, the Government of the United Kingdom do not accept the reservation entered by Viet Nam relating to article XII."

TERRITORIAL APPLICATIONS

Participant	Date of receipt of notification	Territories
Australia	8 July 1949	All territories for the conduct of whose foreign relations Australia is responsible
Belgium	13 Mar. 1952	Belgian Congo, Trust Territory of Rwanda-Urundi
United Kingdom	30 Jan. 1970	Channel Islands, Isle of Man, Dominica, Grenada, St. Lucia, St. Vincent, Bahamas, Bermuda, British Virgin Islands, Falkland Islands and Dependencies,[8] Fiji, Gibraltar, Hong Kong, Pitcairn, St. Helena and Dependencies, Seychelles, Turks and Caicos Islands
		In a notification received by the Secretary-General on 2 June 1970, the Government of the United Kingdom extended the application of the Convention to the Kingdom of Tonga for whose international relations the United Kingdom is or was then responsible
	2 June 1970	Kingdom of Tonga

NOTES

[1] Ratified on behalf of the Republic of China on 19 July 1951. See note concerning signatures, ratifications, accessions, etc. on behalf of China (note 2 in chapter I).

[2] In a note accompanying the instrument of accession, the Government of the Federal Republic of Germany stated that the Convention would also apply to Land Berlin.

With reference to the above-mentioned declaration, a communication from the German Democratic Republic was received by the Secretary-General on 27 December 1973. The text of the communication is identical in essence, *mutatis mutandis,* to that published in note 4 of chapter I.

In this connection, the Secretary-General received from the Governments of France, the United Kingdom of Great Britain and Northern Ireland and the United States of America (17 June

1974 and 8 July 1975), the Federal Republic of Germany (15 July 1974 and 19 September 1975), the Union of Soviet Socialist Republics (12 September 1974 and 8 December 1975), and the Ukrainian Soviet Socialist Republic (19 September 1974), communications identical in essence, *mutatis mutandis,* to the corresponding ones reproduced in note 4 of chapter I.

[3] Accession on behalf of the Republic of South Viet-Nam on 11 August 1950. (For the text of objections to some of the reservations made upon the said accession, see publication, *Multilateral Treaties for which the Secretary-General acts as Depositary* (ST/LEG/SER.D/13, p. 91); also note that the Democratic Republic of Viet-Nam and the Republic of South Viet-Nam (the latter of which replaced the Republic of Viet-Nam) united on 2 July 1976 to constitute a new State, the Socialist Republic of Viet Nam).

[4] The Secretary-General received on 9 November 1981 from the Government of the Democratic Republic of Kampuchea the following objection with regard to the accession by Viet Nam:

> The Government of Democratic Kampuchea, as a party to the Convention on the Prevention and Punishment of the Crime of Genocide, considers that the signing of that Convention by the Government of the Socialist Republic of Viet Nam has no legal force, beause it is no more than a cynical, macabre charade intended to camouflage the foul crimes of genocide committed by the 250,000 soldiers of the Vietnamese invasion army in Kampuchea. It is an odious insult to the memory of the more than 2,500,000 Kampucheans who have been massacred by these same Vietnamese armed forces using conventional weapons, chemical weapons and the weapon of famine, created deliberately by them for the purpose of eliminating all national resistance at its source.

> It is also a gross insult to hundreds of thousands of Laotians who have been massacred or compelled to take refuge abroad since the occupation of Laos by the Socialist Republic of Viet Nam, to the Hmong national minority in Laos, exterminated by Vietnamese conventional and chemical weapons and, finally, to over a million Vietnamese "boat people" who died at sea or sought refuge abroad in their flight to escape the repression carried out in Viet Nam by the Government of the Socialist Republic of Viet Nam.

> This shameless accession by the Socialist Republic of Viet Nam violates and discredits the noble principles and ideals of the United Nations and jeopardizes the prestige and moral authority of our world Organization. It represents an arrogant challenge to the international community, which is well aware of these crimes of genocide committed by the Vietnamese army in Kampuchea, has constantly denounced and condemned them since 25 December 1978, the date on which the Vietnamese invasion of Kampuchea began, and demands that these Vietnamese crimes of genocide be brought to an end by the total withdrawal of the Vietnamese forces from Kampuchea and the restoration of the inalienable right of the people of Kampuchea to decide its own destiny without any foreign interference, as provided in United Nations resolutions 34/22, 35/6 and 36/5.

[5] *International Court of Justice, Report 1951,* p. 15.

[6] *Resolution 598 (VI); Official Records of the General Assembly, Sixth session, Supplement No. 20* (A/2119), p. 84.

[7] By a notification received by the Secretary-General on 29 January 1982, the Government of Cuba withdrew the declaration made on its behalf upon ratification of the said Convention with respect to the reservations to articles IX and XII by Bulgaria, the Byelorussian Soviet Socialist Republic, Czechoslovakia, Poland, Romania, the Ukrainian Soviet Socialist Republic and the Union of Soviet Socialist Republics.

[8] On 3 October 1983, the Secretary-General received from the Government of Argentina the following objection:

[The Government of Argentina makes a] formal objection to the [declaration] of territorial extension issued by the United Kingdom with regard to the Malvinas Islands (and dependencies), which that country is illegally occupying and refers to as the "Falkland Islands."

The Argentine Republic rejects and considers null and void the [said declaration] of territorial extension.

Chapter IX

CONVENTION ON THE NON-APPLICABILITY OF STATUTORY LIMITATIONS TO WAR CRIMES AND CRIMES AGAINST HUMANITY

Adopted by the General Assembly of the United Nations on 26 November 1968

ENTRY INTO FORCE: 11 November 1970, in accordance with article VIII

Participant	Signature	Ratification, accession (a)
Afghanistan		22 July 1983 *a*
Albania		19 May 1971 *a*
Bolivia		6 Oct. 1983 *a*
Bulgaria	21 Jan. 1969	21 May 1969
Byelorussian SSR	7 Jan. 1969	8 May 1969
Cameroon		6 Oct. 1972 *a*
Cuba		13 Sep. 1972 *a*
Czechoslovakia	21 May 1969	13 Aug. 1970
Democratic People's Republic of Korea		8 Nov. 1984 *a*
Democratic Yemen		9 Feb. 1987 *a*
Gambia		29 Dec. 1978 *a*
German Democratic Republic		27 Mar. 1973 *a*
Guinea		7 June 1971 *a*
Hungary	25 Mar. 1969	24 June 1969
India		12 Jan. 1971 *a*
Kenya		1 May 1972 *a*
Lao People's Democratic Republic		28 Dec. 1984 *a*
Mexico	3 July 1969	
Mongolia	31 Jan. 1969	21 May 1969
Nicaragua		3 Sep. 1986 *a*
Nigeria		1 Dec. 1970 *a*

Participant	Signature	Ratification, accession (a)
Philippines		15 May 1973 *a*
Poland	16 Dec. 1968	14 Feb. 1969
Romania	17 Apr. 1969	15 Sep. 1969
Rwanda		16 Apr. 1975 *a*
Saint Vincent and the Grenadines		9 Nov. 1981 *a*
Tunisia		15 June 1972 *a*
Ukrainian SSR	14 Jan. 1969	19 June 1969
Union of Soviet Socialist Republics	6 Jan. 1969	22 Apr. 1969
Viet Nam		6 May 1983 *a*
Yugoslavia	16 Dec. 1968	9 June 1970

DECLARATIONS

(Unless otherwise indicated, the declarations were made
upon ratification or accession.)

Afghanistan

Since the provisions of articles V and VII of the said Convention, according to which some States cannot become a party to the Convention, are not in conformity with the universal character of the Convention, the Presidium of the Revolutionary Council of the Democratic Republic of Afghanistan states that, on the basis of the principle of the sovereign equality of States, the Convention should remain open to all States.

Albania

The Government of the People's Republic of Albania states that the provisions of articles V and VII of the Convention on the Non-Applicability of Statutory Limitations to War Crimes and Crimes against Humanity are unacceptable because, in preventing a number of States from becoming parties to the Convention, they are discriminatory in nature and thus violate the principle of the sovereign equality of States and are incompatible with the spirit and purposes of the Convention.

Bulgaria

The People's Republic of Bulgaria deems it necessary at the same time to declare that the provisions of articles V and VII of the Convention on the Non-Applicability of Statutory Limitations to War Crimes and Crimes against Humanity, which prevent a number of States from signing the Convention or acceding to it, are contrary to the principle of the sovereign equality of States.

Byelorussian Soviet Socialist Republic

The Byelorussian Soviet Socialist Republic declares that the provisions of articles V and VII of the Convention on the Non-Applicability of Statutory Limitations to War Crimes and Crimes against Humanity, which prevent certain States from signing the Convention or acceding to it, are contrary to the principle of the sovereign equality of States.

Cuba

The Government of the Republic of Cuba declares that it regards the provisions of articles V and VII of the Convention on the Non-Applicability of Statutory Limitations to War Crimes and Crimes against Humanity as discriminatory and contrary to the principle of the sovereign equality of States.

Czechoslovakia

"The Czechoslovak Socialist Republic declares that the provisions of articles V and VII of the Convention on the Non-Applicability of Statutory Limitations to War Crimes and Crimes against Humanity, adopted by the General Assembly of the United Nations on 26 November 1968, are in contradiction with the principle that all States have the right to become parties to multilateral treaties governing matters of general interest."

German Democratic Republic

The German Democratic Republic deems it necessary to state that articles V and VII of the Convention deprive a number of States of the opportunity to become parties to the Convention. As the Convention regulates matters affecting the interests of all States, it should be open to participation by all States whose policies are guided by the purposes and principles of the Charter of the United Nations.

Guinea

The Government of the Republic of Guinea considers that the dispositions of articles V and VII of the Convention on the Non-Applicability of Statutory Limitations to War Crimes and Crimes against Humanity, adopted by the General Assembly of the United Nations on 26 November 1968, make it impossible for a number of States to become parties to the Convention and are therefore of a discriminatory character which is contradictory to the object and aims of this Convention.

The Government of the Republic of Guinea is of the opinion that, in accordance with the principle of sovereign equality of States, the Convention should be open to all States without any discrimination and limitation.

Hungary

"The Government of the Hungarian People's Republic declares that the provisions contained in articles V and VII of the Convention on the Non-Applicability of Statutory Limitations to War Crimes and Crimes against Humanity adopted by the General Assembly of the United Nations on 26 November 1968, which deny the possibility to certain States to become signatories to the Convention are of discriminatory nature, violate the principle of sovereign equality of States and are more particularly incompatible with the objectives and purposes of the said Convention."

Lao People's Democratic Republic

The Lao People's Democratic Republic accedes to the above-mentioned Convention and undertakes to implement faithfully all its clauses, except for the provisions of articles V and VII of the Convention on the Non-Applicability of Statutory Limitations to War Crimes and Crimes against Humanity adopted by the United Nations General Assembly on 26 November 1968, which contravene the principle of the sovereign equality of States. The Convention should be open to universal participation in accordance with the purposes and principles of the Charter of the United Nations.

Mongolia

"The Mongolian People's Republic deems it necessary to state that the provisions of articles V and VII of the Convention on the Non-Applicability of Statutory Limitations to War Crimes and Crimes against Humanity have a discriminatory nature and seek to preclude certain States from participation in the Convention and declares that as the Convention deals with matters affecting the interests of all States it should be open to participation by all States without any discrimination or restriction."

Poland

"The Polish People's Republic considers that the dispositions of articles V and VII of the Convention on the Non-Applicability of Statutory Limitations to War Crimes and Crimes against Humanity, adopted by the General Assembly on 26 November 1968, make it impossible for a number of States to become parties to the Convention and are therefore of a discriminatory character which is contradictory to the object and aims of this Convention.

The Polish People's Republic is of the opinion that, in accordance with the principle of sovereign equality of States, the Convention should be open to all States without any discrimination and limitation."

Romania

The State Council of the Socialist Republic of Romania states that the provisions of articles V and VII of the Convention on the Non-Applicability of Statutory Limitations to War Crimes and Crimes against Humanity are not compatible with the principle that multilateral international treaties, the subject and purpose of which concern the international community as a whole, should be open for universal participation.

Ukrainian Soviet Socialist Republic

The Ukrainian Soviet Socialist Republic declares that the provisions of articles V and VII of the Convention on the Non-Applicability of Statutory Limitations to War Crimes and Crimes against Humanity, which prevent certain States from signing the Convention or acceding to it, are contrary to the principle of the sovereign equality of States.

Union of Soviet Socialist Republics

The Union of Soviet Socialist Republics declares that the provisions of articles V and VII of the Convention on the Non-Applicability of Statutory Limitations to War Crimes and Crimes against Humanity, which prevent certain States from signing the Convention or acceding to it, are contrary to the principle of the sovereign equality of States.

Viet Nam

The Government of the Socialist Republic of Viet Nam deems it necessary to state in accordance with the principle of sovereign equality of States that the Convention should be open to all States without any discrimination and limitation.

Chapter X

SLAVERY CONVENTION

Signed at Geneva on 25 September 1926[1],

ENTRY INTO FORCE: 9 March 1927 (article 12).

RATIFICATIONS OR DEFINITIVE ACCESSIONS (*a*)

Afghanistan . . . .   9 Nov. 1935 *a*
Austria . . . .   19 Aug. 1927
United States of America . . . .   21 Mar. 1929 *a*
   Subject to the reservation that the Government of the
   United States, adhering to its policy of opposition
   to forced or compulsory labour except as punishment for crime of which the person concerned has
   been duly convicted, adheres to the Convention
   except as to the first subdivision of the second
   paragraph of article 5, which reads as follows:
      "(I) Subject to the transitional provisions laid
   down in paragraph (2) below, compulsory or forced
   labour may only be exacted for public purposes."[2]
Belgium . . . .   23 Sep. 1927
Great Britain and Northern Ireland . . . .   18 June 1927
   Burma[3]
   The Convention is not binding upon Burma in respect of article 3 in so far as that article may require
   her to enter into any convention whereby vessels by
   reason of the fact that they are owned, fitted out or
   commanded by Burmans, or of the fact that one-
   half of the crew is Burman, are classified as native

---

* For notes, see end of chapter.

vessels or are denied any privilege, right or immunity enjoyed by similar vessels of other States signatories of the Convention or are made subject to any liability or disability to which similar ships of these other States are not subject.

Canada	6 Aug. 1928
Australia	18 June 1927
New Zealand	18 June 1927
Union of South Africa (including *South West Africa*)	18 June 1927
Ireland	18 June 1930 *a*
India	18 June 1927

The signature of the Convention is not binding in respect of article 3 in so far as that article may require India to enter into any convention whereby vessels, by reason of the fact that they are owned, fitted out or commanded by Indians, or of the fact that one-half of the crew is Indian, are classified as native vessels, or are denied any privilege, right or immunity enjoyed by similar vessels of other States signatories of the Convention or are made subject to any liability or disability to which similar ships of such other States are not subject.

Bulgaria	9 Mar. 1927
China[4]	22 Apr. 1937
Cuba	6 July 1931
Czechoslovakia	10 Oct. 1930
Denmark	17 May 1927
Ecuador	26 Mar. 1928 *a*
Egypt	25 Jan. 1928 *a*
Estonia	16 May 1929
Finland	29 Sep. 1927
France	28 Mar. 1931
Syria and *Lebanon*	25 June 1931 *a*
Germany	12 Mar. 1929
Greece	4 July 1930
Haiti	3 Sep. 1927 *a*
Hungary[5]	17 Feb. 1933 *a*
Iraq	18 Jan. 1929 *a*
Italy	25 Aug. 1928
Latvia	9 July 1927
Liberia	17 May 1930
Mexico	8 Sep. 1934 *a*

Monaco	17 Jan. 1928 *a*
The Netherlands (including *Netherlands Indies, Surinam* and *Curaçao*)	7 Jan. 1928
Nicaragua	3 Oct. 1927 *a*
Norway	10 Sep. 1927
Poland	17 Sep. 1930
Portugal	4 Oct. 1927
Romania	22 June 1931
Spain	12 Sep. 1927

For Spain and the *Spanish Colonies,* with the exception
of the Spanish Protectorate of Morocco.

Sudan	15 Sep. 1927 *a*
Sweden	17 Dec. 1927
Switzerland	1 Nov. 1930 *a*
Turkey	24 July 1933 *a*
Yugoslavia	28 Sep. 1929

SIGNATURES OR ACCESSIONS (*a*) NOT YET PERFECTED BY RATIFICATION

Albania[6]

Colombia

Dominican Republic *a*

Iran

> *Ad referendum* and interpreting article 3 as without power to compel Iran to bind herself by any arrangement or convention which would place her ships of whatever tonnage in the category of native vessels provided for by the Convention on the Trade in Arms.

Lithuania

Panama

Uruguay

ACTIONS SUBSEQUENT TO THE ASSUMPTION OF DEPOSITARY FUNCTIONS BY THE SECRETARY-GENERAL OF THE UNITED NATIONS

Participant	*Accession, succession* (d)
Bahamas	10 June 1976 *d*
Bangladesh	7 Jan. 1985
Barbados	22 July 1976 *d*
Benin	4 Apr. 1962 *d*
Bolivia	6 Oct. 1983
Cameroon	7 Mar. 1962 *d*
Central African Republic	4 Sep. 1962 *d*
Congo	15 Oct. 1962 *d*
Côte d'Ivoire	8 Dec. 1961 *d*
Fiji	12 June 1972 *d*
German Democratic Republic[7]	
Ghana	3 May 1963 *d*
Guatemala	11 Nov. 1983
Guinea	30 Mar. 1962 *d*
Israel	6 Jan. 1955
Mali	2 Feb. 1973 *d*
Mauritania	6 June 1986
Morocco	11 May 1959 *d*[8]
Niger	25 Aug. 1961 *d*
Saint Vincent and the Grenadines	9 Nov. 1981
Senegal	2 May 1963 *d*
Solomon Islands	3 Sep. 1981 *d*
Suriname	12 Oct. 1979 *d*
Togo	27 Feb. 1962 *d*

NOTES

[1] Registered No. 1414. League of Nations, *Treaty Series,* vol. 60, p. 253.

[2] This accession, given subject to reservation, has been communicated to the signatory States for acceptance.

[3] As mentioned in the latest official list of the League of Nations, Burma, which was formerly a part of India, was separated from the latter on 1 April 1937 and had possessed since that time the status of an overseas territory of the United Kingdom. It was as such that Burma continued to be bound by a ratification or accession recorded on behalf of India before the date above-mentioned.

[4] See note concerning signatures, ratifications, accessions, etc., on behalf of China (note 2 in chapter I).

[5] See League of Nations, *Treaty Series,* vol. 130, p. 444.

[6] The Government of Albania deposited on 2 July 1957 the instrument of accession to the Convention as amended by the Protocol of 7 December 1953 (see chapter XII).

[7] In a notification received on 16 July 1974 the Government of the German Democratic Republic stated that the German Democratic Republic had declared the reapplication of the Convention as of 22 December 1958.

In this connection, the Secretary-General received, on 2 March 1976, the following communication from the Government of the Federal Republic of Germany:

With reference to the communication by the German Democratic Republic of 17 June 1974, concerning the application, as from 22 December 1958, of the Slavery Convention of 25 September 1926, the Government of the Federal Republic of Germany declares that in the relation between the Federal Republic of Germany and the German Democratic Republic the declaration of application has no retroactive effect beyond 21 June 1973.

Subsequently, in a communication received on 17 June 1976, the Government of the German Democratic Republic declared:

"The Government of the German Democratic Republic takes the view that, in accordance with the applicable rules of international law and the international practice of States, the regulations on the reapplication of agreements concluded under international law are an internal affair of the successor State concerned. Accordingly, the German Democratic Republic was entitled to determine the date of reapplication of the Slavery Convention of 25 September 1926, to which it established its status as a party by way of succession."

[8] By virtue of its acceptance of the Protocol of amendment on 7 December 1953.

Chapter XI

PROTOCOL AMENDING THE SLAVERY CONVENTION SIGNED AT GENEVA ON 25 SEPTEMBER 1926

Adopted by the General Assembly of the United Nations on 23 October 1953

ENTRY INTO FORCE: 7 December 1953, in accordance with article III.[1, *]

Participant	Signature	*Definitive signature* (s), *acceptance*, *succession* (d)
Afghanistan		16 Aug. 1954 *s*
Australia		9 Dec. 1953 *s*
Austria	7 Dec. 1953	16 July 1954
Bahamas		10 June 1976 *d*
Bangladesh		7 Jan. 1985
Barbados		22 July 1976 *d*
Belgium	24 Feb. 1954	13 Dec. 1962
Bolivia		6 Oct. 1983
Burma	14 Mar. 1956	29 Apr. 1957
Cameroon		27 June 1984
Canada		17 Dec. 1953 *s*
China [2]		
Cuba		28 June 1954 *s*
Denmark		3 Mar. 1954 *s*
Ecuador	7 Sep. 1954	17 Aug. 1955
Egypt	15 June 1954	29 Sep. 1954
Fiji		12 June 1972 *d*
Finland		19 Mar. 1954
France	14 Jan. 1954	14 Feb. 1963
German Democratic Republic .		16 July 1974

---

* For notes, see end of chapter.

Participant	Signature	Definitive signature (s), acceptance, succession (d)
Germany, Federal Republic of .		29 May 1973[3]
Greece	7 Dec. 1953	12 Dec. 1955
Guatemala		11 Nov. 1983
Guinea		12 July 1962
Hungary		26 Feb. 1958
India		12 Mar. 1954 s
Iraq		23 May 1955
Ireland		31 Aug. 1961
Israel		12 Sep. 1955
Italy		4 Feb. 1954 s
Liberia		7 Dec. 1953 s
Mali		2 Feb. 1973
Mauritania		6 June 1986
Mexico		3 Feb. 1954 s
Monaco	28 Jan. 1954	12 Nov. 1954
Morocco		11 May 1959
Netherlands	15 Dec. 1953	7 July 1955
New Zealand		16 Dec. 1953 s
Nicaragua		14 Jan. 1986
Niger		7 Dec. 1964
Norway	24 Feb. 1954	11 Apr. 1957
Romania		13 Nov. 1957 s
Saint Vincent and the Grenadines		9 Nov. 1981
Solomon Islands		3 Sep. 1981 d
South Africa		29 Dec. 1953 s
Spain		10 Nov. 1976 s
Sweden		17 Aug. 1954 s
Switzerland		7 Dec. 1953 s
Syrian Arab Republic		4 Aug. 1954
Turkey		14 Jan. 1955 s
United Kingdom		7 Dec. 1953 s
United States of America	16 Dec. 1953	7 Mar. 1956
Yugoslavia	11 Feb. 1954	21 Mar. 1955

TERRITORIAL APPLICATIONS

Participant	*Date of receipt of notification*	*Territories*
Netherlands . . .	7 July 1955	Netherlands Antilles, Netherlands New Guinea, Surinam.

NOTES

[1] The amendments set forth in the Annex to the Protocol entered into force on 7 July 1955, in accordance with article III of the Protocol.

[2] Signed and ratified on behalf of the Republic of China on 7 December 1953 and 14 December 1955 respectively. See note concerning signatures, ratifications, accessions, etc. on behalf of China (note 2 in chapter I).

[3] With the following declaration:

"... The said Protocol shall also apply to Berlin (West) with effect from the date on which it enters into force for the Federal Republic of Germany."

In this connection, the Secretary-General received on 4 December 1973 from the Permanent Mission of the Union of Soviet Socialist Republics to the United Nations the following communication:

"The 1926 Slavery Convention, as amended by the 1953 Protocol, deals with matters relating to the territories under the sovereignty of the countries parties to the Convention within the limits of which they exercise jurisdiction. As is well known, the Western Sectors of Berlin are not integral parts of the Federal Republic of Germany and cannot be governed by it. In that connection, the Soviet Union regards the above-mentioned statement by the Federal Republic of Germany as unlawful and as having no legal force, with all the consequences flowing therefrom, since the extension of the validity of the Convention to the Western Sectors of Berlin raises questions relating to their status, thus conflicting with the relevant provisions of the Quadripartite Agreement of 3 September 1971."

The Government of the German Democratic Republic, upon acceptance of the Protocol on 16 July 1974, made a declaration which is identical in essence to the above-quoted declaration.

The following communication on the same subject was received on 17 July 1974 from the Governments of France, the United Kingdom and the United States of America:

"In a communication to the Government of the Union of Soviet Socialist Republics which is an integral part (Annex IV A) of the Quadripartite Agreement of 3 September 1971, the Governments of France, the United Kingdom of Great Britain and Northern Ireland and the United States of America reaffirmed that, provided that matters of security and status are not affected, international agreements and arrangements entered into by the Federal Republic of Germany may be extended to the Western Sectors of Berlin in accordance with established procedures. For its part, the Government of the Union of Soviet Socialist Republics, in a communication to the Governments of France, the United Kingdom and the United States which is similarly an integral part (Annex IV B) of the Quadripartite Agreement of 3 September 1971, affirmed that it would raise no objection to such extension.

"The purpose and effect of the established procedures referred to above, which were specifically endorsed in Annex IV A and B to the Quadripartite Agreement, are precisely to ensure that agreements and arrangements to be extended to the Western Sectors of Berlin are extended in such a way that questions of security and status remain unaffected and to take account of the fact that these Sectors continue not to be a constituent part of the Federal Republic of Germany and not to be governed by it. The extension of the Convention of 1926, as amended by the Protocol of 1953, to the Western Sectors of Berlin received the prior authorization under these established procedures, of the authorities of France, the United Kingdom and the United States. The rights and responsibilities of the Governments of those three countries remain unaffected thereby. There is thus no question that the extension to the Western Sectors of Berlin of the Convention of 1926, as amended by the Protocol of 1953, is in any way inconsistent with the Quadripartite Agreement.

"Accordingly, the application to the Western Sectors of Berlin of the Convention of 1926, as amended by the Protocol of 1953, continues in full force and effect."

Subsequently, the Secretary-General received on 27 August 1974 from the Government of the Federal Republic of Germany a declaration to the effect that the said Government shared the position set out in the above-quoted declaration, and that the extension of the Protocol to Berlin (West) would continue in full force and effect.

In reference to the declaration by the Government of the German Democratic Republic, communications were received by the Secretary-General from the Governments of France, the United Kingdom of Great Britain and Northern Ireland and the United States of America (8 July 1975) and from the Government of the Federal Republic of Germany (19 September 1975), which are identical in substance, *mutatis mutandis,* to the corresponding communications reproduced in note 4 in chapter I.

Chapter XII

SLAVERY CONVENTION SIGNED AT GENEVA ON 25 SEPTEMBER 1926 AS AMENDED BY THE PROTOCOL

Done at New York on 7 December 1953

ENTRY INTO FORCE: 7 July 1955, the date on which the amendments, set forth in the annex to the Protocol of 7 December 1953, entered into force in accordance with article III of the Protocol.

Participant	Definitive signature or participation in the Convention of 1926 and in the Protocol of 7 December 1953	Ratification, accession (a), succession (d), to the Convention as amended
Afghanistan	16 Aug. 1954	
Albania		2 July 1957 *a*
Algeria		20 Nov. 1963 *a*
Australia	9 Dec. 1953	
Austria	16 July 1954	
Bahamas	10 June 1976	
Bangladesh	7 Jan. 1985	
Barbados	22 July 1976	
Belgium	13 Dec. 1962	
Bolivia	6 Oct. 1983	
Brazil		6 Jan. 1966 *a*
Burma	29 Apr. 1957	
Byelorussian SSR		13 Sep. 1956 *a*
Cameroon	27 June 1984	
Canada	17 Dec. 1953	
China [1], *		

___

* For notes, see end of chapter.

Participant	Definitive signature or participation in the Convention of 1926 and in the Protocol of 7 December 1953	Ratification, accession (a), succession (d), to the Convention as amended
Cuba	28 June 1954	
Cyprus		21 Apr. 1986 d
Democratic Yemen		9 Feb. 1987 a
Denmark	3 Mar. 1954	
Ecuador	17 Aug. 1955	
Egypt	29 Sep. 1954	
Ethiopia		21 Jan. 1969
Fiji	12 June 1972	
Finland	19 Mar. 1954	
France	14 Feb. 1963	
German Democratic Republic[2]	16 July 1974	
Germany, Federal Republic of	29 May 1973	
Greece	12 Dec. 1955	
Guatemala	11 Nov. 1983	
Guinea	12 July 1962	
Hungary	26 Feb. 1958	
India	12 Mar. 1954	
Iraq	23 May 1955	
Ireland	31 Aug. 1961	
Israel	12 Sep. 1955	
Italy	4 Feb. 1954	
Jamaica		30 July 1964 d
Jordan		5 May 1959 a
Kuwait		28 May 1963 a
Lesotho		4 Nov. 1974 d
Liberia	7 Dec. 1953	
Libyan Arab Jamahiriya		14 Feb. 1957 a
Madagascar		12 Feb. 1964 a
Malawi		2 Aug. 1965 a
Mali	2 Feb. 1973	
Malta		3 Jan. 1966 d
Mauritania	6 June 1986	
Mauritius		18 July 1969 d
Mexico	3 Feb. 1954	
Monaco	12 Nov. 1954	
Mongolia		20 Dec. 1968 a
Morocco	11 May 1959	
Nepal		7 Jan. 1963 a

Participant	Definitive signature or participation in the Convention of 1926 and in the Protocol of 7 December 1953	Ratification, accession (a), succession (d), to the Convention as amended
Netherlands	7 July 1955	
New Zealand	16 Dec. 1953	
Nicaragua	14 Jan. 1986	
Niger	7 Dec. 1964	
Nigeria		26 June 1961 d
Norway	11 Apr. 1957	
Pakistan		30 Sep. 1955 a
Papua New Guinea		27 Jan. 1982 a
Philippines		12 July 1955 a
[Republic of South Viet-Nam]		14 Aug. 1956 a[3]
Romania	13 Nov. 1957	
Saint Vincent and the Grenadines		9 Nov. 1981
Saudi Arabia		5 July 1973 a
Sierra Leone		13 Mar. 1962 d
Solomon Islands	3 Sep. 1981	
South Africa	29 Dec. 1953	
Spain	10 Nov. 1976	
Sri Lanka		21 Mar. 1958 a
Sudan		9 Sep. 1957 d
Sweden	17 Aug. 1954	
Switzerland	7 Dec. 1953	
Syrian Arab Republic	4 Aug. 1954	
Trinidad and Tobago		11 Apr. 1966 d
Tunisia		15 July 1966 a
Turkey	14 Jan. 1955	
Uganda		12 Aug. 1964 a
Ukrainian SSR		27 Jan. 1959 a
Union of Soviet Socialist Republics		8 Aug. 1956 a
United Kingdom	7 Dec. 1953	
United Republic of Tanzania		28 Nov. 1962 a
United States of America	7 Mar. 1956	
Yugoslavia	21 Mar. 1955	
Zambia		26 Mar. 1973 d

NOTES

[1] Signed on behalf of the Republic of China on 14 December 1955. See note concerning signatures, ratifications, accessions, etc. on behalf of China (note 2 in chapter I).

[2] A notification of reapplication of the Convention of 25 September 1926 was received on 16 July 1974 from the Government of the German Democratic Republic. As an instrument of acceptance of the amending Protocol of 7 December 1953 was deposited with the Secretary-General on the same date on behalf of the Government of the German Democratic Republic, the latter has been applying the Convention as amended since 16 July 1974 (see also note 7 in chapter X).

[3] The Democratic Republic of Viet-Nam and the Republic of South Viet-Nam (the latter of which replaced the Republic of Viet-Nam) united on 2 July 1976 to constitute a new State, the Socialist Republic of Viet Nam).

At the time of preparing this publication no indication had been received from the Government of the Socialist Republic of Viet Nam regarding its position with respect to a possible succession.

Chapter XIII

SUPPLEMENTARY CONVENTION ON THE ABOLITION OF SLAVERY, THE SLAVE TRADE, AND INSTITUTIONS AND PRACTICES SIMILAR TO SLAVERY

Done at Geneva on 7 September 1956

ENTRY INTO FORCE: 30 April 1957, in accordance with article 13.

Note: The Convention was adopted by the United Nations Conference of Plenipotentiaries on a Supplementary Convention on the Abolition of Slavery, the Slave Trade, and Institutions and Practices Similar to Slavery. The Conference was convened pursuant to resolution 608 (XXI) [1, *] of 30 April 1956 of the Economic and Social Council of the United Nations, and met at the European Office of the United Nations in Geneva from 13 August to 4 September 1956. In addition to the Convention, the Conference adopted the Final Act and two resolutions for the texts of which, see United Nations, *Treaty Series,* vol. 226, p. 3.

Participant	Signature	Ratification, accession (a), succession (d)
Afghanistan		16 Nov. 1966 *a*
Albania		6 Nov. 1958 *a*
Algeria		31 Oct. 1963 *a*
Argentina		13 Aug. 1964 *a*
Australia	7 Sep. 1956	6 Jan. 1958
Austria		7 Oct. 1963 *a*
Bahamas		10 June 1976 *d*
Bangladesh		5 Feb. 1985 *a*
Barbados		9 Aug. 1972 *d*
Belgium	7 Sep. 1956	13 Dec. 1962
Bolivia		6 Oct. 1983 *a*
Brazil		6 Jan. 1966 *a*

* For notes, see end of chapter.

Participant	Signature	Ratification, accession (a), succession (d)
Bulgaria	26 June 1957	21 Aug. 1958
Byelorussian SSR	7 Sep. 1956	5 June 1957
Cameroon		27 June 1984 *a*
Canada	7 Sep. 1956	10 Jan. 1963
Central African Republic		30 Dec. 1970 *a*
China [2]		
Congo		25 Aug. 1977 *a*
Côte d'Ivoire		10 Dec. 1970 *a*
Cuba	10 Jan. 1957	21 Aug. 1963
Cyprus		11 May 1962 *d*
Czechoslovakia	7 Sep. 1956	13 June 1958
Democratic Kampuchea		12 June 1957 *a*
Denmark	27 June 1957	24 Apr. 1958
Djibouti		21 Mar. 1979 *a*
Dominican Republic		31 Oct. 1962 *a*
Ecuador		29 Mar. 1960 *a*
Egypt		17 Apr. 1958 *a*
El Salvador	7 Sep. 1956	
Ethiopia		21 Jan. 1969 *a*
Fiji		12 June 1972 *d*
Finland		1 Apr. 1959 *a*
France	7 Sep. 1956	26 May 1964
German Democratic Republic .		16 July 1974 *a*
Germany, Federal Republic of [3] .	7 Sep. 1956	14 Jan. 1959
Ghana		3 May 1963 *a*
Greece	7 Sep. 1956	13 Dec. 1972
Guatemala	7 Sep. 1956	11 Nov. 1983
Guinea		14 Mar. 1977 *a*
Haiti	7 Sep. 1956	12 Feb. 1958
Hungary	7 Sep. 1956	26 Feb. 1958
Iceland		17 Nov. 1965 *a*
India	7 Sep. 1956	23 June 1960
Iran (Islamic Republic of)		30 Dec. 1959 *a*
Iraq	7 Sep. 1956	30 Sep. 1963
Ireland		18 Sep. 1961 *a*
Israel	7 Sep. 1956	23 Oct. 1957
Italy	7 Sep. 1956	12 Feb. 1958
Jamaica		30 July 1964 *d*
Jordan		27 Sep. 1957 *a*
Kuwait		18 Jan. 1963 *a*

Participant	Signature	Ratification, accession (a), succession (d)
Lao People's Democratic Republic		9 Sep. 1957 *a*
Lesotho		4 Nov. 1974 *d*
Liberia	7 Sep. 1956	
Luxembourg	7 Sep. 1956	1 May 1967
Madagascar		29 Feb. 1972 *a*
Malawi		2 Aug. 1965 *a*
Malaysia		18 Nov. 1957 *a*
Mali		2 Feb. 1973 *a*
Malta		3 Jan. 1966 *d*
Mauritania		6 June 1986 *a*
Mauritius		18 July 1969 *d*
Mexico	7 Sep. 1956	30 June 1959
Mongolia		20 Dec. 1968 *a*
Morocco		11 May 1959 *a*
Nepal		7 Jan. 1963 *a*
Netherlands	7 Sep. 1956	3 Dec. 1957
New Zealand		26 Apr. 1962 *a*
Nicaragua		14 Jan. 1986 *a*
Niger		22 July 1963 *a*
Nigeria		26 June 1961 *d*
Norway	7 Sep. 1956	3 May 1960
Pakistan	7 Sep. 1956	20 Mar. 1958
Peru	7 Sep. 1956	
Philippines		17 Nov. 1964 *a*
Poland	7 Sep. 1956	10 Jan. 1963
Portugal	7 Sep. 1956	10 Aug. 1959
[Republic of South Viet-Nam][4]	7 Sep. 1956	
Romania	7 Sep. 1956	13 Nov. 1957
Saint Vincent and the Grenadines		9 Nov. 1981 *a*
San Marino	7 Sep. 1956	29 Aug. 1967
Saudi Arabia		5 July 1973 *a*
Senegal		19 July 1979 *a*
Sierra Leone		13 Mar. 1962 *d*
Singapore		28 Mar. 1972 *d*
Solomon Islands		3 Sep. 1981 *d*
Spain		21 Nov. 1967 *a*
Sri Lanka	5 June 1957	21 Mar. 1958
Sudan	7 Sep. 1956	9 Sep. 1957

Participant	Signature	Ratification, accession (a), succession (d)
Suriname		12 Oct. 1979 *d*
Sweden		28 Oct. 1959 *a*
Switzerland		28 July 1964 *a*
Syrian Arab Republic [5]		17 Apr. 1958 *a*
Togo		8 July 1980 *a*
Trinidad and Tobago		11 Apr. 1966 *d*
Tunisia		15 July 1966 *a*
Turkey	28 June 1957	17 July 1964
Uganda		12 Aug. 1964 *a*
Ukrainian SSR	7 Sep. 1956	3 Dec. 1958
Union of Soviet Socialist Republics	7 Sep. 1956	12 Apr. 1957
United Kingdom	7 Sep. 1956	30 Apr. 1957
United Republic of Tanzania . .		28 Nov. 1962
United States of America		6 Dec. 1967
Yugoslavia	7 Sep. 1956	20 May 1958
Zaire		28 Feb. 1975
Zambia		26 Mar. 1973

TERRITORIAL APPLICATIONS

Participant	Date of receipt of notification	Territories
Australia	6 Jan. 1958	All the Non-Self-Governing, Trust and other non-metropolitan Territories for the international relations of which Australia is responsible
France	26 May 1964	All the territories of the Republic (Metropolitan France, overseas departments and territories)
Italy	12 Feb. 1958	Somaliland under Italian Administration
Netherlands . . .	3 Dec. 1957	Surinam, the Netherlands Antilles and Netherlands New Guinea
New Zealand . .	26 Apr. 1962 *a*	The Cook Islands (including Niue) and the Tokelau Islands

Participant	Date of receipt of notification	Territories
United Kingdom .	30 Apr. 1957	The Channel Islands and the Isle of Man
United States of America	6 Dec. 1967a	All territories for the international relations of which the United States of America is responsible

TERRITORIAL APPLICATIONS UNDER PARAGRAPH 2 OF ARTICLE 12 OF THE CONVENTION

Participant	Date of receipt of notification	Territories
United Kingdom .	6 Sep. 1957	Aden, Bahamas, Barbados, Basutoland, Bechuanaland, Bermuda, British Guiana, British Honduras, Brunei, Cyprus, Falkland Islands,[6] Fiji, Gambia, Gibraltar, Hong Kong, Jamaica, Kenya, Antigua, Montserrat, St. Kitts-Nevis, Virgin Islands, Malta, Mauritius, North Borneo, St. Helena, Sarawak, Seychelles, Sierra Leone, Singapore, Somaliland Protectorate, Swaziland, Tanganyika, Gilbert and Ellice Islands, Solomon Islands Protectorate, Grenada, St. Lucia, St. Vincent, Zanzibar, Federation of Rhodesia and Nyasaland,[7] Bahrain, Qatar, The Trucial States (Abu Dhabi, Ajman, Dubai, Fujairah, Ras al Khaimah, Sharjah and Ummal Qaiwain)
	18 Oct. 1957	Dominica and Tonga
	21 Oct. 1957	Kuwait
	30 Oct. 1957	Uganda
	14 Nov. 1957	Trinidad and Tobago
	1 July 1957	The Federation of Nigeria

NOTES

[1] *Official Records of the Economic and Social Council, Twenty-first Session, Supplement No. 1* (E/2889), p. 7.

[2] Signed and ratified on behalf of the Republic of China on 23 May 1957 and 28 May 1959 respectively. See note concerning signatures, ratifications, accessions, etc. on behalf of China (note 2 in chapter I).

With reference to the above-mentioned ratification, communications have been addressed to the Secretary-General by the Permanent Missions to the United Nations of Hungary, Poland and the Union of Soviet Socialist Republics, on the one hand, and of China on the other hand. For the nature of these communications, see also note 2 in chapter I.

[3] A note accompanying the instrument of ratification contains a statement that "the Supplementary Convention . . . also applies to Land Berlin at from the date on which the Convention enters into force in the Federal Republic of Germany".

With reference to the above-mentioned statement, communications have been addressed to the Secretary-General by the Governments of Czechoslovakia, Poland, Romania, the Union of Soviet Socialist Republics on the one hand, and by the Government of the Federal Republic of Germany on the other hand. The said communications are identical in essence, *mutatis mutandis,* to those referred to in note 4 of chapter I.

[4] See note 3 in chapter VIII.

[5] Accession by the United Arab Republic.

By a communication dated 24 February 1958, the Minister for Foreign Affairs of the United Arab Republic notified the Secretary-General of the United Nations of the establishment by Egypt and Syria of a single State, the United Arab Republic. Subsequently, in a note dated 1 March 1958, the Ministry for Foreign Affairs of the United Arab Republic informed the Secretary-General of the following: ". . . It is to be noted that the Government of the United Arab Republic declares that the Union henceforth is a single Member of the United Nations, bound by the provisions of the Charter and that all international treaties and agreements concluded by Egypt or Syria with other countries will remain valid within the regional limits prescribed on their conclusion and in accordance with the principles of international law."

In a cable dated 8 October 1961, the Prime Minister and Minister for Foreign Affairs of the Syrian Arab Republic informed the President of the General Assembly of the United Nations that Syria had resumed her former status as an independent State and requested that the United Nations take note of the resumed membership in the United Nations of the Syrian Arab Republic. This request was brought to the attention of Member States by the President of the General Assembly at its 1035th plenary meeting on 13 October 1961. At the 1036th plenary meeting which took place on the same date, the President of the General Assembly stated that no objection having been received on the part of any Member State the delegation of the Syrian Arab Republic has taken its seat in the Assembly as a Member of the United Nations with all the obligations and rights that go with that status. In a letter addressed to the Secretary-General on 19 July 1962, the Permanent Representative of Syria to the United Nations communicated to him the text of *décret-loi* No. 25 promulgated by the President of the Syrian Arab Republic on 13 June 1962 and stated the following:

"It follows from article 2 of the text in question that obligations contracted by the Syrian Arab Republic under multilateral agreements and conventions during the period of the Union with Egypt remain in force in Syria. The period of the Union between Syria and Egypt extends from 22 February 1958 to 27 September 1961."

Finally, in a communication dated 2 September 1971, the Permanent Representative of the Arab Republic of Egypt to the United Nations informed the Secretary-General that the United

Arab Republic had assumed the name of Arab Republic of Egypt (Egypt), and, in a communication dated 13 September 1971, the Permanent Mission of the Syrian Arab Republic stated that the official name of Syria was "Syrian Arab Republic".

Accordingly, in so far as concerns any action taken by Egypt or subsequently by the United Arab Republic in respect of any instrument concluded under the auspices of the United Nations, the date of such action is shown in the list of States opposite the name of Egypt. The dates of actions taken by Syria prior to the formation of the United Arab Republic are shown opposite the name of the Syrian Arab Republic, as also are the dates of receipt of instruments of accession or notification of application to the Syrian Province deposited on behalf of the United Arab Republic during the time when the Syrian Arab Republic formed part of the United Arab Republic.

[6] On 3 October 1983, the Secretary-General received from the Government of Argentina the following objection:

[The Government of Argentina makes a] formal objection to the [declaration] of territorial extension issued by the United Kingdom with regard to the Malvinas Islands (and dependencies), which that country is illegally occupying and refers to as the "Falkland Islands".

The Argentine Republic rejects and considers null and void the [said declaration] of territorial extension.

[7] The Federation of Rhodesia and Nyasaland was dissolved immediately before 1 January 1964. In reply to the Secretariat's inquiry as to the legal effect of that dissolution, in so far as concerns the application in the territories formerly constituting the Federation, i.e., Northern Rhodesia, Nyasaland and Southern Rhodesia, of certain multilateral treaties deposited with the Secretary-General which had been extended by the Government of the United Kingdom of Great Britain and Northern Ireland to the Federation or to any of the territories concerned prior to the formation of the Federation, and of the International Convention to Facilitate the Importation of Commercial Samples and Advertising Material done at Geneva on 7 November 1952, to which the Federation acceded in its capacity of a Contracting party to the General Agreement on Tariffs and Trade, the Government of the United Kingdom in a communication received on 16 April 1964, provided the following clarification:

"Her Majesty's Government consider that in general, multilateral treaties applicable to the Federation of Rhodesia and Nyasaland continued to apply to the constituent territories of the former Federation on its dissolution. Multilateral treaties under which the Federation enjoyed membership of international organisations fall in a special category; their continued application to the constituent territories of the former Federation depends in each case on the terms of the treaty. Her Majesty's Government regard all the conventions listed in the Secretariat's letter of 26 February as applying to the constituent territories of the former Federation since its dissolution, but the accession by the Federation to the International Convention to Facilitate the Importation of Commercial Samples and Advertising Material has not led to this result as article XIII of the Convention allows Her Majesty's Government to extend provisions of the Convention to the three constituent territories of the former Federation if considered desirable.

"With regard to the final query by the Secretariat, I am to reply that extensions prior to the inauguration of the Federation do, of course, continue to apply to the constituent territories."

Northern Rhodesia and Nyasaland have since become independent States under the names of Zambia and Malawi, respectively.

Chapter XIV

CONVENTION FOR THE SUPPRESSION OF THE TRAFFIC IN PERSONS AND OF THE EXPLOITATION OF THE PROSTITUTION OF OTHERS

Adopted by the General Assembly of the United Nations on 2 December 1949

ENTRY INTO FORCE: 25 July 1951, in accordance with article 24.

Participant	Signature	Ratification, accession (a)
Afghanistan		21 May 1985 *a*
Albania		6 Nov. 1958 *a*
Algeria		31 Oct. 1963 *a*
Argentina		15 Nov. 1957 *a*
Bangladesh		11 Jan. 1985 *a*
Belgium		22 June 1965 *a*
Bolivia		6 Oct. 1983 *a*
Brazil	5 Oct. 1951	12 Sep. 1958
Bulgaria		18 Jan. 1955 *a*
Burkina Faso		27 Aug. 1962 *a*
Burma	14 Mar. 1956	
Byelorussian SSR		24 Aug. 1956 *a*
Cameroon		19 Feb. 1982 *a*
Central African Republic		29 Sep. 1981 *a*
Congo		25 Aug. 1977 *a*
Cuba		4 Sep. 1952 *a*
Cyprus		5 Oct. 1983 *a*
Czechoslovakia		14 Mar. 1958 *a*
Denmark	12 Feb. 1951	

Participant	Signature	Ratification, accession (a)
Djibouti		21 Mar. 1979 *a*
Ecuador	24 Mar. 1950	3 Apr. 1979
Egypt		12 June 1959 *a*
Ethiopia		10 Sep. 1981 *a*
Finland	27 Feb. 1953	8 June 1972
France		19 Nov. 1960 *a*
German Democratic Republic		16 July 1974 *a*
Guinea		26 Apr. 1962 *a*
Haiti		26 Aug. 1953 *a*
Honduras	13 Apr. 1954	
Hungary		29 Sep. 1955 *a*
India	9 May 1950	9 Jan. 1953
Iran (Islamic Republic of)	16 July 1953	
Iraq		22 Sep. 1955 *a*
Israel		28 Dec. 1950 *a*
Italy		18 Jan. 1980 *a*
Japan		1 May 1958 *a*
Jordan		13 Apr. 1976 *a*
Kuwait		20 Nov. 1968 *a*
Lao People's Democratic Republic		14 Apr. 1978 *a*
Liberia	21 Mar. 1950	
Libyan Arab Jamahiriya		3 Dec. 1956 *a*
Luxembourg	9 Oct. 1950	5 Oct. 1983
Malawi		13 Oct. 1965 *a*
Mali		23 Dec. 1964 *a*
Mauritania		6 June 1986 *a*
Mexico		21 Feb. 1956 *a*
Morocco		17 Aug. 1973 *a*
Niger		10 June 1977 *a*
Norway		23 Jan. 1952 *a*
Pakistan	21 Mar. 1950	11 July 1952
Philippines	20 Dec. 1950	19 Sep. 1952
Poland		2 June 1952 *a*
Republic of Korea		13 Feb. 1962 *a*
Romania		15 Feb. 1955 *a*
Senegal		19 July 1979 *a*
Singapore		26 Oct. 1966 *a*
South Africa	16 Oct. 1950	10 Oct. 1951
Spain		18 June 1962 *a*
Sri Lanka		15 Apr. 1958 *a*

Participant	Signature	Ratification, accession (a)
Syrian Arab Republic		12 June 1959 a [1],*
Ukrainian SSR		15 Nov. 1954 a
Union of Soviet Socialist Republics		11 Aug. 1954 a
Venezuela		18 Dec. 1968 a
Yugoslavia	6 Feb. 1951	26 Apr. 1951

DECLARATIONS AND RESERVATIONS

(Unless otherwise indicated the declarations and reservations were made upon ratification or accession.)

Afghanistan

Reservation:

"Whereas, the Government of the Democratic Republic of Afghanistan does not agree with the procedure of referring disputes arising between the parties to the Convention relating to its interpretation or application, to the International Court of Justice, at the request of any one of the parties to the dispute, therefore, it does not undertake any commitment regarding observation of article 22 of the present Convention."

Albania

Declaration:

Thanks to the conditions created by the popular democratic régime in Albania, the offences covered by this Convention do not find favourable ground for development there, since the social conditions which give rise to such offences have been eliminated. Nevertheless, in view of the importance of the campaign against these offences in the countries where they still exist and the international importance of that campaign, the People's Republic of Albania has decided to accede to the Convention for the Suppression of the Traffic in Persons and of the Exploitation of the Prostitution of Others adopted on 2 December 1949 at the fourth session of the United Nations General Assembly.

---

* For notes, see end of chapter.

Reservation to article 22:

The People's Republic of Albania does not consider itself bound by the provision of article 22 which stipulates that any dispute between the parties to the Convention relating to its interpretation, application or execution shall, at the request of any one of the parties to the dispute, be referred to the International Court of Justice. The People's Republic of Albania declares that with respect to the competence of the International Court in that connection, it will continue to maintain as in the past that for any dispute to be referred to the International Court of Justice for decision the agreement of all the parties to the dispute shall be necessary in each individual case.

Algeria

The People's Democratic Republic of Algeria does not consider itself bound by the provision of article 22 of the Convention, which provides for the compulsory competence of the International Court of Justice and declares that the agreement of all the parties to the dispute shall be necessary in each individual case for any dispute to be referred to the International Court of Justice for decision.

Bulgaria [2]

Declaration:

The offences referred to in the Convention are unknown under the socialist régime of the People's Republic of Bulgaria, for the conditions favouring them have been eliminated. Nevertheless, since it is important to counteract these offences in the countries where they still exist, and since it is important to the international community that such action should be taken, the People's Republic of Bulgaria has decided to accede to the Convention for the Suppression of the Traffic in Persons and of the Exploitation of the Prostitution of Others adopted by the fourth session of the General Assembly of the United Nations on 2 December 1949.

Reservation to article 22:

The People's Republic of Bulgaria declares, with respect to the competence of the International Court of Justice in disputes relating to the interpretation or application of the Convention, that the consent of all the parties to the dispute is necessary in each particular case before any dispute whatsoever can be referred to the Court.

Byelorussian Soviet Socialist Republic [2, 3]

The Byelorussian Soviet Socialist Republic does not consider itself bound by the provision of article 22, which provides that any dispute between the parties to the present Convention relating to its interpretation or application shall, at the request of any one of the parties to the dispute, be referred to the International Court of Justice, and declares that with respect to the competence of the International Court to adjudicate disputes relating to the interpretation or application of the Convention, the Byelorussian Soviet Socialist Republic will take the position that for any dispute to be referred to the International Court of Justice for decision the agreement of all the parties to the dispute shall be necessary in each individual case.

Ethiopia

Reservation:

"Socialist Ethiopia does not consider itself bound by article 22 of the Convention."

Finland

Reservation to article 9:

"Finland reserves itself the right to leave the decision whether its citizens will or will not be prosecuted for a crime committed abroad to Finland's competent authority."

France

The Government of the French Republic declares that, until further notice, this Convention will only be applicable to the metropolitan territory of the French Republic.

German Democratic Republic

Reservation:

The German Democratic Republic does not consider itself bound by the provision of article 22 of the Convention, according to which disputes concerning the interpretation or application of the Convention which have not been settled through negotiation shall, at the request of any one of the parties to the dispute, be referred to the International Court of Justice for decision, unless the parties have agreed on another way of adjustment. With regard to the competence of the International Court of Justice the German Democratic Republic takes the view that in every single case the consent of all the parties to the dispute shall be necessary to submit a particular dispute to the International Court of Justice for decision.

Declaration:

The German Democratic Republic, in its attitude towards article 23 of the Convention, in so far as it concerns the application of the Convention to colonial and other dependent territories, is guided by the stipulations of the United Nations Declaration on the Granting of Independence to Colonial Countries and Peoples [Res. 1514 (XV) of 14 December 1960], which sets forth the need for an early and unconditional elimination of colonialism in all its forms and manifestations.

Hungary[2, 3]

"The Presidential Council of the Hungarian People's Republic declares explicit reservation concerning article 22 of the Convention being its view that the jurisdiction of the International Court of Justice may be based solely on the previous voluntary submission of all parties interested."

Lao People's Democratic Republic

The Lao People's Democratic Republic does not consider itself bound by the provision of article 22 which states that disputes between the parties to the Convention relating to its interpretation or application shall, at the request of any one of the parties to the dispute, be referred to the International Court of Justice. The Lao People's Democratic Republic declares that, with respect to the competence of the International Court concerning disputes relating to the interpretation and application of the Convention, for any dispute to be referred to the International Court of Justice the agreement of all the parties to the dispute is necessary.

Malawi

"The Government of Malawi accedes to this Convention with the exception of article 22 thereof, the effects of which are reserved."

Romania[2]

Reservation to article 22:

The People's Republic of Romania does not consider itself bound by the provision of article 22 which provides that disputes between Contracting parties concerning the interpretation or application of this Convention shall, at the request of any one of the parties to the dispute, be referred to the International Court of Justice for decision, and declares that for any dispute to be referred to the International Court of Justice for decision the agreement of all parties to the dispute shall be necessary in each individual case.

Ukrainian Soviet Socialist Republic

Declaration:

In the Ukrainian Soviet Socialist Republic the social conditions which give rise to the offences covered by the Convention have been eliminated. Nevertheless, in view of the international importance of suppressing these offences, the Government of the Ukrainian Soviet Socialist Republic has decided to accede to the Convention for the Suppression of the Traffic in Persons and of the Exploitation of the Prostitution of Others adopted on 2 December 1949 at the fourth session of the United Nations General Assembly.

Reservation to article 22:

The Ukrainian Soviet Socialist Republic does not consider itself bound by the provision of article 22, which provides that any dispute between the parties to the present Convention relating to its interpretation or application shall, at the request of any one of the parties to the dispute, be referred to the International Court of Justice, and declares that with respect to the competence of the International Court to adjudicate disputes relating to the interpretation or application of the Convention, the Ukrainian Soviet Socialist Republic will take the position that for any dispute to be referred to the International Court of Justice for decision the agreement of all the parties to the dispute shall be necessary in each individual case.

Union of Soviet Socialist Republics

Declaration:

In the Soviet Union the social conditions which give rise to the offences covered by the Convention have been eliminated. Nevertheless, in view of the international importance of suppressing these offences, the Government of the Soviet Union has decided to accede to the Convention for the Suppression of the Traffic in Persons and of the Exploitation of the Prostitution of Others adopted on 2 December 1949 at the fourth session of the United Nations General Assembly.

Reservation to article 22:

The Soviet Union does not consider itself bound by the provision of article 22, which provides that any dispute between the parties to the present Convention relating to its interpretation or application shall, at the request of any one of the parties to the dispute, be referred to the International Court of Justice, and declares that with respect to the competence of the International Court to adjudicate disputes relating to the interpretation or application of the Convention, the Soviet Union will take the position that for any dispute to be referred to the International Court of Justice for decision the agreement of all the parties to the dispute shall be necessary in each individual case.

NOTES

[1] Accession by the United Arab Republic. See note 5 in chapter XIII.

[2] The Government of Haiti informed the Secretary-General that it considers that in case of dispute it should be possible for either of the Contracting parties concerned, without previous agreement between them, to refer a dispute to the International Court of Justice and that consequently it does not accept the reservation entered into by Bulgaria.

The Government of South Africa informed the Secretary-General that it regards article 22 as fundamental to the Convention and cannot, therefore, accept the reservation entered into by Bulgaria.

Similar communications were received by the Secretary-General from those two Governments in respect of the reservations made by the Governments of the Byelorussian Soviet Socialist Republic, Hungary and Romania.

[3] The Government of the Philippines informed the Secretary-General that it objects to the reservations made by the Governments of the Byelorussian Soviet Socialist Republic and Hungary because it feels that the reference to the International Court of Justice of any dispute relating to the interpretation or application of the Convention should not be made dependent on the consent of all parties.

Chapter XV

CONVENTION AGAINST TORTURE AND OTHER CRUEL, INHUMAN OR DEGRADING TREATMENT OR PUNISHMENT

Adopted by the General Assembly of the United Nations on 10 December 1984

ENTRY INTO FORCE: 26 June 1987, in accordance with article 27 (1).

Participant	Signature	Ratification, accession (a)
Afghanistan	4 Feb. 1985	1 Apr. 1987
Algeria	26 Nov. 1985	
Argentina	4 Feb. 1985	24 Sep. 1986
Australia	10 Dec. 1985	
Austria	14 Mar. 1985	29 July 1987
Belgium	4 Feb. 1985	
Belize		17 Mar. 1986 *a*
Bolivia	4 Feb. 1985	
Brazil	23 Sep. 1985	
Bulgaria	10 June 1986	16 Dec. 1986
Byelorussian SSR	19 Dec. 1985	13 Mar. 1987
Cameroon		19 Dec. 1986 *a*
Canada	23 Aug. 1985	24 June 1987
China	12 Dec. 1986	
Colombia	10 Apr. 1985	
Costa Rica	4 Feb. 1985	
Cuba	27 Jan. 1986	
Cyprus	9 Oct. 1985	
Czechoslovakia	8 Sep. 1986	
Denmark	4 Feb. 1985	27 May 1987

Participant	Signature	Ratification, accession (a)
Dominican Republic	4 Feb. 1985	
Ecuador	4 Feb. 1985	
Egypt		25 June 1986 *a*
Finland	4 Feb. 1985	
France	4 Feb. 1985	18 Feb. 1986
Gabon	21 Jan. 1986	
Gambia	23 Oct. 1985	
German Democratic Republic .	7 Apr. 1986	
Germany, Federal Republic of .	13 Oct. 1986	
Greece	4 Feb. 1985	
Guinea	30 May 1986	
Hungary	28 Nov. 1986	15 Apr. 1987
Iceland	4 Feb. 1985	
Indonesia	23 Oct. 1985	
Israel	22 Oct. 1986	
Italy	4 Feb. 1985	
Liechtenstein	27 June 1985	
Luxembourg	22 Feb. 1985	
Mexico	18 Mar. 1985	23 Jan. 1986
Morocco	8 Jan. 1986	
Netherlands	4 Feb. 1985	
New Zealand	14 Jan. 1986	
Nicaragua	15 Apr. 1985	
Norway	4 Feb. 1985	9 July 1986
Panama	22 Feb. 1985	24 Aug. 1987
Peru	29 May 1985	
Philippines		18 June 1986 *a*
Poland	13 Jan. 1986	
Portugal	4 Feb. 1985	
Senegal	4 Feb. 1985	21 Aug. 1986
Sierra Leone	18 Mar. 1985	
Spain	4 Feb. 1985	
Sudan	4 June 1986	
Sweden	4 Feb. 1985	8 Jan. 1986
Switzerland	4 Feb. 1985	2 Dec. 1986
Togo	25 Mar. 1987	
Tunisia	26 Aug. 1987	
Uganda		3 Nov. 1986 *a*
Ukrainian SSR	27 Feb. 1986	24 Feb. 1987
Union of Soviet Socialist Republics	10 Dec. 1985	3 Mar. 1987

Participant	Signature	Ratification, accession (a)
United Kingdom	15 Mar. 1985	
Uruguay	4 Feb. 1985	24 Oct. 1986
Venezuela	15 Feb. 1985	

DECLARATIONS AND RESERVATIONS

(Unless otherwise indicated, the declarations and reservations were made upon ratification or accession.)

Afghanistan

While ratifying the above-mentioned Convention, the Democratic Republic of Afghanistan, invoking article 28, paragraph 1, of the Convention, does not recognize the authority of the Committee against Torture as foreseen in article 20 of the Convention.

Also according to article 30, paragraph 2, the Democratic Republic of Afghanistan will not be bound to honour the provision of paragraph 1 of the same article since according to that paragraph the compulsory submission of disputes in connection with interpretation or the implementation of the provisions of this Convention by one of the parties concerned to the International Court of Justice is deemed possible. Concerning this matter, it declares that for the settlement of disputes between the States parties, such disputes may be referred to arbitration or to the International Court of Justice with the consent of all the parties concerned and not by one of the parties.

Bulgaria

Upon signature and confirmed upon ratification:

1. Pursuant to article 28 of the Convention, the People's Republic of Bulgaria states that it does not recognize the competence of the Committee against Torture provided for in article 20 of the Convention, as it considers that the provisions of article 20 are not consistent with the principle of respect for sovereignty of the States parties to the Convention.

2. Pursuant to article 30, paragraph 2, of the Convention, the People's Republic of Bulgaria states that it does not consider itself bound by the

provision of article 30, paragraph 1, of the Convention, establishing compulsory jurisdiction of international arbitration or the International Court of Justice in the settlement of disputes between States parties to the Convention. The People's Republic of Bulgaria maintains its position that disputes between two or more States can be submitted for consideration and settlement by international arbitration or the International Court of Justice only provided all parties to the dispute, in each individual case, have explicitly agreed to that.

Byelorussian Soviet Socialist Republic

Upon signature and confirmed upon ratification:

1. The Byelorussian Soviet Socialist Republic does not recognize the competence of the Committee against Torture as defined by article 20 of the Convention.

2. The Byelorussian Soviet Socialist Republic does not consider itself bound by the provision of article 30, paragraph 1, of the Convention.

China

Upon signature:

"(1) The Chinese Government does not recognize the competence of the Committee against Torture as provided for in article 20 of the Convention.

"(2) The Chinese Government does not consider itself bound by article 30, paragraph 1, of the Convention."

Czechoslovakia

Upon signature:

"The Czechoslovak Socialist Republic does not recognize the competence of the Committee against Torture as defined by article 20 of the Convention and it does not consider itself bound by the provision of article 30, paragraph 1, of the Convention."

France

Reservation:

The Government of France declares [...] that it shall not be bound by the provision of paragraph 2 of [article 30].

German Democratic Republic

Upon signature:

The German Democratic Republic declares in accordance with article 28, paragraph 1, of the Convention that it does not recognize the competence of the Committee against Torture provided for in article 20.

The German Democratic Republic declares in accordance with article 30, paragraph 2, of the Convention that it does not consider itself bound by paragraph 1 of this article.

Germany, Federal Republic of

Upon signature:

The Government of the Federal Republic of Germany reserves the right to communicate, upon ratification, such reservations or declarations of interpretation as are deemed necessary especially with respect to the applicability of article 3.

Hungary

Upon signature:

"The Hungarian People's Republic does not recognize the competence of the Committee against Torture as defined by article 20 of the Convention.

The Hungarian People's Republic does not consider itself bound by the provision of article 30, paragraph 1, of the Convention.

Morocco

Upon signature:

In accordance with article 28, paragraph 1, the Government of the Kingdom of Morocco declares that it does not recognize the competence of the Committee against Torture provided for in article 20.

In accordance with article 30, paragraph 2, the Government of the Kingdom of Morocco declares further that it does not consider itself bound by paragraph 1 of the same article.

Panama

The Convention against Torture and Other Cruel, Inhuman or Degrading Treatment or Punishment has been ratified with the declaration that the Republic of Panama does not consider itself bound by article 30, paragraph 1, of said Convention.

Poland

Upon signature:

Under article 28, the Polish People's Republic does not consider itself bound by article 20 of the Convention.

Furthermore, the Polish People's Republic does not consider itself bound by article 30, paragraph 1, of the Convention.

Togo

Upon signature:

The Government of the Togolese Republic reserves the right to formulate, upon ratifying the Convention, any reservations or declarations which it might consider necessary.

Tunisia

Upon signature:

The Government of Tunisia reserves the right to make at some later stage any reservation or declaration which it deems necessary in particular with regard to articles 20 and 21 of said Convention.

Ukrainian Soviet Socialist Republic

Upon signature:

1. The Ukrainian Soviet Socialist Republic does not recognize the competence of the Committee against Torture as defined by article 20 of the Convention.

2. The Ukrainian Soviet Socialist Republic does not consider itself bound by the provision of article 30, paragraph 1, of the Convention.

Union of Soviet Socialist Republics

Upon signature:

[*Same reservations,* mutatis mutandis, *as those made by the Byelorussian Soviet Socialist Republic.*]

United Kingdom of Great Britain and Northern Ireland

Upon signature:

"The United Kingdom reserves the right to formulate, upon ratifying the Convention, any reservations or interpretative declarations which it might consider necessary."

DECLARATIONS RECOGNIZING THE COMPETENCE OF THE COMMITTEE AGAINST TORTURE UNDER ARTICLES 21 AND 22

Argentina

. . . The Argentine Republic recognizes the competence of the Committee against Torture to receive and consider communications to the effect that a State party claims that another State party is not fulfilling its obligations under this Convention. It also recognizes the competence of the Committee to receive and consider communications from or on behalf of individuals subject to its jurisdiction who claim to be victims of a violation by a State party of the provisions of the Convention.

Denmark

"The Government of Denmark declares, pursuant to article 21, paragraph 1, of the Convention that Denmark recognizes the competence of the Committee against Torture to receive and consider communications to the effect that a State party claims that another State party is not fulfilling its obligations under this Convention.

"The Government of Denmark also declares, pursuant to article 22, paragraph 1, of the Convention that Denmark recognizes the competence of the Committee to receive and consider communications from or on behalf of individuals subject to its jurisdiction who claim to be victims of a violation by a State party of the provisions of the Convention."

France

The Government of France declares [...] that it recognizes the competence of the Committee against Torture to receive and consider communications to the effect that a State party claims that another State party is not fulfilling its obligations under the Convention.

The Government of France declares [...] that it recognizes the competence of the Committee against Torture to receive and consider communications from or on behalf of individuals subject to its jurisdiction who claim to be victims of a violation by a State party of the provisions of the Convention.

Norway

". . . Norway recognizes the competence of the Committee against Torture to receive and consider communications to the effect that a State party claims that another State party is not fulfilling its obligations under this Convention.

". . . Norway recognizes the competence of the Committee to receive and consider communications from or on behalf of individuals subject to its jurisdiction who claim to be victims of a violation by a State party of the provisions of the Convention."

Sweden

"Sweden recognizes the competence of the Committee against Torture to receive and consider communications to the effect that a State party claims that another State party is not fulfilling its obligations under this Convention.

"Sweden recognizes the competence of the Committee to receive and consider communications from or on behalf of individuals subject to its jurisdiction who claim to be victims of a violation by a State party of the provisions of the Convention."

Switzerland

(*a*) Pursuant to the Federal Decree of 6 October 1986 on the approval of the Convention against Torture and Other Cruel, Inhuman or Degrading Treatment or Punishment, the Federal Council declares, in accordance with article 21, paragraph 1, of the Convention, that Switzerland recognizes the competence of the Committee against Torture to receive and consider communications to the effect that a State party claims that Switzerland is not fulfilling its obligations under this Convention.

(*b*) Pursuant to the above-mentioned Federal Decree, the Federal Council declares, in accordance with article 22, paragraph 1, of the Convention, that Switzerland recognizes the competence of the Committee to receive and consider communications from or on behalf of individuals subject to its jurisdiction who claim to be victims of a violation by Switzerland of the provisions of the Convention.

Chapter XVI

CONVENTION ON THE NATIONALITY
OF MARRIED WOMEN

Adopted by the General Assembly of the United Nations on 29 January 1957

ENTRY INTO FORCE: 11 August 1958, in accordance with article 6.

Participant	Signature	Ratification, accession (a), succession (d)
Albania		27 July 1960 *a*
Argentina		10 Oct. 1963 *a*
Australia		14 Mar. 1961 *a*
Austria		19 Jan. 1968 *a*
Bahamas		10 June 1976 *d*
Barbados		26 Oct. 1979 *a*
Belgium	15 May 1972	
Brazil	26 July 1966	4 Dec. 1968
Bulgaria		22 June 1960 *a*
Byelorussian SSR	7 Oct. 1957	23 Dec. 1958
Canada	20 Feb. 1957	21 Oct. 1959
Chile	18 Mar. 1957	
China [1], *		
Colombia	20 Feb. 1957	
Cuba	20 Feb. 1957	5 Dec. 1957
Cyprus		26 Apr. 1971 *d*
Czechoslovakia	3 Sep. 1957	5 Apr. 1962
Denmark	20 Feb. 1957	22 June 1959
Dominican Republic	20 Feb. 1957	10 Oct. 1957
Ecuador	16 Jan. 1958	29 Mar. 1960
Fiji		12 June 1972 *d*
Finland		15 May 1968 *a*

* For notes, see end of chapter.

Participant	Signature	Ratification, accession (a), succession (d)
German Democratic Republic .		27 Dec. 1973 a
Germany, Federal Republic of .		7 Feb. 1974 a[2]
Ghana		15 Aug. 1966 a
Guatemala	20 Feb. 1957	13 July 1960
Guinea	19 Mar. 1975	
Hungary	5 Dec. 1957	3 Dec. 1959
Iceland		18 Oct. 1977 a
India	15 May 1957	
Ireland	24 Sep. 1957	25 Nov. 1957
Israel	12 Mar. 1957	7 June 1957
Jamaica		30 July 1964 d
Lesotho		4 Nov. 1974 d
Luxembourg	11 Sep. 1975	22 July 1977
Malawi		8 Sep. 1966 a
Malaysia		24 Feb. 1959 a
Mali		2 Feb. 1973 a
Malta		7 June 1967 d
Mauritius		18 July 1969 d
Mexico		4 Apr. 1979 a
Netherlands		8 Aug. 1966 a
New Zealand	7 July 1958	17 Dec. 1958
Nicaragua		9 Jan. 1986 a
Norway	9 Sep. 1957	20 May 1958
Pakistan	10 Apr. 1958	
Poland		3 July 1959 a
Portugal	21 Feb. 1957	
Romania		2 Dec. 1960 a
Sierra Leone		13 Mar. 1962 d
Singapore		18 Mar. 1966 d
Sri Lanka		30 May 1958 a
Swaziland		18 Sep. 1970 a
Sweden	6 May 1957	13 May 1958
Trinidad and Tobago		11 Apr. 1966 d
Tunisia		24 Jan. 1968 a
Uganda		15 Apr. 1965 a
Ukrainian SSR	15 Oct. 1957	3 Dec. 1958
Union of Soviet Socialist Republics	6 Sep. 1957	17 Sep. 1958
United Kingdom[3]	[20 Feb. 1957]	[28 Aug. 1957]
United Republic of Tanzania . .		28 Nov. 1962 a

Participant	Signature	Ratification, accession (a), succession (d)
Uruguay	20 Feb. 1957	
Venezuela		31 May 1983 *a*
Yugoslavia	27 Mar. 1957	13 Mar. 1959
Zambia		22 Jan. 1975 *d*

DECLARATIONS AND RESERVATIONS
(Unless otherwise indicated, the declarations and reservations were made upon ratification, accession or succession.)

Argentina

Article 7: The Argentine Government expressly reserves the rights of the Republic with respect to the Islas Malvinas (Falkland Islands), the South Sandwich Islands and the lands included within the Argentine Antarctic Sector, declaring that they do not constitute a colony or possession of any nation but are part of Argentine territory and lie within its dominion and sovereignty.

Article 10: The Argentine Government reserves the right not to submit disputes directly or indirectly linked with the territories under Argentine sovereignty to the procedure indicated in this article.

Brazil

"Reservation is made concerning application of article 10."

Chile

The Government of Chile makes a reservation with regard to article 10, in the sense that it does not accept the compulsory jurisdiction of the International Court of Justice for the purpose of the settlement of disputes which may arise between Contracting States concerning the interpretation or application of the present Convention.

German Democratic Republic

Reservation:

The German Democratic Republic does not consider itself bound by the provision of article 10, according to which a dispute between the States parties to the Convention in respect of the interpretation and application of the present Convention which has not been settled through negotiation is to be submitted to the International Court of Justice for decision at the request of one of the parties to the dispute, unless the parties have agreed on another way of adjustment. The German Democratic Republic declares that, with regard to the competence of the International Court of Justice for disputes in respect of the interpretation and application of the Convention, it is of the opinion that in every single case the consent of all the parties to the dispute shall be necessary to submit a particular dispute to the International Court of Justice for decision.

Declaration:

The German Democratic Republic considers that articles 4 and 5 of the Convention are inconsistent with the principle that all States pursuing their policies in accordance with the purposes and principles of the Charter of the United Nations shall have the right to become parties to conventions affecting the interests of all States.

Guatemala

Article 10 of the said Convention shall, by reason of constitutional requirements, be applied without prejudice to article 149, paragraph 3 (*b*) of the Constitution of the Republic.

India

"With the following reservation as to article 10:

"Any dispute which may arise between any two or more Contracting States concerning the interpretation or application of the present Convention which is not settled by negotiations shall, with the consent of the parties to the dispute, be referred to the International Court of Justice for decision unless the parties agree to another mode of settlement."

Tunisia

[Article 10] For any dispute to be referred to the International Court of Justice, the agreement of all the parties to the dispute shall be necessary in every case.

Uruguay

On behalf of Uruguay we hereby make a reservation to the provisions of article 3 which has a bearing on the application of the Convention. The Constitution of Uruguay does not authorize the granting of nationality to an alien unless he is the child of a Uruguayan father or mother, in which case he may become a natural citizen. This case apart, an alien who fulfils the constitutionality and legal conditions may be granted only legal citizenship, and not nationality.

Venezuela

[*See chapter XXI.*]

TERRITORIAL APPLICATIONS
(Declarations made upon ratification or accession (*a*)
under article 7, paragraph 1, of the Convention.)

Participant	Date of receipt of notification	Territories
Australia	14 Mar. 1961 *a*	All the non-metropolitan territories for the international relations of which Australia is responsible
Netherlands	8 Aug. 1966	Netherlands Antilles, Surinam
New Zealand	17 Dec. 1958	The Cook Islands (including Niue), the Tokelau Islands, and the Trust Territory of Western Samoa
United Kingdom[3] . .	28 Aug. 1957	The Channel Islands and the Isle of Man

NOTIFICATIONS UNDER ARTICLE 7, PARAGRAPH 2,
OF THE CONVENTION

	Date of receipt of notification	*Territories*
Participant		
United Kingdom[3] ..	18 Mar. 1958	Aden, the Bahamas, Barbados, Basutoland, Bechuanaland, Bermuda, British Guiana, British Honduras, British Solomon Islands, British Somaliland, Cyprus, Falkland Islands, Fiji, Gambia, Gibraltar, Gilbert and Ellice Islands, Hong Kong, Jamaica, Kenya, the Leeward Islands (Antigua, Montserrat, St. Christopher-Nevis), the British Virgin Islands, Malta, Mauritius, North Borneo, St. Helena, Sarawak, the Seychelles, Sierra Leone, Singapore, Swaziland, Tanganyika, Trinidad and Tobago, Uganda, the Windward Islands (Dominica, Grenada, St. Lucia, St. Vincent), Zanzibar
	19 May 1958	The Federation of Rhodesia and Nyasaland[3]
	3 Nov. 1960	Tonga
	1 Oct. 1962	Brunei

NOTES

[1] Signed and ratified on behalf of the Republic of China on 20 February 1957 and 22 September 1958 respectively. See note concerning signatures, ratifications, accessions, etc. on behalf of China (note 2 in chapter I).

With reference to the above-mentioned ratification, communications have been addressed to the Secretary-General by the Permanent Missions to the United Nations of India, Poland, and the Union of Soviet Socialist Republics, on the one hand, and of China on the other hand. For the nature of these communications, see also note 2 in chapter I.

[2] With the following declaration:

". . . The said Convention shall also apply to Berlin (West) with effect from the date on which it enters into force for the Federal Republic of Germany."

In this respect, the Secretary-General received the following communications:

Union of Soviet Socialist Republics (communication received on 24 May 1974):

The Soviet Government does not object to the extension to the Western Sectors of Berlin of the Convention on the Nationality of Married Women provided that this is done in accordance with the Quadripartite Agreement of 3 September 1971 and that matters of security and status shall not thereby be affected. In this connection, the Soviet Government would like to draw attention to the fact that the Western Sectors of Berlin are not a constituent part of the Federal Republic of Germany, that the permanent residents of the Western Sectors of Berlin are not nationals of the Federal Republic of Germany and that representation abroad of the interests of the Western Sectors of Berlin by the Federal Republic of Germany is permissible only to the extent specified in the Quadripartite Agreement of 3 September 1971 (annex IV).

Czechoslovakia (communication received on 30 May 1974):

"The Government of the Czechoslovak Socialist Republic declares, in accordance with the Four-Power Agreement of 3 September 1971, that West Berlin is not a part of the Federal Republic of Germany and neither can it be administered by it.

"The declaration of the Government of the Federal Republic of Germany contained in its instrument of accession to the above-mentioned Convention, that the validity of the Convention shall also apply to West Berlin is contradictory to the Four-Power Agreement stipulating that the agreements concerning the security and the statute of West Berlin cannot be expanded by the Federal Republic of Germany to West Berlin.

"Therefore, the declaration of the Government of the Federal Republic of Germany cannot have any legal effect."

German Democratic Republic (communication received on 16 July 1974):

With regard to the application of the Convention to Berlin (West) and in accordance with the Quadripartite Agreement of 3 September 1971 between the Governments of the Union of Soviet Socialist Republics, the United Kingdom of Great Britain and Northern Ireland, the United States of America and the French Republic, the German Democratic Republic declares that Berlin (West) is not a constituent part of the Federal Republic of Germany and is not to be governed by it. The declaration by the Federal Republic of Germany to the effect that this Convention will also apply to Berlin (West) is at variance with the Quadripartite Agreement, which states that treaties affecting matters of security and of the status of Berlin (West) may not be applied to Berlin (West) by the Federal Republic of Germany.

Ukrainian SSR (communication received on 6 August 1974):

The Ukrainian Soviet Socialist Republic refrains from raising an objection to the extension to Berlin (West) of the Convention on the Nationality of Married Women only on the understanding that this action is being taken in conformity with the Quadripartite Agreement of 3 September 1971 and will not affect matters of security and status. In this connection, the Ukrainian Soviet Socialist Republic wishes to direct attention to the fact that the Western Sectors of Berlin are not a constituent part of the Federal Republic of Germany, permanent residents of Berlin (West) are not nationals of the Federal Republic of Germany and representation abroad of the interests of Berlin (West) by the Federal Republic of Germany is permitted only to the extent defined by the Quadripartite Agreement of 3 September 1971 (annex IV).

France, United Kingdom of Great Britain and Northern Ireland and United States of America (communications received on 8 July 1975 — in relation to the communications by Czechoslovakia and by the German Democratic Republic):

"The communications mentioned in the notes listed above refer to the Quadripartite Agreement of 3 September 1971. This Agreement was concluded in Berlin between the Governments of the French Republic, the Union of Soviet Socialist Republics, the United Kingdom of Great Britain and Northern Ireland and the United States of America. The Governments sending these communications are not parties to the Quadripartite Agreement and are therefore not competent to make authoritative comments on its provisions.

"The Governments of France, the United Kingdom and the United States wish to bring the following to the attention of the States parties to the instruments referred to in the above-mentioned communications. When authorizing the extension of these instruments to the Western Sectors of Berlin, the authorities of the Three Powers, acting in the exercise of their supreme authority, ensured in accordance with established procedures that those instruments are applied in the Western Sectors of Berlin in such a way as not to affect matters of security and status.

"Accordingly, the application of these instruments to the Western Sectors of Berlin continues in full force and effect.

"The Governments of France, the United Kingdom and the United States do not consider it necessary to respond to any further communications of a similar nature by States which are not signatories to the Quadripartite Agreement. This should not be taken to imply any change in the position of those Governments in this matter."

Federal Republic of Germany (communication received on 19 September 1975 — in relation to the communications by Czechoslovakia and by the German Democratic Republic):

Declaration identical in essence, *mutatis mutandis,* to the one of the same date, reproduced in note 4 of chapter I.

[3] On 24 December 1981, the Secretary-General received from the Government of the United Kingdom of Great Britain and Northern Ireland a notification of denunciation of the said Convention.

The notification specifies that the denunciation is effected on behalf of the United Kingdom of Great Britain and of the following territories for the international relations of which the United Kingdom is responsible and to which the Convention was extended in accordance with the provisions of article 7: Bailiwick of Jersey, Bailiwick of Guernsey, Isle of Man, Saint Christopher-Nevis, Anguilla, Bermuda, British Indian Ocean Territory, British Virgin Islands, Cayman Islands, Falkland Islands, Gibraltar, Hong Kong, Montserrat, Pitcairn, Saint Helena and Dependencies, Turks and Caicos Islands, State of Brunei, United Kingdom Sovereign Bases Areas of Akrotiri and Dhekelia in the Island of Cyprus.

In accordance with the provision of article 9 (2) of the Convention, the denunciation will take effect one year after the date of receipt of the said notification, that is to say, on 24 December 1982.

Chapter XVII

CONVENTION ON THE REDUCTION OF STATELESSNESS

Concluded at New York on 30 August 1961

ENTRY INTO FORCE: 13 December 1975, in accordance with article 18.

Note: The Convention was adopted and opened for signature by the United Nations Conference on the Elimination or Reduction of Future Statelessness, convened by the Secretary-General of the United Nations pursuant to General Assembly resolution 896 (IX)[1,*] of 4 December 1954. The Conference met at the European Office of the United Nations at Geneva from 24 March to 18 April 1959 and reconvened at the Headquarters of the United Nations at New York from 15 to 28 August 1961.

Participant	*Signature*	*Ratification, accession* (a), *succession* (d)
Australia		13 Dec. 1973 *a*
Austria		22 Sep. 1972 *a*
Bolivia		6 Oct. 1983 *a*
Canada		17 July 1978 *a*
Costa Rica		2 Nov. 1977 *a*
Denmark		11 July 1977 *a*
Dominican Republic	5 Dec. 1961	
France	31 May 1962	
Germany, Federal Republic of[2]		31 Aug. 1977 *a*
Ireland		18 Jan. 1973 *a*
Israel	30 Aug. 1961	
Kiribati		29 Nov. 1983 *d*
Netherlands	30 Aug. 1961	13 May 1985[3]
Niger		17 June 1985 *a*
Norway		11 Aug. 1971 *a*
Sweden		19 Feb. 1969 *a*
United Kingdom	30 Aug. 1961	29 Mar. 1966

* For notes, see end of chapter.

DECLARATIONS AND RESERVATIONS

(Unless otherwise indicated, the declarations and
reservations were made upon ratification, accession
or succession.)

Austria

Declarations concerning article 8, paragraph 3 (*a*) (i) and (ii):

"Austria declares to retain the right to deprive a person of his nationality, if such person enters, on his own free will, the military service of a foreign State.

"Austria declares to retain the right to deprive a person of his nationality, if such person being in the service of a foreign State, conducts himself in a manner seriously prejudicial to the interests or to the prestige of the Republic of Austria."

France

At the time of signature of this Convention, the Government of the French Republic declares that it reserves the right to exercise the power available to it under article 8 (3) on the terms laid down in that paragraph, when it deposits the instrument of ratification of the Convention.

The Government of the French Republic also declares, in accordance with article 17 of the Convention, that it makes a reservation in respect of article 11, and that article 11 will not apply so far as the French Republic is concerned.

The Government of the French Republic further declares, with respect to article 14 of the Convention, that in accordance with article 17 it accepts the jurisdiction of the Court only in relation to States parties to this Convention which shall also have accepted its jurisdiction subject to the same reservations; it also declares that article 14 will not apply when there exists between the French Republic and another party to this Convention an earlier treaty providing another method for the settlement of disputes between the two States.

Germany, Federal Republic of

The Federal Republic of Germany will apply the said Convention:

(*a*) in respect of elimination of statelessness, to persons who are stateless under the terms of article 1, paragraph 1, of the Convention relating to the Status of Stateless Persons of 28 September 1954;

(*b*) in respect of prevention of statelessness and retention of nationality, to German nationals within the meaning of the Basic Law (Constitution) for the Federal Republic of Germany.

Ireland

"In accordance with article 8, paragraph 3, of the Convention Ireland retains the right to deprive a naturalized Irish citizen of his citizenship pursuant to section 19 (1) (*b*) of the Irish Nationality and Citizenship Act, 1956, on grounds specified in the aforesaid paragraph."

Niger

Reservations:

With reservations in respect of articles 11, 14 and 15.

United Kingdom of Great Britain and Northern Ireland

"On depositing this instrument I have the honour, on instructions from Her Majesty's Principal Secretary of State for Foreign Affairs, to declare on behalf of the United Kingdom and in accordance with article 8, paragraph 3 (*a*), of the Convention that, notwithstanding the provision of article 8, paragraph 1, the United Kingdom retains the right to deprive a naturalized person of his nationality on the following grounds, being grounds existing in United Kingdom law at the present time: that, inconsistently with his duty of loyalty to Her Britannic Majesty, the person

"(i) has, in disregard of an express prohibition of Her Britannic Majesty, rendered or continued to render services to, or received or continued to receive emoluments from, another State, or

"(ii) has conducted himself in a manner seriously prejudicial to the vital interests of Her Britannic Majesty."

TERRITORIAL APPLICATIONS
(Declarations made upon signature (*s*) or ratification under article 15 of the Convention.)

Participant	Date of receipt of notification	Territories
France	31 May 1962 *s*	The Convention will apply to the Overseas Departments and the Overseas Territories of the French Republic.
United Kingdom	29 Mar. 1966	(*a*) The Convention shall apply to the following non-metropolitan territories for the international relations of which the United Kingdom is responsible: Antigua, Bahamas, Barbados, Basutoland, Bechuanaland, Bermuda, British Guiana, British Honduras, British Solomon Islands Protectorate, Cayman Islands, Channel Islands, Dominica, Falkland Islands, Fiji, Gibraltar, Gilbert and Ellice Islands, Grenada, Hong Kong, Isle of Man, Mauritius, Montserrat, St. Helena, St. Kitts, St. Lucia, St. Vincent, Seychelles, Swaziland, Turks and Caicos Islands, Virgin Islands. (*b*) The Convention shall not apply to Aden and the Protectorate of South Arabia; Brunei; Southern Rhodesia; and Tonga, whose consent to the application of the Convention has been withheld.

NOTES

[1] *Official Records of the General Assembly, Ninth Session, Supplement No. 21* (A/2890), p. 49.

[2] In a communication accompanying the instrument of accession the Government of the Federal Republic of Germany declared that the said Convention shall also apply to Berlin (West) with effect from the day on which it enters into force for the Federal Republic of Germany.

[3] For the Kingdom in Europe and the Netherlands Antilles.

Chapter XVIII

CONVENTION RELATING TO THE STATUS OF STATELESS PERSONS

Done at New York on 28 September 1954

ENTRY INTO FORCE: 6 June 1960, in accordance with article 39.

Note: The Convention was adopted by the United Nations Conference on the Status of Stateless Persons, held at the Headquarters of the United Nations in New York from 13 to 23 September 1954. The Conference was convened pursuant to resolution 526A(XVII)[1.] * of 26 April 1954 of the Economic and Social Council of the United Nations. For the Final Act, recommendation and resolution adopted by the Conference, see United Nations, *Treaty Series,* vol. 360, p. 117.

Participant	Signature	Ratification, accession (a), succession (d)
Algeria		15 July 1964 *a*
Argentina		1 June 1972 *a*
Australia		13 Dec. 1973 *a*
Barbados		6 Mar. 1972 *d*
Belgium	28 Sep. 1954	27 May 1960
Bolivia		6 Oct. 1983 *a*
Botswana		25 Feb. 1969 *d*
Brazil	28 Sep. 1954	
Colombia	30 Dec. 1954	
Costa Rica	28 Sep. 1954	2 Nov. 1977
Denmark	28 Sep. 1954	17 Jan. 1956
Ecuador	28 Sep. 1954	2 Oct. 1970
El Salvador	28 Sep. 1954	
Fiji		12 June 1972 *d*
Finland		10 Oct. 1968 *a*
France	12 Jan. 1955	8 Mar. 1960

---

* For notes, see end of chapter.

Participant	Signature	Ratification, accession (a), succession (d)
Germany, Federal Republic of .	28 Sep. 1954	26 Oct. 1976[2]
Greece		4 Nov. 1975 a
Guatemala	28 Sep. 1954	
Guinea		21 Mar. 1962 a
Holy See	28 Sep. 1954	
Honduras	28 Sep. 1954	
Ireland		17 Dec. 1962 a
Israel	1 Oct. 1954	23 Dec. 1958
Italy	20 Oct. 1954	3 Dec. 1962
Kiribati		29 Nov. 1983 d
Lesotho		4 Nov. 1974 d
Liberia		11 Sep. 1964 a
Liechtenstein	28 Sep. 1954	
Luxembourg	28 Oct. 1955	27 June 1960
Madagascar		[20 Feb. 1962 a][3]
Netherlands	28 Sep. 1954	12 Apr. 1962
Norway	28 Sep. 1954	19 Nov. 1956
Philippines	22 June 1955	
Republic of Korea		22 Aug. 1962 a
Sweden	28 Sep. 1954	2 Apr. 1965
Switzerland	28 Sep. 1954	3 July 1972
Trinidad and Tobago		11 Apr. 1966 d
Tunisia		29 July 1969 a
Uganda		15 Apr. 1965 a
United Kingdom	28 Sep. 1954	16 Apr. 1959
Yugoslavia		9 Apr. 1959 a
Zambia		1 Nov. 1974 d

DECLARATIONS AND RESERVATIONS

(Unless otherwise indicated, the declarations and
reservations were made upon ratification, accession
or succession.)

Argentina

The application of this Convention in territories whose sovereignty is the
subject of discussion between two or more States, irrespective of whether they

are parties to the Convention, cannot be construed as an alteration, renunciation or relinquishment of the position previously maintained by each of them.

Barbados

"The Government of Barbados ... declares with regard to the reservations made by the United Kingdom on notification of the territorial application of the Convention to the West Indies (including Barbados) on 19 March 1962 that it can only undertake that the provisions of articles 23, 24, 25 and 31 will be applied in Barbados so far as the law allows.

"The application of the Convention to Barbados was also made subject to reservations to articles 8, 9, and 26 which are hereby withdrawn."

Botswana[4]

"(*a*) Article 31 of the said Convention shall not oblige Botswana to grant to a stateless person a status more favourable than that accorded to aliens in general;

"(*b*) Articles 7 (2) and 12 (1) of the Convention shall be recognized as recommendations only."

Costa Rica

Reservation made upon signature[5]

Denmark[6]

Denmark is not bound by article 24, paragraph 3:

The provisions of article 24, paragraph 1, under which stateless persons are in certain cases placed on the same footing as nationals, shall not oblige Denmark to grant stateless persons in every case exactly the same remuneration as that provided by law for nationals, but only to grant them what is required for their support.

'Article 31 shall not oblige Denmark to grant to stateless persons a status more favourable than that accorded to aliens in general.

El Salvador

Upon signature:

El Salvador signs the present Convention with the reservation that the expression "treatment as favourable as possible", referred to in those of its provisions to which reservations may be made, must not be understood to include the special treatment which has been or may be granted to the nationals of Spain, the Latin Amercian countries in general, and in particular to the countries which constituted the United Provinces of Central America and now form the Organization of Central American States.

Fiji

The Government of Fiji stated that the first and third reservations made by the United Kingdom are affirmed but have been redrafted as more suitable to the application of Fiji in the following terms:

"1. The Government of Fiji understands articles 8 and 9 as not preventing them from taking in time of war or other grave and exceptional circumstances measures in the interests of national security in the case of a stateless person on the ground of his former nationality. The provision of article 8 shall not prevent the Government of Fiji from exercising any rights over property or interests which they may acquire or have acquired as an Allied or Associated Power under a Treaty of Peace or other agreement or arrangement for the restoration of peace which has been or may be completed as a result of the Second World War. Furthermore, the provision of article 8 shall not affect the treatment to be accorded to any property or interests which, at the date of entry into force of this Convention in respect of Fiji, were under the control of the Government of the United Kingdom of Great Britain and Northern Ireland or of the Government of Fiji respectively by reason of a state of war which existed between them and any other State.

"2. The Government of Fiji cannot undertake to give effect to the obligations contained in article 25, paragraphs 1 and 2, and can only undertake to apply the provision of paragraph 3 so far as the law allows.

"*Commentary:* No arrangements exist in Fiji for the administrative assistance for which provisions are made in article 25 nor have any such arrangements been found necessary in the case of stateless persons. Any need for the documents or certificates mentioned in paragraph 2 of that article would be met by affidavit.

"Any other reservation made by the United Kingdom to the abovementioned Convention is withdrawn."

Finland[7]

"(1) A general reservation to the effect that the application of those provisions of the Convention which grant to stateless persons the most favourable treatment accorded to nationals of a foreign country shall not be affected by the fact that special rights and privileges are now or may in future be accorded by Finland to the nationals of Denmark, Iceland, Norway and Sweden or to the nationals of any one of those countries;

"(2) A reservation to article 7, paragraph 2, to the effect that Finland is not prepared, as a general measure, to grant stateless persons who fulfil the conditions of three years residence in Finland an exemption from any legislative reciprocity which Finnish law may have stipulated as a condition governing an alien's eligibility for same right or privilege;

"(3) A reservation to article 8 to the effect that that article shall not be binding on Finland;

"(4) . . .

"(5) A reservation to article 24, paragraph 1 (*b*) and paragraph 3, to the effect that they shall not be binding on Finland;

"(6) A reservation to article 25, to the effect that Finland does not consider itself bound to cause a certificate to be delivered by a Finnish authority, in the place of the authorities of a foreign country, if the documentary records necessary for the delivery of such certificate do not exist in Finland;

"(7) A reservation with respect to the provision contained in article 28. Finland does not accept the obligations stipulated in the said article, but is prepared to recognize travel documents issued by other Contracting States pursuant to this article."

France

The provision of article 10, paragraph 2, is regarded by the French Government as applying only to stateless persons who were forcibly displaced from French territory, and who have, prior to the date of entry into force of this Convention, returned there direct from the country to which they were forced to proceed, without in the meantime having received authorization to reside in the territory of any other State.

Germany, Federal Republic of

1. Article 23 will be applied without restriction only to stateless persons who are also refugees within the meaning of the Convention relating to the

Status of Refugees of 28 July 1951 and the Protocol relating to the Status of Refugees of 31 January 1967, but otherwise only to the extent provided for under national legislation;

2. Article 27 will not be applied.

Guatemala

Upon signature:

Guatemala signs the present Convention with the reservation that the expression "treatment as favourable as possible", referred to in those of its provisions to which reservations may be made, must not be understood to include the special treatment which has been or may be granted to the nationals of Spain, the Latin American countries in general, and in particular to the countries which constituted the United Provinces of Central America and now form the Organization of Central American States.

Holy See

"The Convention will be applied in the form compatible with the special nature of the State of the Vatican City and without prejudice to the norms that grant access thereunto and sojourn therein."

Honduras

Upon signature:

Honduras signs the present Convention with the reservation that the expression "treatment as favourable as possible", referred to in those of its provisions to which reservations may be made, must not be understood to include the special treatment which has been or may be granted to the nationals of Spain, the Latin American countries in general, and in particular to the countries which constituted the United Provinces of Central America and now form the Organization of Central American States.

Ireland

Declaration:

"The Government of Ireland understand the words 'public order' and 'in accordance with due process of law', as they appear in article 31 of the

Convention, to mean respectively, 'public policy' and 'in accordance with the procedure provided by law'."

Reservation:

"With regard to article 29 (1), the Government of Ireland do not undertake to accord to stateless persons treatment more favourable than that accorded to aliens generally with respect to:

"(*a*) The stamp duty chargeable in Ireland in connection with conveyances, transfers and leases of lands, tenements and hereditaments, and

"(*b*) Income tax (including Surtax)."

Italy[8]

The provisions of articles 17 and 18 are recognized as recommendations only.

Kiribati

Reservations:

[The following reservations originally made by the United Kingdom were reformulated as follows in terms suited to their direct application to Kiribati]:

"1. The Government of Kiribati understands articles 8 and 9 as not preventing them from taking in time of war or other grave and exceptional circumstances measures in the interests of national security in the case of a stateless person on the ground of his former nationality. The provision of article 8 shall not prevent the Government of Kiribati from exercising any rights over property or interests which they may acquire or have acquired as an Allied or Associated Power under a Treaty of Peace or other agreement or arrangement for the restoration of peace which has been or may be completed as a result of the Second World War. Furthermore, the provision of article 8 shall not affect the treatment to be accorded to any property or interests which, at the date of entry into force of this Convention in respect of the Gilbert Islands, were under the control of the Government of the United Kingdom of Great Britain and Northern Ireland by reason of a state of war which exists or existed between them and any other State.

"2. The Government of Kiribati can only undertake to apply the provision of article 24, paragraph 1, subparagraph (*b*), so far as the law allows.

"3.   The Government of Kiribati cannot undertake to give effect to the obligations contained in article 25, paragraphs 1 and 2, and can only undertake to apply the provision of paragraph 3 so far as the law allows."

Lesotho [9]

"1. In accordance with article 38 of the Convention, the Government of the Kingdom of Lesotho declares that it understands articles 8 and 9 as not preventing it from taking in time of war or other grave and exceptional circumstances measures in the interest of national security in the case of a stateless person on the ground of his former nationality. The provision of article 8 shall not prevent the Government of the Kingdom of Lesotho from exercising any rights over property or interests which they may acquire or have acquired as an Allied or Associated Power under a Treaty of Peace or other agreement or arrangement for the restoration of peace which has been or may be completed as a result of the Second World War. Furthermore, the provision of article 8 shall not affect the treatment to be accorded to any property or interests which, at the date of entry into force of this Convention in respect of Lesotho, were under the control of the Government of the United Kingdom of Great Britain and Northern Ireland or of the Government of Lesotho by reason of a state of war which existed between them and any other State.

"2. The Government of the Kingdom of Lesotho cannot undertake to give effect to the obligations contained in article 25, paragraphs 1 and 2, and can only undertake to apply the provision of paragraph 3 so far as the laws of Lesotho allow.

"3. The Government of the Kingdom of Lesotho shall not be bound under article 31 to grant to a stateless person a status more favourable than that accorded to aliens generally."

Netherlands

The Government of the Kingdom reserves the right not to apply the provision of article 8 of the Convention to stateless persons who previously possessed enemy nationality or the equivalent thereof with respect to the Kingdom of the Netherlands;

With reference to article 26 of the Convention, the Government of the Kingdom reserves the right to designate a place of principal residence for certain stateless persons or groups of stateless persons in the public interest.

Philippines

Upon signature:

"(*a*) As regards article 17, paragraph 1, granting stateless persons the right to engage in wage-earning employment, my Government finds that this provision conflicts with the Philippine Immigration Act of 1940, as amended, which classifies as excludable aliens under Section 29 those coming to the Philippines to perform unskilled labour, and permits the admission of pre-arranged employees under Section 9 (*g*) only when there are no persons in the Philippines willing and competent to perform the labour or service for which the admission of aliens is desired.

"(*b*) As regards article 31, paragraph 1, to the effect that 'the Contracting States shall not expel a stateless person lawfully in their territory, save on grounds of national security or public order', this provision would unduly restrict the power of the Philippine Government to deport undesirable aliens under Section 37 of the same Immigration Act which states the various grounds upon which aliens may be deported.

"Upon signing the Convention on behalf of the Philippine Government, I am therefore hereby registering its non-conformity to the provisions of article 17, paragraph 1, and article 31, paragraph 1, thereof, for the reasons stated in (*a*) and (*b*) above."

Sweden [10]

(1) ...

(2) To article 8. This article will not be binding on Sweden.

(3) To article 12, paragraph 1. This paragraph will not be binding on Sweden.

(4) To article 24, paragraph 1 (*b*). Notwithstanding the rule concerning the treatment of stateless persons as nationals, Sweden will not be bound to accord to stateless persons the same treatment as is accorded to nationals in respect of the possibility of entitlement to a national pension under the provisions of the National Insurance Act; and likewise to the effect that, in so far as the right to a supplementary pension under the said Act and the computation of such pension in certain respects are concerned, the rules applicable to Swedish nationals shall be more favourable than those applied to other insured persons.

(5) To article 24, paragraph 3. The provision of this paragraph will not be binding on Sweden.

(6) To article 25, paragraph 2. Sweden does not consider itself obliged to cause a Swedish authority, in lieu of a foreign authority, to deliver certificates for the issuance of which there is insufficient documentation in Sweden.

United Kingdom of Great Britain and Northern Ireland

Declaration:

"I have the honour further to state that the Government of the United Kingdom deposit the present instrument of ratification on the understanding that the combined effects of articles 36 and 38 permit them to include in any declaration or notification made under article 36, paragraph 1, or article 36, paragraph 2, respectively, any reservation consistent with article 38 which the Government of the territory concerned might desire to make."

Reservations:

"When ratifying the Convention relating to the Status of Stateless Persons which was opened for signature at New York on 28 September 1954, the Government of the United Kingdom have deemed it necessary to make certain reservations in accordance with article 38, paragraph 1, thereof, the text of which is reproduced below:

"(1) The Government of the United Kingdom of Great Britain and Northern Ireland understand articles 8 and 9 as not preventing them from taking in time of war or other grave and exceptional circumstances measures in the interests of national security in the case of a stateless person on the ground of his former nationality. The provision of article 8 shall not prevent the Government of the United Kingdom of Great Britain and Northern Ireland from exercising any rights over property or interests which they may acquire or have acquired as an Allied or Associated Power under a Treaty of Peace or other agreement or arrangement for the restoration of peace which has been or may be completed as a result of the Second World War. Furthermore, the provision of article 8 shall not affect the treatment to be accorded to any property or interests which, at the date of entry into force of this Convention for the United Kingdom of Great Britain and Northern Ireland, are under the control of the Government of the United Kingdom of Great Britain and Northern Ireland by reason of a state of war which exists or existed between them and any other State.

"(2) The Government of the United Kingdom of Great Britain and Northern Ireland, in respect of such of the matters referred to in article 24, paragraph 1, subparagraph (*b*) as fall within the scope of the National Health

Service, can only undertake to apply the provision of that paragraph so far as the law allows.

"(3) The Government of the United Kingdom of Great Britain and Northern Ireland cannot undertake to give effect to the obligations contained in article 25, paragraphs 1 and 2, and can only undertake to apply the provision of paragraph 3 so far as the law allows."

Commentary:

"In connection with article 24, paragraph 1, subparagraph (*b*), which relates to certain matters within the scope of the National Health Service, the National Health Service (Amendment) Act 1949 contains powers for charges to be made to persons not ordinarily resident in Great Britain (which category would include some stateless persons) who receive treatment under the Service. These powers have not yet been exercised but it may be necessary to exercise them at some future date. In Northern Ireland the Health Services are restricted to persons ordinarily resident in the country except where regulations are made to extend the Services to others. For these reasons, the Government of the United Kingdom, while prepared in the future, as in the past, to give the most sympathetic consideration to the situation of stateless persons, find it necessary to make reservation to article 24, paragraph 1, subparagraph (*b*).

"No arrangements exist in the United Kingdom for the administrative assistance for which provision is made in article 25 nor have any such arrangements been found necessary in the case of stateless persons. Any need for the documents or certifications mentioned in paragraph 2 of that article would be met by affidavit."

Zambia[11]

"Article 22 (1):

"The Government of the Republic of Zambia considers article 22, paragraph 1, to be a recommendation only, and not a binding obligation to accord to stateless persons national treatment with respect to elementary education;

"Article 26:

"The Government of the Republic of Zambia reserves the right under article 26 to designate a place or places of residence for stateless persons;

"Article 28:

"The Government of the Republic of Zambia does not consider itself bound under article 28 to issue a travel document with a return clause in cases where a country of second asylum has accepted or indicated its willingness to accept a stateless person from Zambia;

"*Article 31:*

"The Government of the Republic of Zambia shall not undertake under article 31 to grant treatment more favourable than that accorded to aliens generally with respect to expulsion."

TERRITORIAL APPLICATIONS

Participant	Date of receipt of notification	Territories
France	8 Mar. 1960	Departments of Algeria, of the Oases and of Saoura, Guadeloupe, Martinique and Guiana and the five Overseas Territories (New Caledonia and Dependencies, French Polynesia, French Somaliland, the Comoro Archipelago and the Islands of St. Pierre and Miquelon)
Netherlands[12] . .	12 Apr. 1962	Surinam and Netherlands New Guinea
United Kingdom	16 Apr. 1959	The Channel Islands and the Isle of Man
	7 Dec. 1959	High Commission Territories of Basutoland,[13] Bechuanaland Protectorate[4] and Swaziland
	9 Dec. 1959	Federation of Rhodesia and Nyasaland[14, 15]
	19 Mar. 1962	Aden Colony, Bermuda, Malta, Sarawak, Seychelles, St. Helena, Uganda,[16] Virgin Islands and Zanzibar
		British Guiana, British Honduras, British Solomon Islands Protectorate, Falkland Islands, Fiji,[17] Gambia, Gilbert and Ellice Islands, Hong Kong, Kenya, Mauritius, North Borneo, State of Singapore and the West Indies

DECLARATIONS AND RESERVATIONS MADE ON NOTIFICATIONS OF TERRITORIAL APPLICATIONS

United Kingdom of Great Britain and Northern Ireland

Channel Islands and Isle of Man

"(i) The Government of the United Kingdom of Great Britain and Northern Ireland understand articles 8 and 9 as not preventing the taking in the Isle of Man and in the Channel Islands, in time of war or other grave and exceptional circumstances, of measures in the interests of national security in the case of a stateless person on the ground of his former nationality. The provision of article 8 shall not prevent the Government of the United Kingdom of Great Britain and Northern Ireland from exercising any rights over property or interests which they may acquire or have acquired as an Allied or Associated Power under a Treaty of Peace or other agreement or arrangement for the restoration of peace which has been or may be completed as a result of the Second World War. Furthermore, the provision of article 8 shall not affect the treatment to be accorded to any property or interests which, at the date of entry into force of this Convention for the Isle of Man and the Channel Islands, are under the control of the Government of the United Kingdom of Great Britain and Northern Ireland by reason of a state of war which exists or existed between them and any other State.

"(ii) The Government of the United Kingdom of Great Britain and Northern Ireland can only undertake that the provisions of article 24, paragraph 1, subparagraph (*b*), and of paragraph 2 of that article, will be applied in the Channel Islands so far as the law allows, and that the provision of that subparagraph, in respect of such matters referred to therein as fall within the scope of the Isle of Man Health Service, will be applied in the Isle of Man so far as the law allows.

"(iii) The Government of the United Kingdom of Great Britain and Northern Ireland cannot undertake that effect will be given in the Isle of Man and the Channel Islands to article 25, paragraphs 1 and 2, and can only undertake that the provision of paragraph 3 will be applied in the Isle of Man and the Channel Islands so far as the law allows."

High Commission Territories of Basutoland,[13] Bechuanaland Protectorate[4] and Swaziland

[*Same reservations, in essence, as those made for the Channel Islands and the Isle of Man, under Nos. (i) and (iii).*]

Federation of Rhodesia and Nyasaland[14]

[*Same reservation, in essence, as that made for the Channel Islands and the Isle of Man, under No. (iii).*]

British Guiana, British Solomon Islands Protectorate, Falkland Islands, Gambia, Gilbert and Ellice Islands, Kenya, Mauritius

[*Same reservations, in essence, as those made for the Channel Islands and the Isle of Man, under Nos. (i) and (iii).*]

British Honduras, Hong Kong

[*Same reservations, in essence, as those made for the Channel Islands and the Isle of Man, under Nos. (i) and (iii).*]

North Borneo

[*Same reservations, in essence, as those made for the Channel Islands and the Isle of Man.*]

Fiji[17]

(i) The Government of the United Kingdom of Great Britain and Northern Ireland understand articles 8 and 9 as not preventing the taking in Fiji, in time of war or other grave and exceptional circumstances, of measures in the interests of national security in the case of a stateless person on the ground of his former nationality.

(ii) The Government of the United Kingdom of Great Britain and Northern Ireland, in respect of the provision of article 24, paragraph 1, sub-paragraph (*b*), can only undertake that effect will be given in Fiji to the provision of that paragraph so far as the law allows.

(iii) The Government of the United Kingdom of Great Britain and Northern Ireland cannot undertake that effect will be given in Fiji to article 25, paragraphs 1 and 2, and can only undertake that the provisions of paragraph 3 will be applied in Fiji so far as the law allows.

The State of Singapore

The Government of the United Kingdom of Great Britain and Northern Ireland cannot undertake that effect will be given in the State of Singapore to article 23.

The West Indies

The Government of the United Kingdom of Great Britain and Northern Ireland cannot undertake that effect will be given in the West Indies to articles 8, 9, 23, 24, 25, 26 and 31.

NOTES

[1] *Official Records of the Economic and Social Council, Seventeenth Session, Supplement No. 1* (E/2596), p. 12.

[2] Instrument received by the Secretary-General on 2 August 1976 and supplemented by notification of reservation received on 26 October 1976, the date on which the instrument is deemed to have been deposited.

In a letter accompanying the instrument of ratification, the Government of the Federal Republic of Germany declared that the said Convention shall also apply to Berlin (West) with effect from the date on which it enters into force for the Federal Republic of Germany.

With reference to the above-mentioned declaration, the Secretary-General received on 13 October 1976 from the Government of the Union of Soviet Socialist Republics the following communication:

> The Convention relating to the Status of Stateless Persons of 28 September 1954 affects, in its substance, matters relating to the status of West Berlin. The USSR therefore regards the declaration made by the Federal Republic of Germany concerning the application of the said Convention to West Berlin as illegal and as having no legal force, since, under the Quadripartite Agreement of 3 September 1971, the treaty obligations of the Federal Republic of Germany affecting matters of security and status cannot be applied to West Berlin.

[3] By a notification received by the Secretary-General on 2 April 1965, the Government of Madagascar denounced the Convention; the denunciation took effect on 2 April 1966.

[4] In the notification of succession, the Government of Botswana also maintained the reservations made by the Government of the United Kingdom of Great Britain and Northern Ireland on extension of the Convention to the Bechuanaland Protectorate.

[5] The reservation was not maintained upon ratification. For the text of the reservation, see United Nations, *Treaty Series*, vol. 360, p. 196.

[6] In a communication received on 23 August 1962, the Government of Denmark informed the Secretary-General of its decision to withdraw as from 1 October 1961 the reservation to article 14 of the Convention.

In a communication received on 25 March 1968, the Government of Denmark informed the Secretary-General of its decision to withdraw as from that date, the reservation to article 24, paragraph 2, of the Convention.

For the text of the reservations withdrawn by the above communications, see United Nations, *Treaty Series*, vol. 360, p. 132.

[7] In a communication received on 30 September 1970, the Government of Finland notified the Secretary-General of its decision to withdraw the reservation formulated in its instrument of accession to article 12, paragraph 1, of the Convention. For the text of the said reservation, see United Nations, *Treaty Series*, vol. 648, p. 368.

[8] In a communication received on 25 January 1968, the Government of Italy notified the Secretary-General of the withdrawal of the reservations made at the time of signature to articles 6, 7 (2), 8, 19, 22 (2), 23, 25 and 32 (see United Nations, *Treaty Series*, vol. 189, p. 192).

[9] Reservations 1 and 2 had been formulated by the Government of the United Kingdom in respect of the territory of Basutoland. Reservation 3 constitutes a new reservation, which was made subject to the provision of article 39 (2) of the Convention.

[10] In a communication received on 25 November 1966, the Government of Sweden has notified the Secretary-General that it has decided, in accordance with article 38, paragraph 2, of the Convention, to withdraw some of its reservations to article 24, paragraph 1 (*b*), and the reservation to article 24, paragraph 2, of the Convention. In a communication received on 5 March 1970, the Government of Sweden notified the Secretary-General of the withdrawal of its reservation to article 7, paragraph 2, of the Convention. For the text of the reservations to article 24, paragraph 1 (*b*), as originally formulated by the Government of Sweden in its instrument of ratification, and of the reservation to article 7, paragraph 2, see United Nations, *Treaty Series*, vol. 529, p. 362.

[11] In its notification of succession, the Government of Zambia declared that it withdrew the reservations made by the Government of the United Kingdom upon extension of the Convention by the latter to the former Federation of Rhodesia and Nyasaland. The reservations reproduced herein are new reservations, which were made subject to the provision of article 39 (2) of the Convention.

[12] In the note accompanying the instrument of ratification, the Government of the Netherlands stated, with reference to article 36, paragraph 3, of the Convention, that "if at any time the Government of the Netherlands Antilles agrees to the extension of the Convention to its territory, the Secretary-General shall be notified thereof without delay. Such notification will contain the reservations, if any, which the Government of the Netherlands Antilles might wish to make with respect to local requirements in accordance with article 38 of the Convention.

[13] See succession by Lesotho.

[14] See note 7 in chapter XIII.

[15] In a letter addressed to the Secretary-General on 22 March 1968, the President of the Republic of Malawi, referring to the Convention relating to the Status of Stateless Persons, done at New York on 28 September 1954, stated the following:

"In my letter to you of 24 November 1964, concerning the disposition of Malawi's inherited treaty obligations, my Government declared that with respect to multilateral treaties which had been applied or extended to the former Nyasaland Protectorate, any party to such a treaty could on the basis of reciprocity rely as against Malawi on the terms of that treaty until Malawi notified its depositary of what action it wished to take by way of confirmation of termination, confirmation of succession, or accession.

"I am to inform you as depositary of this Convention that the Government of Malawi now wishes to terminate any connection with this Convention which it might have inherited. The Government of Malawi considers that any legal relationship with the aforementioned Convention relating to the Status of Stateless Persons, New York, 1954, which might have devolved upon it by way of succession from the ratification of the United Kingdom, is terminated as of this date."

[16] See accession by Uganda.

[17] See succession by Fiji.

Chapter XIX

CONVENTION RELATING TO THE STATUS
OF REFUGEES

Signed at Geneva on 28 July 1951

ENTRY INTO FORCE: 22 April 1954, in accordance with article 43.

Note: The Convention was adopted by the United Nations Conference of Plenipotentiaries
on the Status of Refugees and Stateless Persons, held at Geneva from 2 to 25 July 1951. The
Conference was convened pursuant to resolution 429 (V),[1, *] adopted by the General Assembly of
the United Nations on 14 December 1950.

Participant	Signature	Ratification, accession (a), succession (d)
Algeria		21 Feb. 1963 *d*
Angola		23 June 1981 *a*
Argentina		15 Nov. 1961 *a*
Australia		22 Jan. 1954 *a*
Austria	28 July 1951	1 Nov. 1954
Belgium	28 July 1951	22 July 1953
Benin		4 Apr. 1962 *d*
Bolivia		9 Feb. 1982 *a*
Botswana		6 Jan. 1969 *a*
Brazil	15 July 1952	16 Nov. 1960
Burkina Faso		18 June 1980 *a*
Burundi		19 July 1963 *a*
Cameroon		23 Oct. 1961 *d*
Canada		4 June 1969 *a*
Central African Republic		4 Sep. 1962 *d*
Chad		19 Aug. 1981 *a*
Chile		28 Jan. 1972 *a*

---

* For notes, see and of chapter.

Participant	Signature	Ratification, accession (a), succession (d)
China		24 Sep. 1982 *a*
Colombia	28 July 1951	10 Oct. 1961
Congo		15 Oct. 1962 *d*
Costa Rica		28 Mar. 1978 *a*
Côte d'Ivoire		8 Dec. 1961 *d*
Cyprus		16 May 1963 *d*
Denmark	28 July 1951	4 Dec. 1952
Djibouti		9 Aug. 1977 *d*
Dominican Republic		4 Jan. 1978 *a*
Ecuador		17 Aug. 1955 *a*
Egypt		22 May 1981 *a*
El Salvador		28 Apr. 1983 *a*
Equatorial Guinea		7 Feb. 1986 *a*
Ethiopia		10 Nov. 1969 *a*
Fiji		12 June 1972 *d*
Finland		10 Oct. 1968 *a*
France	11 Sep. 1952	23 June 1954
Gabon		27 Apr. 1964 *a*
Gambia		7 Sep. 1966 *d*
Germany, Federal Republic of [2]	19 Nov. 1951	1 Dec. 1953
Ghana		18 Mar. 1963 *a*
Greece	10 Apr. 1952	5 Apr. 1960
Guatemala		22 Sep. 1983 *a*
Guinea		28 Dec. 1965 *d*
Guinea-Bissau		11 Feb. 1976 *a*
Haiti		25 Sep. 1984 *a*
Holy See	21 May 1952	15 Mar. 1956
Iceland		30 Nov. 1955 *a*
Iran (Islamic Republic of)		28 July 1976 *a*
Ireland		29 Nov. 1956 *a*
Israel	1 Aug. 1951	1 Oct. 1954
Italy	23 July 1952	15 Nov. 1954
Jamaica		30 July 1964 *d*
Japan		3 Oct. 1981 *a*
Kenya		16 May 1966 *a*
Lesotho		14 May 1981 *a*
Liberia		15 Oct. 1964 *a*
Liechtenstein	28 July 1951	8 Mar. 1957
Luxembourg	28 July 1951	23 July 1953
Madagascar		18 Dec. 1967 *a*

Participant	Signature	Ratification, accession (a), succession (d)
Mali		2 Feb. 1973 *d*
Malta		17 June 1971 *a*
Mauritania		5 May 1987 *a*
Monaco		18 May 1954 *a*
Morocco		7 Nov. 1956 *d*
Mozambique		16 Dec. 1983 *a*
Netherlands	28 July 1951	3 May 1956
New Zealand		30 June 1960 *a*
Nicaragua		28 Mar. 1980 *a*
Niger		25 Aug. 1961 *d*
Nigeria		23 Oct. 1967 *a*
Norway	28 July 1951	23 Mar. 1953
Panama		2 Aug. 1978 *a*
Papua New Guinea		17 July 1986 *a*
Paraguay		1 Apr. 1970 *a*
Peru		21 Dec. 1964 *a*
Philippines		22 July 1981 *a*
Portugal		22 Dec. 1960 *a*
Rwanda		3 Jan. 1980 *a*
Sao Tome and Principe . . .		1 Feb. 1978 *a*
Senegal		2 May 1963 *d*
Seychelles		23 Apr. 1980 *a*
Sierra Leone		22 May 1981 *a*
Somalia		10 Oct. 1978 *a*
Spain		14 Aug. 1978 *a*
Sudan		22 Feb. 1974 *a*
Suriname		29 Nov. 1978 *d*
Sweden	28 July 1951	26 Oct. 1954
Switzerland	28 July 1951	21 Jan. 1955
Togo		27 Feb. 1962 *d*
Tunisia		24 Oct. 1957 *d*
Turkey	24 Aug. 1951	30 Mar. 1962
Tuvalu		7 Mar. 1986 *d*[3]
Uganda		27 Sep. 1976 *a*
United Kingdom	28 July 1951	11 Mar. 1954
United Republic of Tanzania . .		12 May 1964 *a*
Uruguay		22 Sep. 1970 *a*
Yemen		18 Jan. 1980 *a*
Yugoslavia	28 July 1951	15 Dec. 1959
Zaire		19 July 1965 *a*

		Ratification, *accession* (a), *succession* (d)
Participant	*Signature*	
Zambia		24 Sep. 1969 *d*
Zimbabwe		25 Aug. 1981 *a*

DECLARATIONS UNDER SECTION B OF
ARTICLE 1 OF THE CONVENTION

(Unless otherwise indicated in a footnote, the declarations
were received upon ratification, accession or succession.)

(a) *"Events occurring in Europe before 1 January 1951"*

Brazil	Malta
Congo	Monaco
Italy	Paraguay
Madagascar	Turkey

(b) *"Events occurring in Europe or elsewhere*
before 1 January 1951"

Algeria	Cyprus
Angola	Denmark
Argentina [4]	Djibouti
Australia [5]	Dominican Republic
Austria	Ecuador [5]
Belgium	Egypt
Benin [5]	El Salvador
Bolivia	Equatorial Guinea
Botswana [6]	Ethiopia
Burundi	Fiji
Cameroon [5]	Finland
Canada	France [5]
Central African Republic [5]	Gabon
Chad	Gambia
Chile [5]	Germany, Federal Republic of
China	Ghana
Colombia [4]	Greece
Costa Rica	Guatemala
Côte d'Ivoire [5]	Guinea

Guinea-Bissau
Haiti
Holy See[5]
Iceland
Iran (Islamic Republic of)[5]
Ireland
Israel
Jamaica
Japan
Kenya
Lesotho
Liberia
Liechtenstein
Luxembourg[5]
Mali
Mauritania
Morocco
Mozambique
Netherlands
New Zealand
Nicaragua
Niger[5]
Nigeria
Norway
Panama
Papua New Guinea
Peru[5]

Philippines
Portugal
Rwanda
Sao Tome and Principe
Senegal[5]
Seychelles
Sierra Leone
Somalia
Spain
Sudan[5]
Suriname
Sweden
Switzerland
Togo[5]
Tunisia
Tuvalu
Uganda
United Kingdom
United Republic of Tanzania
Upper Volta
Uruguay
Yemen
Yugoslavia
Zaire
Zambia
Zimbabwe

DECLARATIONS OTHER THAN THOSE MADE UNDER SECTION B OF ARTICLE 1 AND RESERVATIONS

(Unless otherwise indicated, the declarations and
reservations were made upon ratification, accession
or succession. For objections thereto and territorial
applications, see hereinafter.)

Angola

Declarations:

The Government of the People's Republic of Angola also declares that the provisions of the Convention shall be applicable in Angola provided that they are not contrary to or incompatible with the constitutional and legal provisions in force in the People's Republic of Angola, especially as regards articles 7, 13, 15, 18 and 24 of the Convention. Those provisions shall not be construed so as to accord to any category of aliens resident in Angola more extensive rights than are enjoyed by Angolan citizens.

The Government of the People's Republic of Angola also considers that the provisions of articles 8 and 9 of the Convention cannot be construed so as to limit its right to adopt in respect of a refugee or group of refugees such measures as it deems necessary to safeguard national interests and to ensure respect for its sovereignty, whenever circumstances so require.

Reservations:

Ad *article 17:* The Government of the People's Republic of Angola accepts the obligations set forth in article 17, provided that:

(*a*) Paragraph 1 of this article shall not be interpreted to mean that refugees must enjoy the same privileges as may be accorded to nationals of countries with which the People's Republic of Angola has signed special co-operation agreements;

(*b*) Paragraph 2 of this article shall be construed as a recommendation and not as an obligation.

Ad *article 26:* The Government of the People's Republic of Angola reserves the right to prescribe, transfer or circumscribe the place of residence of certain refugees or groups of refugees, and to restrict their freedom of movement, whenever considerations of national or international order make it advisable to do so.

Australia[7]

Austria[8]

The Convention is ratified:

(*a*) Subject to the reservation that the Republic of Austria regards the provisions of article 17, paragraphs 1 and 2 (excepting, however, the phrase "who was already exempt from them at the date of entry into force of this Convention for the Contracting State concerned, or . . ." in the latter paragraph), not as a binding obligation, but merely as a recommendation.

(*b*) Subject to the reservation that the provision of article 22, paragraph 1, shall not be applicable to the establishment and maintenance of private elementary schools, that the "public relief and assistance" referred to in article 23 shall be interpreted solely in the sense of allocations from public welfare funds (Armenversorgung), and that the "documents or certifications" referred to in article 25, paragraphs 2 and 3, shall be construed to mean the identity certificates provided for in the Convention of 30 June 1928 relating to refugees.

Belgium

1. In all cases where the Convention grants to refugees the most favourable treatment accorded to nationals of a foreign country, this provision shall not be interpreted by the Belgian Government as necessarily involving the régime accorded to nationals of countries with which Belgium has concluded regional, customs, economic or political agreements.

2. Article 15 of the Convention shall not be applicable in Belgium; refugees lawfully staying in Belgian territory will enjoy the same treatment, as regards the right of association, as that accorded to aliens in general.

Botswana

"Subject to the reservations of articles 7, 17, 26, 31, 32 and 34 and article 12, paragraph 1, of the Convention."

Brazil[9]

"Refugees will be granted the same treatment accorded to nationals of foreign countries in general, with the exception of the preferential treatment extended to nationals of Portugal through the Friendship and Consultation Treaty of 1953 and Article 199 of the Brazilian Constitutional Amendment No. 1 of 1969".

Canada

Reservations to articles 23 and 24:

"Canada interprets the phrase 'lawfully staying' as referring only to refugees admitted for permanent residence: refugees admitted for temporary residence will be accorded the same treatment with respect to the matters dealt with in articles 23 and 24 as is accorded visitors generally".

Chile

(1) With the reservation that, with reference to the provision of article 34, the Government of Chile will be unable to grant to refugees facilities greater that those granted to aliens in general, in view of the liberal nature of Chilean naturalization laws;

(2) With the reservation that the period specified in article 17, paragraph 2 (*a*), shall, in the case of Chile, be extended from three to ten years;

(3) With the reservation that article 17, paragraph 2 (*c*), shall apply only if the refugee is the widow or the widower of a Chilean spouse;

(4) With the reservation that the Government of Chile cannot grant a longer period for compliance with an expulsion order than that granted to other aliens in general under Chilean law.

China

Reservations:

Article 14

"In the territory of any other Contracting State, he shall be accorded the same protection as is accorded in that territory to nationals of the country in which he has his habitual residence."

Article 16
Application excluded.

Cyprus [10]

With confirmation of the reservations made by the Government of the United Kingdom upon application of the Convention to the territory of Cyprus.

Denmark [11]

25 March 1968

Rewording of the reservation:

"The obligation in article 17, paragraph 1, to accord to refugees lawfully staying in Denmark the most favourable treatment accorded to nationals of a foreign country as regards the right to engage in wage-earning employment shall not be construed to mean that refugees shall be entitled to the privileges which in this respect are accorded to nationals of Finland, Iceland, Norway and Sweden."

Ecuador

With respect to article 1, relating to the definition of the term "refugee", the Government of Ecuador declares that its accession to the Convention relating to the Status of Refugees does not imply its acceptance of the conventions which have not been expressly signed and ratified by Ecuador.

With respect to article 15, Ecuador further declares that its acceptance of the provisions contained therein shall be limited in so far as those provisions are in conflict with the constitutional and statutory provisions in force prohibiting aliens, and consequently refugees, from being members of political bodies.

Egypt

The Government of Egypt accedes to the Convention with reservations in respect of article 12 (1), articles 20 and 22 (1), and articles 23 and 24.

Clarifications (received on 24 September 1981):

1. Egypt formulated a reservation to article 12 (1) because it is in contradiction with the internal laws of Egypt. This article provides that the personal status of a refugee shall be governed by the law of the country of his domicile or, failing this, of his residence. This formula contradicts article 25 of the Egyptian civil code, which reads as follows:

"The judge declares the applicable law in the case of persons without nationality or with more than one nationality at the same time. In the case of persons where there is proof, in accordance with Egyptian law, of Egyptian nationality, and at the same time in accordance with the law of one or more foreign countries, of nationality of that country or countries, the Egyptian law must be applied."

The competent Egyptian authorities are not in a position to amend this article (25) of the civil code.

2. Concerning articles 20, 22, paragraph 1, 23 and 24 of the Convention of 1951, the competent Egyptian authorities had reservations because these articles consider the refugee as equal to the national.

We made this general reservation to avoid any obstacle which might affect the discretionary authority of Egypt in granting privileges to refugees on a case-by-case basis.

Ethiopia

"The provisions of articles 8, 9, 17 (2) and 22 (1) of the Convention are recognized only as recommendations and not as legally binding obligations."

Fiji

The Government of Fiji stated that the first and fourth reservations made by the United Kingdom are affirmed but have been redrafted as more suitable to the application of Fiji in the following terms:

"1. The Government of Fiji understands articles 8 and 9 as not preventing them from taking in time of war or other grave and exceptional circumstances measures in the interests of national security in the case of a refugee on the ground of his nationality. The provision of article 8 shall not prevent the Government of Fiji from exercising any rights over property and interests which they may acquire or have acquired as an Allied or Associated Power under a Treaty of Peace or other agreement or arrangement for the restoration of peace which has been or may be completed as a result of the Second World War. Furthermore, the provision of article 8 shall not affect the treatment to be accorded to any property or interests which, at the date of entry into force of this Convention on behalf of Fiji, were under the control of the Government of the United Kingdom of Great Britain and Northern Ireland or of the Government of Fiji respectively by reason of a state of war which existed between them and any other State.

"2. The Government of Fiji cannot undertake to give effect to the obligations contained in article 25, paragraphs 1 and 2, and can only undertake to apply the provisions of paragraph 3 so far as the law allows.

"*Commentary:* No arrangements exist in Fiji for the administrative assistance for which provision is made in article 25 nor have any such arrangements been found necessary in the case of refugees. Any need for the documents or certifications mentioned in paragraph 2 of that article would be met by affidavits.

"Any other reservation made by the United Kingdom to the above-mentioned Convention is withdrawn."

Finland

Reservations:

"(1) A general reservation to the effect that the application of those provisions of the Convention which grant to refugees the most favourable treatment accorded to nationals of a foreign country shall not be affected by the fact that special rights and privileges are now or may in future be accorded by Finland to the nationals of Denmark, Iceland, Norway and Sweden or to the nationals of any one of those countries;

"(2) A reservation to article 7, paragraph 2, to the effect that Finland is not prepared, as a general measure, to grant refugees who fulfil the conditions of three years residence in Finland an exemption from any legislative reciprocity which Finnish law may have stipulated as a condition governing an alien's eligibility for same right or privilege;

"(3) A reservation to article 8 to the effect that that article shall not be binding on Finland;

"(4) A reservation to article 12, paragraph 1, to the effect that the Convention shall not modify the rule of Finnish private international law as now in force, under which the personal status of a refugee is governed by the law of his country of nationality;

"(5) A reservation to article 24, paragraph 1 (*b*) and paragraph 3, to the effect that they shall not be binding on Finland;

"(6) A reservation to article 25, to the effect that Finland does not consider itself bound to cause a certificate to be delivered by a Finnish authority, in the place of the authorities of a foreign country, if the documentary records necessary for the delivery of such certificate do not exist in Finland.

"(7) A reservation with respect to the provisions contained in article 28, paragraph 1. Finland does not accept the obligations stipulated in the said paragraph, but is prepared to recognize travel documents issued by other Contracting States pursuant to this article."

France

In depositing its instrument of ratification, the Government of the French Republic, acting in accordance with article 42 of the Convention, makes the following statements:

(*a*) It considers that article 29, paragraph 2, does not prevent the application in French territory of the provisions of the Act of 7 May 1934 authorizing the levying of the Nansen tax for the support of refugee welfare, resettlement and relief work.

(*b*) Article 17 in no way prevents the application of the laws and regulations establishing the proportion of alien workers that employers are authorized to employ in France or affects the obligations of such employers in connection with the employment of alien workers.

Gambia [12]

Greece [13]

In cases or circumstances which, in its opinion, would justify exceptional procedure for reasons of national security or public order, the Hellenic Government reserves the right to derogate from the obligations imposed by the provisions of article 26.

As far as wage-earning employment under article 17 is concerned, the Hellenic Government shall not accord to the refugees less rights than those accorded generally to nationals of foreign countries.

Guatemala

Reservation:

The Republic of Guatemala accedes to the Convention relating to the Status of Refugees and its Protocol, with the reservation that it will not apply provisions of those instruments in respect of which the Convention allows reservations if those provisions contravene constitutional precepts in Guatemala or norms of public order under domestic law.

Declaration:

The expression "treatment as favourable as possible" in all articles of the Convention and of the Protocol in which the expression is used should be interpreted as not including rights which, under law or treaty, the Republic of Guatemala has accorded or is according to nationals of the Central American countries or of other countries with which it has concluded or is entering into agreements of a regional nature.

Holy See

The Holy See, in conformity with the terms of article 42, paragraph 1, of the Convention, makes the reservation that the application of the Convention must be compatible in practice with the special nature of the Vatican City State and without prejudice to the norms governing access to and sojourn therein.

Iran (Islamic Republic of)

1. In all cases where, under the provisions of this Convention, refugees enjoy the most favourable treatment accorded to nationals of a foreign State, the Government of Iran reserves the right not to accord refugees the most favourable treatment accorded to nationals of States with which Iran has concluded regional establishment, customs, economic or political agreements.

2. The Government of Iran considers the stipulations contained in articles 17, 23, 24 and 26 as being recommendations only.

Ireland [14]

. . .

"2. The Government of Ireland understands the words 'public order' in article 32 (1) and the words 'in accordance with due process of law' in article 32 (2) to mean, respectively, 'public policy' and 'in accordance with a procedure provided by law'.

"3. With regard to article 17 the Government of Ireland do not undertake to grant to refugees rights of wage-earning employment more favourable than those granted to aliens generally.

"4. The Government of Ireland undertake to give effect to article 25 only in so far as may be practicable and permissible under the laws of Ireland.

"5. With regard to article 29 (1) the Government of Ireland do not undertake to accord to refugees treatment more favourable than that accorded to aliens generally with respect to

. . .

"(c) Income Tax (including Surtax)."

Israel

. . .

"2. Articles 8 and 12 shall not apply to Israel.

"3. Article 28 shall apply to Israel with the limitations which result from Section 6 of the Passport Law of 5712-1952, according to which the Minister may, at his discretion:

"(*a*) Refuse to grant, or to extend the validity of a passport or laissez-passer;

"(*b*) Attach conditions to the grant or the extension of the validity of a passport or laissez-passer;

"(*c*) Cancel, or shorten the period of validity of a passport or laissez-passer issued, and order the surrender thereof;

"(*d*) Limit, either at or after the issue of a passport or laissez-passer, the range of countries for which it is to be valid.

"4. Permits provided for by article 30 shall be issued by the Minister of Finance at his discretion."

Italy [15]

In signing this Convention, the Government of the Republic of Italy declares that the provisions of articles 17 and 18 are recognized by it as recommendations only.

Jamaica

"The Government of Jamaica confirms and maintains the following reservations, which were made when the Convention was extended to Jamaica by the United Kingdom of Great Britain and Northern Ireland:

"(i) The Government of the United Kingdom understand articles 8 and 9 as not preventing the taking by the above-mentioned territory, in time of war or other grave and exceptional circumstances, of measures in the interests of national security in the case of a refugee on the ground of his nationality. The provision of article 8 shall not prevent the Government of the United Kingdom from exercising any rights over property or interests which they may acquire or have acquired as an Allied or Associated Power under a Treaty of Peace or other agreement or arrangement for the restoration of peace which has been or may be completed as a result of the Second World War. Furthermore, the provision of article 8 shall not affect the treatment to be accorded to any property or interests which, at the date of entry into force of the Convention for the above-mentioned territory, are under the control of the Government of the United Kingdom by reason of a state of war which exists or existed between them and any other State.

"(ii) The Government of the United Kingdom accept article 17, paragraph 2, in its application to the above-mentioned territory with the substitution of 'four years' for 'three years' in subparagraph (*a*) and with the omission of subparagraph (*c*).

"(iii) The Government of the United Kingdom can only undertake that the provisions of article 24, paragraph 1, subparagraph (*b*), and of paragraph 2 of that article will be applied to the above-mentioned territory so far as the law allows.

"(iv) The Government of the United Kingdom cannot undertake that effect will be given in the above-mentioned territory to article 25, paragraphs 1 and 2, and can only undertake that the provision of paragraph 3 will be applied in the above-mentioned territory so far as the law allows."

Liechtenstein

Ad *article 17:* With respect to the right to engage in wage-earning employment, refugees are treated in law on the same footing as aliens in general, on the understanding, however, that the competent authorities shall make every effort in so far as is possible, to apply to them the provisions of this article.

Ad *article 24, paragraph 1* (a) *and* (b), *and paragraph 3:* Provisions relating to aliens in general on training, apprenticeship, unemployment insurance, old-age and survivors insurance shall be applicable to refugees. Nevertheless, in the case of old-age and survivors insurance, refugees residing in Liechtenstein (including their survivors if the latter are considered as refugees) are already entitled to normal old-age or survivors' benefits after paying their contributions for at least one full year, provided that they have resided in Liechtenstein for ten years—of which five years without interruption have immediately preceded the occurrence of the event insured against. Moreover, the one-third reduction in benefits provided in the case of aliens and stateless persons under article 74 of the Act on Old-Age and Survivors Insurance, is not applicable to refugees. Refugees residing in Liechtenstein who, on the occurrence of the event insured against, are not entitled to old-age or survivors' benefits, are paid not only their own contributions but any contributions which may have been made by the employers.

Luxembourg

Upon signature:

Subject to the following reservation: in all cases where this Convention grants to refugees the most favourable treatment accorded to nationals of a foreign country, this provision shall not be interpreted as necessarily involving the régime accorded to nationals of countries with which the Grand Duchy of Luxembourg has concluded regional, customs, economic or political agreements.

1 November 1984

Interpretative statement:

The Grand Duchy of Luxembourg considers that the reservation made by the Republic of Guatemala concerning the Convention relating to the Status of Refugees of 28 July 1951 and the Protocol relating to the Status of Refugees of 31 January 1967 does not affect the obligations of Guatemala deriving from those instruments.

Madagascar

The provision of article 7 (1) shall not be interpreted as requiring the same treatment as is accorded to nationals of countries with which the Malagasy Republic has concluded conventions of establishment or agreements on co-operation;

The provisions of articles 8 and 9 shall not be interpreted as forbidding the Malagasy Government to take, in time of war or other grave and exceptional circumstances, measures with regard to a refugee because of his nationality in the interests of national security.

The provisions of article 17 cannot be interpreted as preventing the application of the laws and regulations establishing the proportion of alien workers that employers are authorized to employ in Madagascar or affecting the obligations of such employers in connection with the employment of alien workers.

Malta

"Article 7, paragraph 2, articles 14, 23, 27 and 28 shall not apply to Malta, and article 7, paragraphs 3, 4 and 5, articles 8, 9, 11, 17, 18, 31, 32 and 34 shall apply to Malta compatibly with its own special problems, its peculiar position and characteristics."

Monaco

Subject to the reservation that the stipulations contained in article 7, paragraph 2, articles 15, 22, paragraph 1, and articles 23 and 24 shall be provisionally considered as being recommendations and not legal obligations.

Mozambique

Reservations:

In respect of articles 13 and 22: The Government of Mozambique will take these provisions as simple recommendations not binding it to accord to refugees the same treatment as is accorded to Mozambicans with respect to elementary education and property.

In respect of articles 17 and 19: The Government of Mozambique will interpret [these provisions] to the effect that it is not required to grant privileges from obligation to obtain a work permit.

As regards article 15: The Government of Mozambique will not be bound to accord to refugees or group of refugees resident in its territory more extensive rights than those enjoyed by nationals with respect to the right of association and it reserves the right to restrict them in the interest of national security.

As regards article 26: The Government of Mozambique reserves its right to designate place or places for principal residence for refugees or to restrict their freedom of movement whenever considerations of national security make it advisable.

As regards article 34: The Government of Mozambique does not consider itself bound to grant to refugees facilities greater than those granted to other categories of aliens in general, with respect to naturalization laws.

Netherlands

Reservation made upon signature and confirmed upon ratification:

This signature is appended subject to the reservation that in all cases where this Convention grants to refugees the most favourable treatment accorded to nationals of a foreign country this provision shall not be interpreted as involving the régime accorded to nationals of countries with which the Netherlands has concluded regional, customs, economic or political agreements.

Declarations:

(1) With reference to article 26 of this Convention, the Netherlands Government reserves the right to designate a place of principal residence for certain refugees or groups of refugees in the public interest.

(2) In the notifications concerning overseas territories referred to in article 40, paragraph 2, of this Convention, the Netherlands Government reserves the right to make a declaration in accordance with section B of article 1 with respect to such territories and to make reservations in accordance with article 42 of the Convention.

Interpretative declaration:

In depositing the instrument of ratification by the Netherlands, ... I declare on behalf of the Netherlands Government that it does not regard the Amboinese who were transported to the Netherlands after 27 December 1949, the date of the transfer of sovereignty by the Kingdom of the Netherlands to the Republic of the United States of Indonesia, as eligible for the status of refugees as defined in article 1 of the said Convention.

New Zealand

"... The Government of New Zealand can only undertake to give effect to the provision contained in article 24, paragraph 2, of the Convention so far as the law of New Zealand allows ..."

Norway [16]

"The obligation stipulated in article 17 (1) to accord to refugees lawfully staying in the country the most favourable treatment accorded to nationals of a foreign country in the same circumstances as regards the right to engage in wage-earning employment, shall not be construed as extending to refugees the benefits of agreements which may in the future be concluded between Norway, Denmark, Finland, Iceland and Sweden, or between Norway and any one of these countries, for the purpose of establishing special conditions for the transfer of labour between these countries."

Papua New Guinea

"The Government of Papua New Guinea in accordance with article 42, paragraph 1, of the Convention makes a reservation with respect to the provisions contained in articles 17 (1), 21, 22 (1), 26, 31, 32 and 34 of the Convention and does not accept the obligations stipulated in these articles."

Portugal

13 July 1976[17]

"In all cases in which the Convention confers upon the refugees the most favoured person status granted to nationals of a foreign country, this clause will not be interpreted in such a way as to mean the status granted by Portugal to the nationals of Brazil."

Rwanda

Reservation to article 26:

For reasons of public policy (*ordre public*), the Rwandese Republic reserves the right to determine the place of residence of refugees and to establish limits to their freedom of movement.

Sierra Leone

"The Government of Sierra Leone wishes to state with regard to article 17 (2) that Sierra Leone does not consider itself bound to grant to refugees the rights stipulated therein."

"Further, with regard to article 17 as a whole, the Government of Sierra Leone wishes to state that it considers the article to be a recommendation only and not a binding obligation."

"The Government of Sierra Leone wishes to state that it does not consider itself bound by the provisions of article 29, and it reserves the right to impose special taxes on aliens as provided for in the Constitution."

Somalia

"The Government of the Somali Democratic Republic acceded to the Convention and Protocol on the understanding that nothing in the said Convention or Protocol will be construed so as to prejudice or adversely affect the national status, or political aspiration of displaced people from Somali Territories under alien domination.

"It is in this spirit, that the Somali Democratic Republic will commit itself to respect the terms and provisions of the said Convention and Protocol."

Spain

(*a*) The expression "the most favourable treatment" shall, in all the articles in which it is used, be interpreted as not including rights which, by law or by treaty, are granted to nationals of Portugal, Andorra, the Philippines or the Latin American countries or to nationals of countries with which international agreements of a regional nature are concluded.

(*b*) The Government of Spain considers that article 8 is not a binding rule but a recommendation.

(*c*) The Government of Spain reserves its position on the application of article 12, paragraph 1. Article 12, paragraph 2, shall be interpreted as referring exclusively to rights acquired by a refugee before he obtained, in any country, the status of refugee.

(*d*) Article 26 of the Convention shall be interpreted as not precluding the adoption of special measures concerning the place of residence of particular refugees, in accordance with Spanish law.

Sudan

With reservation as to article 26.

Sweden [18]

With the following reservations:

First, a general reservation to the effect that the application of those provisions of the Convention which grant to refugees the most favourable treatment accorded to nationals of a foreign country shall not be affected by the fact that special rights and privileges are now or may in future be accorded by Sweden to the nationals of Denmark, Finland, Iceland and Norway or to the nationals of any one of those countries; and, secondly, the following reservations: a reservation to article 8 to the effect that that article shall not be binding on Sweden; a reservation to article 12, paragraph 1, to the effect that the Convention shall not modify the rule of Swedish private international law, as now in force, under which the personal status of a refugee is governed by the law of his country of nationality . . .; a reservation to article 17, paragraph 2, to the effect that Sweden does not consider itself bound to grant a refugee who fulfils any one of the conditions set out in subparagraphs (*a*) to (*c*) an automatic exemption from the obligation to obtain a work permit; a reservation to article 24, paragraph 1 (*b*), to the effect that notwithstanding the principle of national treatment for refugees, Sweden shall not be bound to accord to refugees the same treatment as is accorded to nationals in respect of the possibility of entitlement to a national pension under the provisions of the National Insurance Act; and likewise to the effect that, in so far as the right to a supplementary pension under the said Act and the computation of such pension in certain respects are concerned, the rules applicable to Swedish nationals shall be more favourable than those applied to other insured persons; a reservation to article 24, paragraph 3, to the effect that the provision of this paragraph shall not be binding on Sweden; and a reservation to article 25, to the effect that Sweden does not consider itself bound to cause a certificate to be delivered by a Swedish authority, in the place of the authorities of a foreign country, if the documentary records necessary for the delivery of such a certificate do not exist in Sweden.

Switzerland [19]

Turkey

Upon signature:

The Turkish Government considers that the term "events occurring before 1 January 1951" refers to the beginning of the events. Consequently, since the pressure exerted upon the Turkish minority in Bulgaria, which began before 1 January 1951, is still continuing, the provision of this Convention must also apply to the Bulgarian refugees of Turkish extraction compelled to leave that country as a result of this pressure and who, being unable to enter Turkey, might seek refuge on the territory of another Contracting party after 1 January 1951.

The Turkish Government will, at the time of ratification, enter reservations which it could make under article 42 of the Convention.

Reservation and declaration made upon ratification:

No provision of this Convention may be interpreted as granting to refugees greater rights than those accorded to Turkish citizens in Turkey.

The Government of the Republic of Turkey is not a party to the Arrangements of 12 May 1926 and of 30 June 1928 mentioned in article 1, paragraph A, of this Convention. Furthermore, the 150 persons affected by the Arrangement of 30 June 1928 having been amnestied under Act No. 3527, the provisions laid down in this Arrangement are no longer valid in the case of Turkey. Consequently, the Government of the Republic of Turkey considers the Convention of 28 July 1951 independently of the aforementioned Arrangements ...

The Government of the Republic of Turkey understands that the action of "reavailment" or "reacquisition" as referred to in article 1, paragraph C, of the Convention—that is to say: "If (1) He has voluntarily reavailed himself of the protection of the country of his nationality; or (2) Having lost his nationality, he has voluntarily reacquired it"—does not depend only on the request of the person concerned but also on the consent of the State in question.

Uganda

(1) *In respect of article 7:* "The Government of the Republic of Uganda understands this provision as not conferring any legal, political or other enforceable right upon refugees who, at any given time may be in Uganda. On the basis of this understanding the Government of the Republic of Uganda shall accord refugees such facilities and treatment as the Government of the Republic of Uganda shall in her absolute discretion, deem fit having regard to her own security, economic and social needs."

(2) *In respect of articles 8 and 9:* "The Government of the Republic of Uganda declares that the provisions of articles 8 and 9 are recognized by it as recommendations only."

(3) *In respect of article 13:* "The Government of the Republic of Uganda reserves to itself the right to abridge this provision without recourse to courts of law or arbitral tribunals, national or international, if the Government of the Republic of Uganda deems such abridgement to be in the public interest."

(4) *In respect of article 15:* "The Government of the Republic of Uganda shall in the public interest have the full freedom to withhold any or all rights conferred by this article from any refugees as a class of residents within her territory."

(5) *In respect of article 16:* "The Government of the Republic of Uganda understands article 16, paragraphs 2 and 3 thereof, as not requiring the Government of the Republic of Uganda to accord to a refugee in need of legal assistance, treatment more favourable than that extended to aliens generally in similar circumstances."

(6) *In respect of article 17:* "The obligation specified in article 17 to accord to refugees lawfully staying in the country in the same circumstances shall not be construed as extending to refugees the benefit of preferential treatment granted to nationals of the States who enjoy special privileges on account of existing or future treaties between Uganda and those countries, particularly States of the East African Community and the Organization of African Unity, in accordance with the provisions which govern such charters in this respect."

(7) *In respect of article 25:* "The Government of the Republic of Uganda understands that this article shall not require the Government of the Republic of Uganda to incur expenses on behalf of the refugees in connection with the granting of such assistance except in so far as such assistance is requested by and the resulting expense is reimbursed to the Government of the Republic of Uganda by the United Nations High Commissioner for Refugees or any other agency of the United Nations which may succeed it."

(8) *In respect of article 32:* "Without recourse to legal process the Government of the Republic of Uganda shall, in the public interest, have the unfettered right to expel any refugee in her territory and may at any time apply such internal measures as the Government may deem necessary in the circumstances; so however that, any action taken by the Government of the Republic of Uganda in this regard shall not operate to the prejudice of the provisions of article 33 of this Convention."

United Kingdom of Great Britain and Northern Ireland

(i) The Government of the United Kingdom of Great Britain and Northern Ireland understand articles 8 and 9 as not preventing them from taking in time of war or other grave and exceptional circumstances measures in the interests of national security in the case of a refugee on the ground of his nationality. The provision of article 8 shall not prevent the Government of the United Kingdom of Great Britain and Northern Ireland from exercising any rights over property or interests which they may acquire or have acquired as an Allied or Associated Power under a Treaty of Peace or other agreement or arrangement for the restoration of peace which has been or may be completed as a result of the Second World War. Furthermore, the provision of article 8 shall not affect the treatment to be accorded to any property or interests which, at the date of entry into force of this Convention for the United Kingdom of Great Britain and Northern Ireland, are under the control of the Government of the United Kingdom of Great Britain and Northern Ireland by reason of a state of war which exists or existed between them and any other State.

(ii) The Government of the United Kingdom of Great Britain and Northern Ireland accept article 17, paragraph 2, with the substitution of "four years" for "three years" in subparagraph (*a*) and with the omission of subparagraph (*c*).

(iii) The Government of the United Kingdom of Great Britain and Northern Ireland, in respect of such of the matters referred to in article 24, paragraph 1, subparagraph (*b*), as fall within the scope of the National Health Service, can only undertake to apply the provisions of that paragraph so far as the law allows; and it can only undertake to apply the provision of paragraph 2 of that article so far as the law allows.

(iv) The Government of the United Kingdom of Great Britain and Northern Ireland cannot undertake to give effect to the obligations contained in article 25, paragraphs 1 and 2, and can only undertake to apply the provision of paragraph 3 so far as the law allows.

Commentary:

"In connection with article 24, paragraph 1, subparagraph (*b*), relating to certain matters within the scope of the National Health Service, the National Health Service (Amendment) Act, 1949, contains powers for charges to be made to persons not ordinarily resident in Great Britain (which category would include refugees) who receive treatment under the Service. While these powers have not yet been exercised it is possible that this might have to be done at some future date. In Northern Ireland the Health Services are restricted to persons ordinarily resident in the country except where regulations are made to extend the Service to others. It is for these reasons that the Government of the United Kingdom while they are prepared in the future, as in the past, to give the most sympathetic consideration to the situation of refugees, find it necessary to make a reservation to article 24, paragraph 1, subparagraph (*b*), of the Convention.

The scheme of Industrial Injuries Insurance in Great Britain does not meet the requirements of article 24, paragraph 2, of the Convention. Where an insured person has died as the result of an industrial accident or a disease due to the nature of his employment, benefit cannot generally be paid to his dependants who are abroad unless they are in any part of the British Commonwealth, in the Irish Republic or in a country with which the United Kingdom has made a reciprocal agreement concerning the payment of industrial injury benefits. There is an exception to this rule in favour of the dependants of certain seamen who die as a result of industrial accidents happening to them while they are in the service of British ships. In this matter refugees are treated in the same way as citizens of the United Kingdom and Colonies and by reason of article 24, paragraphs 3 and 4, of the Convention, the dependants of refugees will be able to take advantage of reciprocal agreements which provide for the payment of United Kingdom industrial injury benefits in other countries. By reason of article 24, paragraphs 3 and 4, refugees will enjoy under the scheme of National Insurance and Industrial Injuries Insurance certain rights which are withheld from British subjects who are not citizens of the United Kingdom and Colonies.

No arrangements exist in the United Kingdom for the administrative assistance for which provision is made in article 25 nor have any such arrangements been found necessary in the case of refugees. Any need for the documents or certifications mentioned in paragraph 2 of that article would be met by affidavits."

Zambia

"Subject to the following reservations made pursuant to article 42 (1) of the Convention:

Article 17 (2)

"The Government of the Republic of Zambia wishes to state with regard to article 17, paragraph 2, that Zambia does not consider itself bound to grant to a refugee who fulfils any one of the conditions set out in subparagraphs (*a*) to (*c*) automatic exemption from the obligation to obtain a work permit.

"Further, with regard to article 17 as a whole Zambia does not wish to undertake to grant to refugees rights of wage-earning employment more favourable than those granted to aliens generally."

Article 22 (1)

"The Government of the Republic of Zambia wishes to state that Zambia considers article 22 (1) to be a recommendation only and not a binding obligation to accord to refugees the same treatment as is accorded to nationals with respect to elementary education."

Article 26

"The Government of the Republic of Zambia wishes to state with regard to article 26 that Zambia reserves the right to designate a place or places of residence for refugees."

Article 28

"The Government of the Republic of Zambia wishes to state with regard to article 28 that Zambia considers itself not bound to issue a travel document with a return clause in cases where a country of second asylum has accepted or indicated its willingness to accept a refugee from Zambia."

Zimbabwe

"1. The Government of the Republic of Zimbabwe declares that it is not bound by any of the reservations to the Convention relating to the Status of Refugees, the application of which had been extended by the Government of the United Kingdom to its territory before the attainment of independence.

"2. The Government of the Republic of Zimbabwe wishes to state with regard to article 17, paragraph 2, that it does not consider itself bound to grant a refugee who fulfils any of the conditions set out in subparagraphs (*a*) to (*c*) automatic exemption from the obligation to obtain a work permit. In addition, with regard to article 17 as a whole, the Republic of Zimbabwe does not undertake to grant to refugees rights of wage-earning employment more favourable than those granted to aliens generally.

"3. The Government of the Republic of Zimbabwe wishes to state that it considers article 22 (1) as being a recommendation only and not an obligation to accord to refugees the same treatment as it accords to nationals with respect to elementary education.

"4. The Government of the Republic of Zimbabwe considers articles 23 and 24 as being recommendations only.

"5. The Government of the Republic of Zimbabwe wishes to state with regard to article 26 that it reserves the right to designate a place or places of residence for refugees."

OBJECTIONS

(Unless otherwise indicated, the objections were
made upon ratification, accession or succession.)

Belgium

5 November 1984

[Regarding the reservation made by Guatemala upon accession] [the Belgian Government] considers that it is impossible for the other States parties to determine the scope of a reservation which is expressed in such broad terms and which refers for the most part to domestic law, and that the reservation is thus not acceptable. It therefore voices an objection to the said reservation.

Ethiopia

10 January 1979

"The Provisional Military Government of Socialist Ethiopia wishes to place on record its objection to the declaration [made by Somalia upon accession] and that it does not recognize it as valid on the ground that there are no Somali territories under alien domination."

France

23 October 1984

[*Same declaration,* mutatis mutandis, *as the one made by Belgium.*]

Germany, Federal Republic of

5 December 1984

"The Federal Government views [the reservation made by Guatemala] as being worded in such general terms that its application could conceivably nullify the provisions of the Convention and the Protocol. Consequently, this reservation cannot be accepted."

Greece [14]

Italy

26 November 1984

[The Government of Italy] considers [the reservation made by Guatemala] to be unacceptable since the very general terms in which it is couched and the fact that it refers for the most part to domestic law and leaves it to the Guatemalan Government to decide whether to apply numerous aspects of the Convention make it impossible for other States parties to determine the scope of the reservation.

Luxembourg

[*For an interpretative statement by Luxembourg concerning the reserva-tion by Guatemala, see under "Declarations other than those made under section B of article 1 and Reservations" in this chapter.*]

Netherlands

11 December 1984

"The Government of the Kingdom of the Netherlands is of the opinion that a [the reservation by Guatemala] phrased in such general terms and referring to the domestic law only is undesirable, since its scope is not entirely clear."

TERRITORIAL APPLICATIONS

Participant	*Date of receipt of notification*	*Territories*
Australia	22 Jan. 1954	Norfolk Island, Papua New Guinea and Nauru
Denmark	4 Dec. 1952	Greenland
France	23 June 1954	All territories for the international relations of which France is responsible
Netherlands . . .	29 July 1971	Surinam
United Kingdom	11 Mar. 1954	The Channel Islands and the Isle of Man
	25 Oct. 1956	The following territories with reservations: British Solomon Islands Protectorate, Cyprus, Dominica, Falkland Islands,[20] Fiji, Gambia, Gilbert and Ellice Islands,[3] Grenada, Jamaica, Kenya, Mauritius, St. Vincent, Seychelles, Somaliland Protectorate, Zanzibar and St. Helena
	19 June 1957	British Honduras

Participant	Date of receipt of notification	Territories
	11 July 1960	Federation of Rhodesia and Nyasaland [21, 22]
	11 Nov. 1960	Basutoland, Bechuanaland Protectorate [23] and Swaziland
	4 Sep. 1968	St. Lucia, Montserrat
	20 Apr. 1970	The Bahama Islands

DECLARATIONS AND RESERVATIONS MADE ON NOTIFICATIONS OF TERRITORIAL APPLICATIONS

Denmark

Greenland

Subject to the reservations made on ratification by the Government of Denmark.

Netherlands

Surinam [24]

The extension is subject to the following reservations, which had been made in substance by the Government of the Netherlands upon ratification:

"1. that in all cases where the Convention, in conjunction with the Protocol, grants to refugees the most favourable treatment accorded to nationals of a foreign country, this provision shall not be interpreted as involving the régime accorded to nationals of countries with which the Kingdom of the Netherlands has concluded regional, customs, economic or political agreements which apply to Surinam;

"2. that the Government of Surinam as regards article 26 of the Convention, in conjunction with article 1, paragraph 1, of the Protocol, reserves the right for reasons of public order to appoint for certain refugees or groups of refugees a principal place of residence."

United Kingdom of Great Britain and Northern Ireland

The Channel Islands and the Isle of Man

"(i) The Government of the United Kingdom of Great Britain and Northern Ireland understand articles 8 and 9 as not preventing the taking in the Isle of Man and in the Channel Islands, in time of war or other grave and exceptional circumstances, of measures in the interests of national security in the case of a refugee on the ground of his nationality. The provision of article 8 shall not prevent the Government of the United Kingdom of Great Britain and Northern Ireland from exercising any rights over property or interests which they may acquire or have acquired as an Allied or Associated Power under a Treaty of Peace or other agreement or arrangement for the restoration of peace which has been or may be completed as a result of the Second World War. Furthermore, the provision of article 8 shall not affect the treatment to be accorded to any property or interests which, at the date of the entry into force of this Convention for the Isle of Man and the Channel Islands, are under the control of the Government of the United Kingdom of Great Britain and Northern Ireland by reason of a state of war which exists or existed between them and any other State.

"(ii) The Government of the United Kingdom of Great Britain and Northern Ireland accept article 17, paragraph 2, in its application to the Isle of Man and the Channel Islands with the substitution of 'four years' for 'three years' in subparagraph (*a*) and with the omission of subparagraph (*c*).

"(iii) The Government of the United Kingdom of Great Britain and Northern Ireland can only undertake that the provisions of article 24, paragraph 1, subparagraph (*b*), and article 24, paragraph 2, will be applied in the Channel Islands so far as the law allows, and that the provisions of that subparagraph (*b*), in respect of such matters referred to therein as fall within the scope of the Isle of Man Health Service, and of article 24, paragraph 2, will be applied in the Isle of Man so far as the law allows.

"(iv) The Government of the United Kingdom of Great Britain and Northern Ireland cannot undertake that effect will be given in the Isle of Man and the Channel Islands to article 25, paragraphs 1 and 2, and can only undertake that the provision of paragraph 3 will be applied in the Isle of Man and the Channel Islands so far as the law allows.

"The considerations upon which certain of these reservations are based are similar to those set out in the memorandum relating to the corresponding reservations made in respect of the United Kingdom, which was enclosed in [the] note under reference."

British Solomon Islands Protectorate, Cyprus, [10]
Dominica, Falkland Islands, Fiji, [25] ***Gambia,*** [12]
Gilbert and Ellice Islands, Grenada, Jamaica, [26]
Kenya, [27] ***Mauritius, St. Vincent, Seychelles***
and Somaliland Protectorate

[*Same reservations, in essence, as those made for the Channel Islands and the Isle of Man.*]

Zanzibar and St. Helena

[*Same reservations, in essence, as those made for the Channel Islands and the Isle of Man under Nos. (i), (iii) and (iv).*]

British Honduras

[*Same reservations, in essence, as those made for the Channel Islands and the Isle of Man under No. (i).*]

Federation of Rhodesia and Nyasaland [21, 22]

[*Same reservations, in essence, as those made for the Channel Islands and the Isle of Man.*]

Basutoland, Bechuanaland Protectorate [23] and Swaziland

[*Same reservations, in essence, as those made for the Channel Islands and the Isle of Man under Nos. (i), (iii), and (iv).*]

The Bahama Islands

"Subject to the following reservation in respect of article 17, paragraphs 2 and 3, of the Convention:

"Refugees and their dependants would normally be subject to the same laws and regulations relating generally to the employment of non-Bahamians within the Commonwealth of the Bahama Islands, so long as they have not acquired Bahamian status."

NOTES

[1] *Official Records of the General Assembly, Fifth Session, Supplement No. 20* (A/1775), p. 48.

[2] On 15 December 1955, a communication was received by the Secretary-General from the Government of the Federal Republic of Germany stating that the Convention also applies to Land Berlin as from the date of its entry into force for the Federal Republic of Germany.

[3] In a declaration contained in the notification of succession to the Convention, the Government of Tuvalu confirmed that it regards the Convention [. . .] as continuing in force subject to reservations previously made by the Government of the United Kingdom of Great Britain and Northern Ireland in relation to the Colony of the Gilbert and Ellice Islands.

[4] Colombia, upon signature, and Argentina, upon accession, had specified the article (*a*). The declarations specifying alternative (*b*) were made respectively upon ratification (10 October 1961) and upon subsequent ratification (15 November 1984).

[5] Notifications of the extension of their obligations under the Convention by adopting alternative (*b*) of section B (1) of the Convention were received by the Secretary-General on the dates indicated:

Australia	6 July 1970
Benin	1 Dec. 1967
Cameroon	29 Dec. 1961
Central African Republic	15 Oct. 1962
Chile	28 Jan. 1972
Côte d'Ivoire	20 Dec. 1966
Ecuador	1 Feb. 1972
France	3 Feb. 1971
Holy See	17 Nov. 1961
Iran (Islamic Republic of)	27 Sep. 1976
Luxembourg	22 Aug. 1972
Niger	7 Dec. 1964
Peru	8 Dec. 1980
Portugal	13 July 1976
Senegal	12 Oct. 1964
Sudan	7 Mar. 1974
Togo	23 Oct. 1962

[6] On 21 January 1983, the Secretary-General received from the Government of Botswana the following communication:

"Having simultaneously acceded to the Convention and Protocol [relating to the status of refugees done at New York on 31 January 1967] on 6 January 1969 and in view of the fact that the Protocol provides in article I (2) that 'the term "refugee" shall . . . mean any person within the definition of article 1 of the Convention' as if the words 'As a result of events occurring before 1 January 1951 and . . .' and the words '. . . as a result of such events', in article [I (A) (2)] were omitted and thus modifies in effect the provisions of article 1 of the Convention, it is the position of the Government of Botswana that no separate declaration under article 1 B (1) of the Convention is required in the circumstances."

On the basis of the aforementioned communication, the Secretary-General has included Botswana in the list of States having chosen formula (*b*) under section B of article 1.

Subsequently, in a communication received by the Secretary-General on 29 April 1986, and with reference to article 1 B (1) of the above-mentioned Convention, the Government of Botswana confirmed that it has no objection to be listed among the States applying the Convention without any geographical limitation.

[7] In a communication received on 1 December 1967, the Government of Australia notified the Secretary-General of the withdrawal of the reservations to articles 17, 18, 19, 26 and 32, and, in a communication received by the Secretary-General on 11 March 1971, of the withdrawal of the reservation to article 28, paragraph 1, of the Convention. For the text of those reservations, see United Nations, *Treaty Series*, vol. 189, p. 202.

[8] These reservations replace those made at the time of signature. For the text of reservations made on signature, see United Nations, *Treaty Series*, vol. 189, p. 186.

[9] On 7 April 1972, upon its accession to the Protocol relating to the Status of Refugees done at New York on 31 January 1967, the Government of Brazil withdraws its reservations excluding articles 15 and 17, paragraphs 1 and 3, from its application to the Convention. For the text of the said reservations, see United Nations, *Treaty Series*, vol. 380, p. 430.

[10] On notifying its succession to the Convention, the Government of Cyprus confirmed the reservations made at the time of the extension of the Convention to its territory by the Government of the United Kingdom of Great Britain and Northern Ireland. For the text of those reservations, see under "Declarations and reservations made on notifications of territorial applications" of this chapter.

[11] In a communication received on 23 August 1962, the Government of Denmark informed the Secretary-General of its decision to withdaw as from 1 October 1961 the reservation to article 14 of the Convention.

In a communication received on 25 March 1968, the Government of Denmark informed the Secretary-General of its decision to withdraw as from that date the reservations made on ratification to article 24, paragraphs 1, 2 and 3, and partially the reservation made on ratification to article 17 by rewording the said reservation. For the text of the reservations originally formulated by the Government of Denmark on ratification, see United Nations, *Treaty Series*, vol. 189, p. 198.

[12] On notifying its succession to the Convention, the Government of Gambia confirmed the reservations made at the time of the extension of the Convention to its territory by the Government of the United Kingdom of Great Britain and Northern Ireland.

[13] In a communication received by the Secretary-General on 19 April 1978, the Government of Greece declared that it withdrew the reservations that it had made upon ratification pertaining to articles 8, 11, 13, 24 (3), 26, 28, 31, 32 and 34, and also the objection contained in paragraph 6 of the relevant declaration of reservations by Greece is also withdrawn. For the text of the reservations and objection so withdrawn, see United Nations, *Treaty Series*, vol. 354, p. 402.

[14] In a communication received on 23 October 1968, the Government of Ireland notified the Secretary-General of the withdrawal of two of its reservations in respect of article 29 (1), namely those indicated at (*a*) and (*b*) of paragraph 5 of declarations and reservations contained in the instrument of accession by the Government of Ireland to the Convention. For the text of the withdrawn reservations, see United Nations, *Treaty Series*, vol. 254, p. 412.

[15] In a communication received on 20 October 1964, the Government of Italy has notified the Secretary-General that "it withdraws the reservations made at the time of signature, and confirmed at the time of ratification, to articles 6, 7, 8, 19, 22, 23, 25 and 34 of the Convention [see United Nations, *Treaty Series*, vol. 189, p. 192]. The above-mentioned reservations are inconsistent with the internal provisions issued by the Italian Government since the ratification of the Convention. The Italian Government also adopted in December 1963 provisions which implement the contents of article 17, paragraph 2."

Furthermore, the Italian Government confirms that "it maintains its declaration made in accordance with section B (1) of article 1, and that it recognizes the provisions of articles 17 and 18 as recommendations only".

[16] In a communication received by the Secretary-General on 21 January 1954, the Government of Norway gave notice of the withdrawal, with immediate effect, of the reservation to article 24 of the Convention, "as the Acts mentioned in the said reservation have been amended to accord to refugees lawfully staying in the country the same treatment as is accorded to Norwegian nationals". For the text of that reservation, see United Nations, *Treaty Series*, vol. 189, p. 198.

[17] That text, which was communicated in a notification received on 13 July 1976, replaces the reservations originally made by Portugal upon accession. For the text of the reservations withdrawn, see United Nations, *Treaty Series*, vol. 383, p. 314.

[18] In a communication received on 20 April 1961, the Government of Sweden gave notice of the withdrawal, as from 1 July 1961, of the reservation to article 14 of the Convention.

In a communication received on 25 November 1966, the Government of Sweden has notified the Secretary-General that it has decided, in accordance with article 42, paragraph 2, of the Convention, to withdraw some of its reservations to article 24, paragraph 1 (*b*), by rewording them and to withdraw the reservation to article 24, paragraph 2.

In a communication received on 5 March 1970, the Government of Sweden notified the Secretary-General of the withdrawal of its reservation to article 7, paragraph 2, of the Convention.

For the text of the reservations as originally formulated by the Government of Sweden upon ratification, see United Nations, *Treaty Series*, vol. 200, p. 336.

[19] In a communication received on 18 February 1963, the Government of Switzerland gave notice to the Secretary-General of the withdrawal of the reservation made at the time of ratification to article 24, paragraph 1, subparagraphs (*a*) and (*b*), and paragraph 3, of the Convention, in so far as that reservation concerns old-age and survivors' insurance.

In a communication received on 3 July 1972, the Government of Switzerland gave notice of its withdrawal of the reservation to article 17 formulated in its instrument of ratification of the Convention.

In a communication received on 17 December 1980, the Government of Switzerland gave notice of its withdrawal, in its entirety, of the subsisting reservation formulated in respect of article 24, paragraph 1, subparagraphs (*a*) and (*b*), which encompasses training, apprenticeship and unemployment insurance with effect from 1 January 1981, date of entry into force of the Swiss Law on Asylum of 5 October 1979.

For the text of the reservations made initially, see United Nations, *Treaty Series*, vol. 202, p. 368.

[20] On 30 October 1983, the Secretay-General received from the Government of Argentina the following objection:

> [The Government of Argentina makes a] formal objection to the declaration of territorial extension issued by the United Kingdom with regard to the Malvinas Islands (and dependencies), which that country is illegally occupying and refers to as the "Falkland Islands".

> The Argentine Republic rejects and considers null and void the [declaration] of territorial extension.

See also note 14 in chapter II.

[21] The Federation of Rhodesia and Nyasaland was dissolved immediately before 1 January 1964. In reply to the Secretariat's inquiry as to the legal effect of that dissolution, in so far as

concerns the application in the territories formerly constituting the Federation, i.e., Northern Rhodesia, Nyasaland and Southern Rhodesia, of certain multilateral treaties deposited with the Secretary-General which had been extended by the Government of the United Kingdom of Great Britain and Northern Ireland to the Federation or to any of the territories concerned prior to the formation of the Federation, and of the International Convention to Facilitate the Importation of Commercial Samples and Advertising Material done at Geneva on 7 November 1952, to which the Federation acceded in its capacity of a Contracting party to the General Agreement on Tariffs and Trade, the Government of the United Kingdom in a communication received on 16 April 1964, provided the following clarification:

"Her Majesty's Government consider that in general, multilateral treaties applicable to the Federation of Rhodesia and Nyasaland continued to apply to the constituent territories of the former Federation on its dissolution. Multilateral treaties under which the Federation enjoyed membership of international organizations fall in a special category; their continued application to the constituent territories of the former Federation depends in each case on the terms of the treaty. Her Majesty's Government regard all the conventions listed in the Secretariat's letter of 26 February as applying to the constituent territories of the former Federation since its dissolution, but the accession by the Federation to the International Convention to Facilitate the Importation of Commercial Samples and Advertising Material has not led to this result as article 13 of the Convention allows Her Majesty's Government to extend provisions of the Convention to the three constituent territories of the former Federation if considered desirable."

"With regard to the final query by the Secretariat, I am to reply that extensions prior to the inauguration of the Federation do, of course, continue to apply to the constituent territories."

Northern Rhodesia and Nyasaland have since become independent States under the names of Zambia and Malawi, respectively.

[22] In a letter addressed to the Secretary-General on 22 March 1968, the President of the Republic of Malawi, referring to the Convention relating to the Status of Refugees, done at Geneva on 28 July 1951, stated the following:

"In my letter to you of 24 November 1964, concerning the disposition of Malawi's inherited treaty obligations, my Government declared that with respect to multilateral treaties which had been applied or extended to the former Nyasaland Protectorate, any party to such a treaty could on the basis of reciprocity rely as against Malawi on the terms of such treaty until Malawi notified its depositary of what action it wished to take by way of confirmation of termination, confirmation of succession, or accession.

"I am now to inform you as depositary of this Convention that the Government of Malawi wishes to terminate any connection with this Convention which it might have inherited. The Government of Malawi considers that any legal relationship with the aforementioned Convention relating to the Status of Refugees, Geneva, 1951, which might have devolved upon it by way of succession from the ratification of the United Kingdom, is terminated as of this date."

See succession by Zambia.

[23] See succession by Botswana (formerly Bechuanaland Protectorate).

[24] Upon notifying its succession (29 November 1978) the Government of Suriname informed the Secretary-General that the Republic of Suriname did not succeed to the reservations formulated on 29 July 1951 by the Netherlands when the Convention and Protocol relating to the Status of Refugees were extended to Surinam.

[25] See succession by Fiji.

[26] See succession by Jamaica.

[27] See succession by Kenya.

Chapter XX

PROTOCOL RELATING TO THE STATUS
OF REFUGEES

Done at New York on 31 January 1967

ENTRY INTO FORCE: 4 October 1967, in accordance with article VIII.

Note: On the recommendation of the Executive Committee of the Programme of the United Nations High Commissioner for Refugees, the High Commissioner submitted the draft of the above-mentioned Protocol to the General Assembly of the United Nations, through the Economic and Social Council, in the addendum to his report concerning measures to extend the personal scope of the Convention relating to the Status of Refugees. The Economic and Social Council, in resolution 1186 (XLI)[1.] * of 18 November 1966, took note with approval of the draft Protocol and transmitted the said addendum to the General Assembly. The General Assembly, in resolution 2198 (XXI)[2] of 16 December 1966, took note of the Protocol and requested the Secretary-General "to transmit the text of the Protocol to the States mentioned in article V thereof, with a view to enabling them to accede to the Protocol".

Participant	Accession, succession (d)
Algeria	8 Nov. 1967
Angola	23 June 1981
Argentina	6 Dec. 1967
Australia[3]	13 Dec. 1973
Austria	5 Sep. 1973
Belgium	8 Apr. 1969
Benin	6 July 1970
Bolivia	9 Feb. 1982
Botswana	6 Jan. 1969
Brazil	7 Apr. 1972
Burkina Faso	18 June 1980
Burundi	15 Mar. 1971
Cameroon	19 Sep. 1967
Canada	4 June 1969

* For notes, see end of chapter.

Participant	Accession, succession (d)
Cape Verde	9 July 1987
Central African Republic	30 Aug. 1967
Chad	19 Aug. 1981
Chile	27 Apr. 1972
China	24 Sep. 1982
Colombia	4 Mar. 1980
Congo	10 July 1970
Costa Rica	28 Mar. 1978
Côte d'Ivoire	16 Feb. 1970
Cyprus	9 July 1968
Denmark	29 Jan. 1968
Djibouti	9 Aug. 1977 d
Dominican Republic	4 Jan. 1978
Ecuador	6 Mar. 1969
Egypt	22 May 1981
El Salvador	28 Apr. 1983
Equatorial Guinea	7 Feb. 1986
Ethiopia	10 Nov. 1969
Fiji	12 June 1972 d
Finland	10 Oct. 1968
France	3 Feb. 1971
Gabon	28 Aug. 1973
Gambia	29 Sep. 1967
Germany, Federal Republic of [4]	5 Nov. 1969
Ghana	30 Oct. 1968
Greece	7 Aug. 1968
Guatemala	22 Sep. 1983
Guinea	16 May 1968
Guinea-Bissau	11 Feb. 1976
Haiti	25 Sep. 1984
Holy See	8 June 1967
Iceland	26 Apr. 1968
Iran (Islamic Republic of)	28 July 1976
Ireland	6 Nov. 1968
Israel	14 June 1968
Italy	26 Jan. 1972
Jamaica	30 Oct. 1980
Japan	1 Jan. 1982
Kenya	13 Nov. 1981
Lesotho	14 May 1981

Participant	Accession, succession (d)
Liberia	27 Feb. 1980
Liechtenstein	20 May 1968
Luxembourg	22 Apr. 1971
Mali	2 Feb. 1973
Malta	15 Sep. 1971
Mauritania	5 May 1987
Morocco	20 Apr. 1971
Netherlands[5]	29 Nov. 1968
New Zealand	6 Aug. 1973
Nicaragua	28 Mar. 1980
Niger	2 Feb. 1970
Nigeria	2 May 1968
Norway	28 Nov. 1967
Panama	2 Aug. 1978
Papua New Guinea	17 July 1986
Paraguay	1 Apr. 1970
Peru	15 Sep. 1983
Philippines	22 July 1981
Portugal	13 July 1976
Rwanda	3 Jan. 1980
Sao Tome and Principe	1 Feb. 1978
Senegal	3 Oct. 1967
Seychelles	23 Apr. 1980
Sierra Leone	22 May 1981
Somalia	10 Oct. 1978
Spain	14 Aug. 1978
Sudan	23 May 1974
Suriname	29 Nov. 1978 *d*[6]
Swaziland	28 Jan. 1969
Sweden	4 Oct. 1967
Switzerland	20 May 1968
Togo	1 Dec. 1969
Tunisia	16 Oct. 1968
Turkey	31 July 1968
Tuvalu	7 Mar. 1986 *d*
Uganda	27 Sep. 1976
United Kingdom	4 Sep. 1968
United Republic of Tanzania	4 Sep. 1968
United States of America	1 Nov. 1968
Uruguay	22 Sep. 1970

| | *Accession,* |
Participant	*succession* (d)
Venezuela	19 Sep. 1986
Yemen	18 Jan. 1980
Yugoslavia	15 Jan. 1968
Zaire	13 Jan. 1975
Zambia	24 Sep. 1969
Zimbabwe	25 Aug. 1981

DECLARATIONS AND RESERVATIONS

(Unless otherwise indicated, the declarations and
reservations were made upon accession or succession.
For objections thereto and territorial applications,
see hereinafter.)

Angola

The Government of Angola, in accordance with article VII, paragraph 1,
declares that it does not consider itself bound by article IV of the Protocol,
concerning settlement of disputes relating to the interpretation of the
Protocol.

Botswana

"Subject to the reservation in respect of article IV of the said Protocol
and in respect of the application in accordance with article I thereof of the
provisions of articles 7, 17, 26, 31, 32 and 34, and article 12, paragraph 1, of
the Convention relating to the Status of Refugees, done at Geneva on 28 July
1951."

Burundi

In acceding to this Protocol, the Government of the Republic of Burundi
enters the following reservations:

1. The provisions of article 22 of the Convention are accepted, in respect
of elementary education, only

   (*a*) In so far as they apply to public education, and not to private
   education;

(*b*) On the understanding that the treatment applicable to refugees shall be the most favourable accorded to nationals of other States.

2. The provisions of article 17 (1) and (2) of the Convention are accepted as mere recommendations and, in any event, shall not be interpreted as necessarily involving the régime accorded to nationals of countries with which the Republic of Burundi may have concluded regional, customs, economic or political agreements.

3. The provision of article 26 of the Convention is accepted only subject to the reservation that refugees:

(*a*) Do not choose their place of residence in a region bordering on their country of origin;

(*b*) Refrain, in any event, when exercising their right to move freely, from any activity or incursion of a subversive nature with respect to the country of which they are nationals.

Cape Verde

In all cases where the 1951 Convention relating to the Status of Refugees grants to refugees the most favourable treatment accorded to nationals of a foreign country, this provision shall not be interpreted as involving the régime accorded to nationals of countries with which Cape Verde has concluded regional, customs, economic or political agreements.

Chile

(1) With the reservation that, with reference to the provision of article 34 of the Convention, the Government of Chile will be unable to grant to refugees facilities greater than those granted to aliens in general, in view of the liberal nature of Chilean naturalization laws;

(2) With the reservation that the period specified in article 17, paragraph 2 (*a*), shall, in the case of Chile, be extended from three to ten years;

(3) With the reservation that article 17, paragraph 2 (*c*), shall apply only if the refugee is the widow or the widower of a Chilean spouse;

(4) With the reservation that the Government of Chile cannot grant a longer period for compliance with an expulsion order than that granted to other aliens in general under Chilean law.

China

With a reservation in respect of article IV of the Protocol.

Congo

The Protocol is accepted with the exception of article IV.

El Salvador

With the reservation that the Government of El Salvador will not apply article IV of the Protocol.

Ethiopia

Subject to the following reservation in respect of the application, under article I of the Protocol, of the Convention relating to the Status of Refugees, done at Geneva on 28 July 1951:

"The provisions of articles 8, 9, 17 (2) and 22 (1) of the Convention are recognized only as recommendations and not as legally binding obligations."

Finland

Subject to the reservations made in relation to the Convention relating to the Status of Refugees, in accordance with article I of the Protocol.

Ghana

"The Government of Ghana does not consider itself bound by article IV of the Protocol regarding the settlement of disputes."

Guatemala

[See chapter XIX.]

Israel

"The Government of Israel accedes to the Protocol subject to the same statements and reservations made at the time of ratifying the Convention [relating to the Status of Refugees, done at Geneva on 28 July 1951], in accordance with the provisions of article VII (2) of the Protocol."

Jamaica

1. "The Government of Jamaica understands articles 8 and 9 of the Convention as not preventing it from taking, in time of war or other grave and exceptional circumstances, measures in the interest of national security in the case of a refugee on the ground of his nationality."

2. "The Government of Jamaica can only undertake that the provisions of article 17, paragraph 2, of the Convention will be applied so far as the law of Jamaica allows."

3. "The Government of Jamaica can only undertake that the provisions of article 24 of the Convention will be applied so far as the law of Jamaica allows."

4. "The Government of Jamaica can only undertake that the provisions of article 25, paragraphs 1, 2 and 3, of the Convention will be applied so far as the law of Jamaica allows."

5. "The Government of Jamaica does not accept the obligation imposed by article IV of the Protocol relating to the Status of Refugees with regard to the settlement of disputes."

Luxembourg

[*See chapter XIX.*]

Malta

In accordance with article VII (2), the reservations to the Convention relating to the Status of Refugees of 28 July 1951 by the Government of Malta on deposit of its instrument of accession on 17 June 1971, pursuant to article 42 of the said Convention, are applicable in relation to its obligations under the present Protocol.

Netherlands[6]

"In accordance with article VII of the Protocol, all reservations made by the Kingdom of the Netherlands upon signature and ratification of the Convention relating to the Status of Refugees, which was signed in Geneva on 28 July 1951, are regarded to apply to the obligations resulting from the Protocol."

Peru

Declaration:

[The Government of Peru] hereby expressly declares, with reference to the provisions of article I, paragraph 1, and article II of the aforementioned Protocol, that compliance with the obligations undertaken by virtue of the act of accession to that instrument shall be ensured by the Peruvian State using all the means at its disposal, and the Government of Peru shall endeavour in all cases to co-operate as far as possible with the Office of the United Nations High Commissioner for Refugees.

Portugal

"1. The Protocol will be applied without any geographical limitation.

"2. In all cases in which the Protocol confers upon the refugees the most favoured person status granted to nationals of a foreign country, this clause will not be interpreted in such a way as to mean the status granted by Portugal to the nationals of Brazil or to the nationals of other countries with whom Portugal may establish commonwealth-type relations."

Rwanda

Reservation to article IV:

For the settlement of any dispute between States parties, recourse may be had to the International Court of Justice only with the prior agreement of the Rwandese Republic.

Somalia

[See chapter XIX.]

Swaziland

Reservations:

Subject to the following reservations in respect of the application of the Convention relating to the Status of Refugees, done at Geneva on 28 July 1951, under article I of the Protocol:

"(1) The Government of the Kingdom of Swaziland is not in a position to assume obligations as contained in article 22 of the said Convention, and therefore will not consider itself bound by the provisions therein;

"(2) Similarly, the Government of the Kingdom of Swaziland is not in a position to assume the obligations of article 34 of the said Convention, and must expressly reserve the right not to apply the provisions therein."

Declaration:

"The Government of the Kingdom of Swaziland deems it essential to draw attention to the accession as a Member of the United Nations, and not as a party to the [Convention relating to the Status of Refugees] by reason of succession or otherwise."

Turkey

The instrument of accession stipulates that the Government of Turkey maintains the provisions of the declaration made under article 1, section B, of the Convention relating to the Status of Refugees, done at Geneva on 28 July 1951, according to which it applies the Convention only to persons who have become refugees as a result of events occurring in Europe, and also the reservation clause made upon ratification of the Convention to the effect that no provision of this Convention may be interpreted as granting to refugees greater rights than those accorded to Turkish citizens in Turkey.

Uganda

[See chapter XIX.]

United Kingdom of Great Britain and Northern Ireland

"...

"(*a*) In accordance with the provisions of the first sentence of article VII (4) of the Protocol, the United Kingdom hereby excludes from the application of the Protocol the following territories for the international relations of which it is responsible: Jersey, Southern Rhodesia and Swaziland;

"(*b*) In accordance with the provision of the second sentence of article VII (4) of the said Protocol, the United Kingdom hereby extends the application of the Protocol to the following territories for the international relations of which it is responsible: St. Lucia and Montserrat."

United Republic of Tanzania

"... subject to the reservation hereby made, that the provision of article IV of the Protocol shall not be applicable to the United Republic of Tanzania except within the explicit consent of the Government of the United Republic of Tanzania."

United States of America

With the following reservations in respect of the application, in accordance with article I of the Protocol, of the Convention relating to the Status of Refugees, done at New York on 28 July 1951:

"The United States of America construes article 29 of the Convention as applying only to refugees who are resident in the United States and reserves the right to tax refugees who are not residents of the United States in accordance with its general rules relating to non-resident aliens.

"The United States of America accepts the obligation of article 24, paragraph 1 (*b*), of the Convention except in so far as that paragraph may conflict in certain instances with any provisions of title II (old-age, survivors' and disability insurance) or title XVIII (hospital and medical insurance for the aged) of the Social Security Act. As to any such provision, the United States will accord to refugees lawfully staying in its territory treatment no less favourable than is accorded aliens generally in the same circumstances."

Venezuela

In implementing the provisions of the Protocol which confer on refugees the most favourable treatment accorded to nationals of a foreign country, it shall be understood that such treatment does not include any rights and benefits which Venezuela has granted or may grant regarding entry into or sojourn in Venezuelan territory to nationals of countries with which

Venezuela has concluded regional or subregional integration, customs, economic or political agreements.

The instrument of accession also contains a reservation in respect of article IV.

OBJECTIONS

For the text of objections to the Protocol by **Belgium, Ethiopia, Federal Republic of Germany, France, Italy, Luxembourg** and **Netherlands,** see chapter XIX, page 292.

TERRITORIAL APPLICATIONS

Participant	*Date of receipt of notification*	*Territories*
Netherlands	29 July 1971	Surinam
	4 Feb. 1987	Aruba
United Kingdom . .	20 Apr. 1970	Bahama Islands[7]

NOTES

[1] *Official Records of the Economic and Social Council, Forty-first Session, Supplement No. 14* (E/4264/Add.1), p. 1.

[2] *Official Records of the General Assembly, Twenty-first Session, Supplement No. 16* (A/6316), p. 48.

[3] With the following declaration: "The Government of Australia will not extend the provisions of the Protocol to Papua New Guinea."

[4] In a note accompanying the instrument of accession, the Government of the Federal Republic of Germany declared that the Protocol "shall also apply to Land Berlin with effect from the date on which it enters into force for the Federal Republic of Germany".

With reference to the above-mentioned declaration, communications have been addressed to the Secretary-General by the Governments of Bulgaria and Mongolia. The said communications are identical in essence, *mutatis mutandis,* to the corresponding ones referred to in note 4 of chapter I.

[5] The Kingdom of the Netherlands accedes to the said Protocol so far as the territory of the Kingdom situated in Europe is concerned; and, as from 1 January 1986, to Aruba.

[6] See note 24 in chapter XIX.

[7] Subject to the reservation which was formulated on behalf of the Bahama Islands in respect of the Convention relating to the Status of Refugees.

Chapter XXI

CONVENTION ON THE POLITICAL RIGHTS
OF WOMEN

Adopted by the General Assembly of the United Nations on 20 December 1952

ENTRY INTO FORCE: 7 July 1954, in accordance with article VI.

Participant	Signature	Ratification, accession (a), succession (d)
Afghanistan		16 Nov. 1966 *a*
Albania		12 May 1955 *a*
Angola		17 Sep. 1986 *a*
Argentina	31 Mar. 1953	27 Feb. 1961
Australia		10 Dec. 1974 *a*
Austria	19 Oct. 1959	18 Apr. 1969
Bahamas		16 Aug. 1977 *d*
Barbados		12 Jan. 1973 *a*
Belgium		20 May 1964 *a*
Bolivia	9 Apr. 1953	22 Sep. 1970
Brazil	20 May 1953	13 Aug. 1963
Bulgaria		17 Mar. 1954 *a*
Burma	14 Sep. 1954	
Byelorussian SSR	31 Mar. 1953	11 Aug. 1954
Canada		30 Jan. 1957 *a*
Central African Republic		4 Sep. 1962 *d*
Chile	31 Mar. 1953	18 Oct. 1967
China [1],*		
Colombia		5 Aug. 1986 *a*
Congo		15 Oct. 1962 *d*
Costa Rica	31 Mar. 1953	25 July 1967
Cuba	31 Mar. 1953	8 Apr. 1954

---

* For notes, see end of chapter.

Participant	Signature	Ratification, accession (a), succession (d)
Cyprus	10 Sep. 1968	12 Nov. 1968
Czechoslovakia	31 Mar. 1953	6 Apr. 1955
Democratic Yemen		9 Feb. 1987
Denmark	29 Oct. 1953	7 July 1954
Dominican Republic	31 Mar. 1953	11 Dec. 1953
Ecuador	31 Mar. 1953	23 Apr. 1954
Egypt		8 Sep. 1981 a
El Salvador	24 June 1953	
Ethiopia	31 Mar. 1953	21 Jan. 1969
Fiji		12 June 1972 d
Finland		6 Oct. 1958 a
France	31 Mar. 1953	22 Apr. 1957
Gabon	19 Apr. 1967	19 Apr. 1967
German Democratic Republic		27 Mar. 1973 a
Germany, Federal Republic of		4 Nov. 1970 a²
Ghana		28 Dec. 1965 a
Greece	1 Apr. 1953	29 Dec. 1953
Guatemala	31 Mar. 1953	7 Oct. 1959
Guinea	19 Mar. 1975	24 Jan. 1978
Haiti	23 July 1957	12 Feb. 1958
Hungary	2 Sep. 1954	20 Jan. 1955
Iceland	25 Nov. 1953	30 June 1954
India	29 Apr. 1953	1 Nov. 1961
Indonesia	31 Mar. 1953	16 Dec. 1958
Ireland		14 Nov. 1968 a
Israel	14 Apr. 1953	6 July 1954
Italy		6 Mar. 1968 a
Jamaica		14 Aug. 1966 a
Japan	1 Apr. 1955	13 July 1955
Lao People's Democratic Republic		28 Jan. 1969 a
Lebanon	24 Feb. 1954	5 June 1956
Lesotho		4 Nov. 1974 a
Liberia	9 Dec. 1953	
Luxembourg	4 June 1969	1 Nov. 1976
Madagascar		12 Feb. 1964 a
Malawi		29 June 1966 a
Mali		16 July 1974 a
Malta		9 July 1968 a
Mauritania		4 May 1976 a

Participant	Signature	*Ratification, accession* (a), *succession* (d)
Mauritius		18 July 1969 *d*
Mexico	31 Mar. 1953	23 Mar. 1981
Mongolia		18 Aug. 1965 *a*
Morocco		22 Nov. 1976 *a*
Nepal		26 Apr. 1966 *a*
Netherlands	8 Aug. 1968	30 July 1971
New Zealand		22 May 1968 *a*
Nicaragua		17 Jan. 1957 *a*
Niger		7 Dec. 1964 *d*
Nigeria	11 July 1980	17 Nov. 1980
Norway	18 Sep. 1953	24 Aug. 1956
Pakistan	18 May 1954	7 Dec. 1954
Papua New Guinea		27 Jan. 1982 *a*
Paraguay	16 Nov. 1953	
Peru		1 July 1975 *a*
Philippines	23 Sep. 1953	12 Sep. 1957
Poland	31 Mar. 1953	11 Aug. 1954
Republic of Korea		23 June 1959 *a*
Romania	27 Apr. 1954	6 Aug. 1954
Senegal		2 May 1963 *d*
Sierra Leone		25 July 1962 *a*
Solomon Islands		3 Sep. 1981 *a*[3]
Spain		14 Jan. 1974 *a*
Swaziland		20 July 1970 *a*
Sweden	6 Oct. 1953	31 Mar. 1954
Thailand	5 Mar. 1954	30 Nov. 1954
Trinidad and Tobago		24 June 1966 *a*
Tunisia		24 Jan. 1968 *a*
Turkey	12 Jan. 1954	26 Jan. 1960
Ukrainian SSR	31 Mar. 1953	15 Nov. 1954
Union of Soviet Socialist Republics	31 Mar. 1953	3 May 1954
United Kingdom		24 Feb. 1967 *a*
United Republic of Tanzania . .		19 June 1975 *a*
United States of America		8 Apr. 1976 *a*
Uruguay	26 May 1953	
Venezuela		31 May 1983 *a*
Yugoslavia	31 Mar. 1953	23 June 1954
Zaire		12 Oct. 1977 *a*
Zambia		4 Feb. 1972 *a*

DECLARATIONS AND RESERVATIONS

(Unless otherwise indicated, the declarations and
reservations were made upon ratification, accession
or succession. For objections thereto and territorial
applications, see hereinafter.)

Albania

1. *As regards article VII:* The People's Republic of Albania declares its disagreement with the last sentence of article VII and considers that the juridical effect of a reservation is to make the Convention operative as between the State making the reservation and all other States parties to the Convention, with the exception only of that part thereof to which the reservation relates.

2. *As regards article IX:* The People's Republic of Albania does not consider itself bound by the provision of article IX which provides that disputes between Contracting parties concerning the interpretation or application of this Convention shall, at the request of any one of the parties to the dispute, be referred to the International Court of Justice for decision, and declares that, for any dispute to be referred to the International Court of Justice for decision, the agreement of all the parties to the dispute shall be necessary in each individual case.

Argentina

The Argentine Government reserves the right not to submit to the procedure set out in this article [article IX] any dispute which is directly connected with territories which fall within Argentine sovereignty.

Australia

"The Government of Australia hereby declares that the accession by Australia shall be subject to the reservation that article III of the Convention shall have no application as regards recruitment to and conditions of service in the Defence Forces.

"The Government of Australia furthermore declares that the Convention shall not extend to Papua New Guinea."

Austria

"In ratifying the Convention on the Political Rights of Women the Federal President of the Republic of Austria declares that Austria reserves its right to apply the provision of article III to this Convention, as far as service in the Armed Forces is concerned, within the limits established by national legislation."

Belgium[4]

In exercise of the option available to each State under article VII of the Convention on the Political Rights of Women, the Government of Belgium declares that it submits the following reservations to article III of the Convention:

The Constitution reserves the exercise of royal powers to men.

As regards the exercise of the functions of regency, article III of the Convention shall not prevent the application of the constitutional rules as interpreted by the Belgian State.

Bulgaria

As regards articles VII and IX: [same declaration and reservation as those reproduced under "Albania"].

Byelorussian Soviet Socialist Republic

As regards articles VII and IX: [same declaration and reservation as those reproduced under "Albania"].

Canada

"Inasmuch as under the Canadian constitutional system legislative jurisdiction in respect of political rights is divided between the provinces and the Federal Government, the Government of Canada is obliged, in acceding to this Convention, to make a reservation in respect of rights within the legislative jurisdiction of the provinces."

Czechoslovakia

As regards articles VII and IX: [same declaration and reservation as those reproduced under "Albania"].

Democratic Yemen

(*a*) The People's Democratic Republic of Yemen declares that it does not accept the last sentence of article VII and considers that the juridical effect of a reservation is to make the Convention operative as between the State making the reservation and all other States parties to the Convention with the exception only of that part thereof to which the reservation relates;

(*b*) The People's Democratic Republic of Yemen does not consider itself bound by the text of article IX, which provides that disputes between Contracting parties concerning the interpretation or application of this Convention may, at the request of any one of the parties to the dispute, be referred to the International Court of Justice. It declares that the competence of the International Court of Justice with respect to disputes concerning the interpretation or application of the Convention shall in each case be subject to the express consent of all parties to the dispute.

Denmark

Subject to a reservation with respect to article III of the Convention, in so far as it relates to the right of women to hold military appointments or to act as heads of recruitment services or to serve on recruitment boards.

Ecuador

The Government of Ecuador signs this Convention subject to a reservation with respect to the last phrase in article I, "without any discrimination", since article 22 of the Political Constitution of the Republic specifies that "a vote in popular elections is obligatory for a man and optional for a woman".

Fiji

"The reservations of the United Kingdom (1) (*a*), (*b*), (*d*) and (*f*) are affirmed and are redrafted as more suitable to the situation of Fiji in the following terms:

"Article III is accepted subject to reservations, pending notification of withdrawal of any case, in so far as it relates to:

"(*a*) Succession to the Crown;

"(*b*) Certain offices primarily of a ceremonial signature;

"(*d*) Recruitment to and conditions of service in the Armed Forces;

"(*f*) The employment of married women in the civil service.

"All other reservations made by the United Kingdom are withdrawn."

Finland

As regards article III: "A decree may be issued to the effect that only men or women can be appointed to certain functions, which because of their nature, can be properly discharged either only by men or by women."

France[5]

German Democratic Republic

Reservations:

As regards article VII: The German Democratic Republic declares that it does not consider itself bound by the provision of article VII of the Convention under which the Convention is not to enter into force as between a State party making a reservation and a State party objecting to such reservation. The German Democratic Republic is of the opinion that the Convention should also be effective between the State which has made the reservation and all other States parties, with the exception of that part of the Convention to which the reservation relates.

As regards article IX: The German Democratic Republic does not consider itself bound by the provision of article IX of the Convention, which provides that disputes between Contracting parties concerning the interpretation or application of the Convention are, at the request of any one of the parties to the dispute, to be referred to the International Court of Justice for decision, and declares that, in each individual case, the consent of all parties to such a dispute is necessary in order to refer the dispute to the International Court of Justice for decision.

Declaration:

The German Democratic Republic deems it necessary to state that article IV, paragraph 1, and article V, paragraph 1, of the Convention deprive a number of States of the opportunity to become parties to the Convention. As the Convention regulates matters affecting the interests of all States, it should be open to participation by all States whose policies are guided by the purposes and principles of the Charter of the United Nations.

Germany, Federal Republic of

"The Federal Republic of Germany accedes to the Convention with the reservation that article III of the Convention does not apply to service in the Armed Forces."

Guatemala

1. Articles I, II and III shall apply only to female citizens of Guatemala in accordance with the provisions of article 16, paragraph 2, of the Constitution of the Republic.

2. In order to satisfy constitutional requirements, article IX shall be interpreted subject to the provisions of article 149, paragraph 3 (*b*), of the Constitution of the Republic.

Hungary

As regards articles VII and IX: [*same declaration and reservation as those reproduced under "Albania"*].

India

"Article III of the Convention shall have no application as regards recruitment to, and conditions of service in any of the Armed Forces of India or the Forces charged with the maintenance of public order in India."

Indonesia

"... The last sentence of article VII and the whole of article IX do not apply to Indonesia."

Ireland

"Article III is accepted subject to reservation in so far as it relates to:

"(*a*) The employment of married women in the public service;

"(*b*) The unequal remuneration of women in certain positions in the public service,

"and subject to the following declarations:

"(1) That the exclusion of women from positions of employment for which by objective standards or for physical reasons they are not suitable is not regarded as discriminatory;

"(2) That the fact that jury service is not at present obligatory for women is not regarded as discriminatory."

Italy

"In acceding to the Convention on the Political Rights of Women, open for signature at New York on 31 March 1953, the Italian Government declares that it reserves its rights to apply the provisions of article III as far as service in the Armed Forces and in special armed corps is concerned within the limits established by national legislation."

Lesotho

"Article III is accepted subject to reservation, pending notification of withdrawal in any case, so far as it relates to: matters regulated by Basotho Law and Custom."

Malta

"In acceding to this Convention, the Government of Malta hereby declares that it does not consider itself bound by article III in so far as that article applies to conditions of service in the Public Service and to jury service."

Mauritius

"The Government of Mauritius hereby declares that it does not consider itself bound by article III of the Convention in so far as that article applies to recruitment to and conditions of service in the Armed Forces or to jury service."

Mexico

Declaration:

"It is expressly understood that the Government of Mexico will not deposit its instrument of ratification pending the entry into force of the amendment to the Political Constitution of the United Mexican States, which is now under consideration, providing that citizenship rights shall be granted to Mexican women."

Mongolia

As regards articles IV and V: "The Government of the Mongolian People's Republic declares its disagreement with article IV, paragraph 1, and article V, paragraph 1, and considers that the present Convention should be open to all States for signature or accession.

"As regards articles VII and IX: [same declaration and reservation as those reproduced under "Albania"].

Morocco

The consent of all the parties concerned is required for the referral of any dispute to the International Court of Justice.

Nepal

As regards article IX of the Convention: ". . . any dispute shall be referred for decision to the International Court of Justice only at the request of all the parties to the dispute."

Netherlands

. . .[6]

New Zealand

"Subject to a reservation with respect to article III of the Convention, in so far as it relates to recruitment and conditions of service in the Armed Forces of New Zealand."

Pakistan

"Article III of the Convention shall have no application as regards recruitment to and conditions of services charged with the maintenance of public order or unsuited to women because of the hazards involved."

Poland

As regards articles VII and IX: [same declaration and reservation as those reproduced under "Albania"].

Romania

As regards articles VII and IX: [same declaration and reservation as those reproduced under "Albania"].

Sierra Leone

"In acceding to this Convention, the Government of Sierra Leone hereby declares that it does not consider itself bound by article III in so far as that article applies to recruitment to and conditions of service in the Armed Forces or to jury service."

Solomon Islands

10 May 1982

In relation to the succession: The Government of Solomon Islands declared that Solomon Islands maintains the reservations entered by the United Kingdom save in so far as the same cannot apply to Solomon Islands.

Spain

Articles I and III of the Convention shall be interpreted without prejudice to the provisions which in current Spanish legislation define the status of head of family.

Articles II and III shall be interpreted without prejudice to the norms relating to the office of Head of State contained in the Spanish Fundamental Laws.

Article III shall be interpreted without prejudice to the fact that certain functions, which, by their nature can be exercised satisfactorily only by men or only by women, shall be exercised exclusively by men or by women, as appropriate, in accordance with Spanish legislation.

Swaziland

"(*a*) Article III of the Convention shall have no application as regards remuneration for women in certain posts in the Civil Service of the Kingdom of Swaziland;

"(*b*) The Convention shall have no application to matters which are regulated by Swaziland Law and Custom in accordance with Section 62 (2) of the Constitution of the Kingdom of Swaziland."

Tunisia

[Article IX] For any dispute to be referred to the International Court of Justice, the agreement of all the parties to the dispute shall be necessary in every case.

Ukrainian Soviet Socialist Republic

As regards articles VII and IX: [same declaration and reservation as those reproduced under "Albania"].

Union of Soviet Socialist Republics

As regards articles VII and IX: [same declaration and reservation as those reproduced under "Albania"].

United Kingdom of Great Britain and Northern Ireland

"The United Kingdom of Great Britain and Northern Ireland accedes to the Convention with the following reservations submitted in accordance with article VII:

"(1) Article III is accepted subject to reservations, pending notification of withdrawal in any case, in so far as it relates to:

"(*a*) Succession to the Crown:

"(*b*) Certain offices primarily of a ceremonial nature;

"(*c*) The function of sitting and voting in the House of Lords pertaining to holders of hereditary peerages and holders of certain offices in the Church of England;

"(*d*) Recruitment to and conditions of service in the Armed Forces;

"(*e*) Jury service in Grenada, the Isle of Man and Montserrat, as well as in the Kingdom of Tonga;[7]

"(*f*) [8]

"(*g*) Remuneration for women in the Civil Service of Gibraltar and Hong Kong, as well as of the Protectorate of Swaziland;[9]

"(*h*) The post of Bailiff in Guernsey;

"(*i*) In the State of Brunei, the exercise of the royal powers, jury service or its equivalent and the holding of certain offices governed by Islamic Law.

"(2) The United Kingdom reserves the right to postpone the application of this Convention in respect of women living in the Colony of Aden, having regard to the local customs and traditions. Further, the United Kingdom reserves the right not to apply this Convention to Rhodesia unless and until the United Kingdom informs the Secretary-General of the United Nations that it is in a position to ensure that the obligations imposed by the Convention in respect of that territory can be fully implemented."

Venezuela

Reservation with regard to article IX:

[Venezuela] does not accept the jurisdiction of the International Court of Justice for the settlement of disputes concerning the interpretation or application of this Convention.

OBJECTIONS

Canada

Objection to the reservations made in respect of articles VII and IX by the Governments of Albania, Bulgaria, the Byelorussian Soviet Socialist Republic, Czechoslovakia, Hungary, Poland, Romania, the Ukrainian Soviet Socialist Republic and the Union of Soviet Socialist Republics.

China [10]

Czechoslovakia

Objection to the reservations made by the Government of Spain in respect of articles I, II and III, on the grounds that they are incompatible with the objectives of the Convention.

Denmark

Objection to the reservations in respect of articles VII and IX: [*same States as those listed under "Canada"*].

Dominican Republic

Objection to the reservations made by the Government of the Union of Soviet Socialist Republics in respect of articles VII and IX.

Ethiopia

Objection to the reservations in respect of articles VII and IX: [*same States as those listed under "Canada"*].

Israel

Objection to the reservations in respect of articles VII and IX: [*same States as those listed under "Canada"*].

Norway

Objection to the reservations made by the Government of Guatemala in respect of articles I, II and III.

Objection to the reservations in respect of articles VII and IX: [*same States as those listed under "Canada"*].

Pakistan

Objection to the reservation made by France and recorded in the procès-verbal on signature of the Convention.[5]

Objection to the reservations made by the Government of Guatemala in respect of articles I, II and III.

Objection to the reservations in respect of articles VII and IX: [*same States as those listed under "Canada"*].

Philippines

Objection to the reservations made by the Governments of Albania and Romania in respect of articles VII and IX.

Republic of Korea

Objection to the reservations made by the Government of Mongolia in respect of articles IV, paragraph 1, and V, paragraph 1.

Sweden

Objection to reservations: [*same objections as those listed under "Norway"*].

Yugoslavia

Objection to the reservations made by the Government of Guatemala, in respect of articles I, II and III, as these reservations "are not in accordance with the principles contained in Article I of the Charter of the United Nations and with the aims of the Convention".

TERRITORIAL APPLICATIONS

Participant	Date of receipt of notification	Territories
Netherlands . . .	30 July 1971	Surinam
United Kingdom[11]	24 Feb. 1967	Territories under the territorial sovereignty of the United Kingdom: British Solomon Islands Protectorate, State of Brunei, Protectorate of Swaziland, Kingdom of Tonga

---

NOTES

[1] Signed and ratified on behalf of the Republic of China on 9 June 1953 and 21 December 1953 respectively. See note concerning signatures, ratifications, accessions, etc. on behalf of China (note 2 in chapter I).

With reference to the above-mentioned ratification, communications have been addressed to the Secretary-General by the Permanent Missions to the United Nations of Denmark, Hungary, India, Norway, Poland, Romania and the Union of Soviet Socialist Republics, on the one hand, and of China on the other hand. For the nature of these communications, see also note 2 in chapter I.

[2] In a letter accompanying the instrument of accession, the Government of the Federal Republic of Germany declared that "the said Convention shall also apply to Land Berlin with effect from the date on which it enters into force for the Federal Republic of Germany".

With reference to the above-mentioned declaration, communications were addressed to the Secretary-General by the Governments of Bulgaria, Mongolia, Poland, the Ukrainian Soviet Socialist Republic and the Union of Soviet Socialist Republics. Those communications are identical in essence, *mutatis mutandis,* to those referred to in note 4 of chapter I.

Subsequently, on 27 December 1973, the Secretary-General received from the Government of the German Democratic Republic a communication identical in essence, *mutatis mutandis,* to that reproduced in note 4 of chapter I.

Finally, communications were received on the same subject from the Governments of France, the United Kingdom and the United States of America (on 17 June 1974) and the Federal Republic of Germany (on 15 July 1974): those communications are identical in essence, *mutatis mutandis,* to the corresponding ones reproduced in note 4 of chapter I.

[3] In a communication received on 10 May 1982, the Government of Solomon Islands declared that Solomon Islands maintains the reservations entered by the United Kingdom save in so far as the same cannot apply to Solomon Islands.

[4] By a notification received by the Secretary-General on 19 June 1978 the Government of Belgium withdrew reservation No. 2, relating to article III of the Convention. For the text of the reservation so withdrawn, see United Nations, *Treaty Series,* vol. 496, p. 353.

[5] In a communication received on 26 November 1960 the Government of France gave notice of the withdrawal of the reservation made in the procès-verbal of signature of the Convention. For the text of the reservation, see United Nations, *Treaty Series,* vol. 193, p. 159.

[6] On 17 December 1985, the Secretary-General received from the Government of the Kingdom of the Netherlands a notification of withdrawal of its reservation (the reservation concerned the succession to the Crown) relating to article III of the Convention made upon ratification. For the text of the said reservation, see United Nations, *Treaty Series,* vol. 790, p. 130.

[7] The reservation contained in subparagraph (*e*), as formulated on accession, also applied to the Bahamas. In a communication received on 12 February 1968, the Government of the United Kingdom notified the Secretary-General of the withdrawal of the said reservation in respect of the Bahamas.

[8] In a communication received on 15 October 1974, the Government of the United Kingdom notified the Secretary-General of the withdrawal of the reservation contained in subparagraph (*f*) (employment of married women in Her Majesty's Diplomatic Service and in the Civil Service) in respect of the territories where the reservation was still applicable, that is to say: Northern Ireland, Antigua, Hong Kong and St. Lucia. The same reservation had been withdrawn in respect of St. Vincent by a notification received on 24 November 1967. For the text of the reservation, see United Nations, *Treaty Series,* vol. 590, p. 298.

[9] By a notification received on 15 October 1974, the Government of the United Kingdom notified the Secretary-General of the withdrawal of this reservation in respect of the Seychelles, to which the said reservation applied originally.

[10] Various communications were received by the Secretary-General on behalf of the Republic of China, objecting to the reservations made by the Governments of Albania, Bulgaria, the Byelorussian SSR, Czechoslovakia, Hungary, Poland, Romania, the Ukrainian SSR and the Union of Soviet Socialist Republics. In this connection, see note concerning signatures, ratifications, accessions, etc., on behalf of China, preface, p. v.

[11] For the reservations to article III of the Convention in its application to certain territories, and for the reservations regarding application of the Convention to the Colony of Aden and to Rhodesia, see "United Kingdom" under "Declarations and Reservations" in this chapter.

Chapter XXII

CONVENTION ON CONSENT TO MARRIAGE, MINIMUM AGE FOR MARRIAGE AND REGISTRATION OF MARRIAGES

Adopted by the General Assembly of the United Nations on 7 November 1962

ENTRY INTO FORCE: 9 December 1964, in accordance with article 6.

Participant	Signature	Ratification, accession (a), succession (d)
Argentina		26 Feb. 1970 *a*
Austria		1 Oct. 1969 *a*
Barbados		1 Oct. 1979 *a*
Benin		19 Oct. 1965 *a*
Brazil		11 Feb. 1970 *a*
Burkina Faso		8 Dec. 1964 *a*
Chile	10 Dec. 1962	
China [1, *]		
Cuba	17 Oct. 1963	20 Aug. 1965
Czechoslovakia	8 Oct. 1963	5 Mar. 1965
Democratic Yemen		9 Feb. 1987 *a*
Denmark	31 Oct. 1963	8 Sep. 1964
Dominican Republic		8 Oct. 1964 *a*
Fiji		19 July 1971 *d*
Finland		18 Aug. 1964 *a*
France	10 Dec. 1962	
German Democratic Republic		16 July 1974 *a*
Germany, Federal Republic of		9 July 1969*a*[2]
Greece	3 Jan. 1963	
Guatemala		18 Jan. 1983 *a*
Guinea	10 Dec. 1962	24 Jan. 1978

---

* For notes, see end of chapter.

Participant	Signature	Ratification, accession (a), succession (d)
Hungary		5 Nov. 1975 *a*
Iceland		18 Oct. 1977 *a*
Israel	10 Dec. 1962	
Italy	20 Dec. 1963	
Mali		19 Aug. 1964 *a*
Mexico		22 Feb. 1983 *a*
Netherlands	10 Dec. 1962	2 July 1965
New Zealand	23 Dec. 1963	12 June 1964
Niger		1 Dec. 1964 *a*
Norway		10 Sep. 1964 *a*
Philippines	5 Feb. 1963	21 Jan. 1965
Poland	17 Dec. 1962	8 Jan. 1965
Romania	27 Dec. 1963	
Samoa		24 Aug. 1964 *a*
Spain		15 Apr. 1969 *a*
Sri Lanka	12 Dec. 1962	
Sweden	10 Dec. 1962	16 June 1964
Trinidad and Tobago		2 Oct. 1969 *a*
Tunisia		24 Jan. 1968 *a*
United Kingdom		9 July 1970 *a*
United States of America	10 Dec. 1962	
Venezuela		31 May 1983 *a*
Yugoslavia	10 Dec. 1962	19 June 1964

DECLARATIONS AND RESERVATIONS

(Unless otherwise indicated, the declarations and reservations were made upon ratification, accession or succession.)

Denmark

"With the reservation that article 1, paragraph 2, shall not apply to the Kingdom of Denmark."

Dominican Republic

The Dominican Republic wishes the laws of the Dominican Republic to continue to have precedence in respect of the possibility, provided for in article 1, paragraph 2, of entering into a civil marriage by means of a proxy or procuration. Consequently, it can accept the said provision only with reservations.

Fiji

"The Government of Fiji withdraws the reservation, and declarations in respect of the law of Scotland and in respect of Southern Rhodesia, made on 9 July 1970 by Her Majesty's Government in the United Kingdom, and affirms that the Government of Fiji declares it to be their understanding that:

"(*a*) article 1, paragraph 1, and article 2, second sentence, of the Convention are concerned with the entry into marriage under the laws of a State party and not with the recognition under the laws of one State or territory of the validity of marriages contracted under the laws of another State or territory; and

"(*b*) article 1, paragraph 2, does not require legislative provision to be made where no such legislation already exists, for marriages to be contracted in the absence of one of the parties."

Finland

"With the reservation that article 1, paragraph 2, shall not apply to the Republic of Finland."

Greece

With reservation to article 1, paragraph 2, of the Convention.

Guatemala

Reservation:

With regard to article 1, paragraph 1, of the Convention, Guatemala declares that since its legislation, in respect of its nationals, does not call for the requirements relating to publicity of the marriage and the presence of witnesses for it to be solemnized, it does not consider itself obliged to comply with those requirements where the parties are Guatemalans.

Hungary

In acceding to the Convention, the Presidential Council of the Hungarian People's Republic declares that it does not consider article 1, paragraph 2, of the Convention as binding the Hungarian People's Republic to grant, under the terms thereof, permit of marriage when one of the intending spouses is not present.

Iceland

"Article 1, paragraph 2, shall not apply to the Republic of Iceland."

Netherlands

"In signing the Convention on Consent to Marriage, Minimum Age for Marriage and Registration of Marriages, I the undersigned, Plenipotentiary of the Kingdom of the Netherlands, hereby declare that, in view of the equality which exists, from the standpoint of public law, between the Netherlands, Surinam and the Netherlands Antilles, the Government of the Kingdom reserves the right to ratify the Convention in respect of only one or two parts of the Kingdom and to declare at a later date, by written notification to the Secretary-General, that the Convention is to apply also to the other part or parts of the Kingdom."

Norway

"With the reservation that article 1, paragraph 2, shall not apply to the Kingdom of Norway."

Philippines

"The Convention on Consent to Marriage, Minimum Age for Marriage and Registration of Marriages was adopted for the purpose, among other things, of insuring to all persons complete freedom in the choice of a spouse. The first paragraph of article 1 of the Convention requires that the full and free consent of both parties shall be expressed in the presence of the competent authority and of witnesses.

"Considering the provisions of its Civil Code, the Philippines, in ratifying this Convention interprets the second paragraph of article 1 (which authorizes, in exceptional cases, the solemnization of marriage by proxy) as not imposing upon the Philippines the obligation to allow within its territory the celebration of proxy marriages or marriages of the kind contemplated in that paragraph, where such manner of marriage is not authorized by the laws of the Philippines. Rather, the solemnization within Philippine territory of a marriage in the absence of one of the parties under the conditions stated in said paragraph will be permitted only if so allowed by Philippine law."

Sweden

With reservation to article 1, paragraph 2, of the Convention.

United Kingdom of Great Britain and Northern Ireland [3]

"(a) [3]

"(b) It is the understanding of the Government of the United Kingdom that article 1, paragraph 1, and the second sentence of article 2, of the Convention are concerned with entry into marriage under the laws of a State party and not with the recognition under the laws of one State or territory of the validity of marriages contracted under the laws of another State or territory; nor is article 1, paragraph 1, applicable to marriages by cohabitation with habit and repute under the law of Scotland;

"(c) Article 1, paragraph 2, does not require legislative provision to be made, where no such legislation already exists, for marriages to be contracted in the absence of one of the parties;

"(d) The provisions of the Convention shall not apply to Southern Rhodesia unless and until the Government of the United Kingdom inform the Secretary-General that they are in a position to ensure that the obligations imposed by the Convention in respect of that territory can be fully implemented."

United States of America

"With the understanding that legislation in force in the various States of the United States of America is in conformity with this Convention and that action by the United States of America with respect to this Convention does not constitute acceptance of the provision of article 8 as a precedent for any subsequent instruments."

Venezuela

[*See chapter XXI.*]

TERRITORIAL APPLICATIONS

Participant	Date of receipt of notification	Territories
Netherlands . . .	2 July 1965	Netherlands Antilles, Surinam
United Kingdom	9 July 1970	Associated States (Antigua, Dominica, Grenada, Saint Kitts-Nevis-Anguilla, Saint Lucia and Saint Vincent), State of Brunei, Territories under the territorial sovereignty of the United Kingdom
	15 Oct. 1974	Montserrat[3]

NOTES

[1] Signed on behalf of the Republic of China on 4 April 1963. See note concerning signatures, ratifications, accessions, etc. on behalf of China (note 2 in chapter I).

[2] In a note accompanying the instrument of accession, the Government of the Federal Republic of Germany declared that the Convention "shall also apply to Land Berlin with effect from the date on which it enters into force for the Federal Republic of Germany".

With reference to the above-mentioned declaration, communications have been addressed to the Secretary-General by the Governments of Bulgaria, Czechoslovakia, Hungary, Poland, Romania and the Union of Soviet Socialist Republics. Those communications are identical in essence, *mutatis mutandis,* to those referred to in note 2 of chapter I.

In this respect. the Government of the German Democratic Republic, upon accession to the Convention on 16 July 1974. made a declaration which is identical in essence, *mutatis mutandis,* to the one reproduced in note 2 of chapter I.

In reference to that declaration, communications were received by the Secretary-General from the Governments of France, the United Kingdom of Great Britain and Northern Ireland and the United States of America (8 July 1975) and from the Government of the Federal Republic of Germany (19 September 1975), which are identical in essence, *mutatis mutandis,* to the corresponding communications reproduced in note 2 of chapter I.

[3] In a notification received on 15 October 1974, the Government of the United Kingdom informed the Secretary-General of the withdrawal of the reservation corresponding to subparagraph (*a*). according to which it reserved the right to postpone the application of article 2 of the Convention to Montserrat pending notification to the Secretary-General that the said article would be applied there.

Printed in Switzerland, 03000P United Nations publication
November 1987   Sales No. E.87.XIV.2
Reprinted at United Nations, Geneva
GE.89-16058–June 1989–10,000

ISBN 92-1-154063-1
ISSN 1014-3629

ST/HR/5